Current Controversies in Virtue Theory

Virtue is among the most venerable concepts in philosophy and has recently seen a major revival. However, new challenges to conceptions of virtue have also arisen. In *Current Controversies in Virtue Theory,* five pairs of philosophers square off in cutting-edge debates over central topics in virtue theory: the nature of virtue, the connection between virtue and flourishing, the connection between moral and epistemic virtues, the way in which virtues are acquired, and the possibility of attaining virtue. Mark Alfano guides his readers through these essays (all published here for the first time), with a synthetic introduction, succinct abstracts of each debate, suggested further readings and study questions for each controversy, and a list of further controversies to be explored.

Mark Alfano is Assistant Professor of Philosophy at the University of Oregon. He specializes in moral psychology broadly construed, including virtue theory, decision making, ethics, and experimental philosophy. His first book was *Character as Moral Fiction* (2013). He has also participated in a number of interdisciplinary projects, including a grant-funded investigation of the nature, causes of, and consequences of intellectual humility.

Current Controversies in Philosophy

In venerable Socratic fashion, philosophy proceeds best through reasoned conversation. Current Controversies in Philosophy provides short, accessible volumes that cast a spotlight on ongoing central philosophical conversations. In each book, pairs of experts debate four or five key issues of contemporary concern, setting the stage for students, teachers, and researchers to join the discussion. Short chapter descriptions precede each chapter, and an annotated bibliography and study questions conclude each debate. In addition, each volume includes both a general introduction and a supplemental guide to further controversies. Combining timely debates with useful pedagogical aids allows the volumes to serve as clear and detailed snapshots, for all levels of readers, of some the most exciting work happening in philosophy today.

Series Editor

John Turri
University of Waterloo

Volumes in the Series

Published

Current Controversies in Virtue Theory
Edited by Mark Alfano

Current Controversies in Epistemology
Edited by Ram Neta

Current Controversies in Experimental Philosophy
Edited by Edouard Machery and Elizabeth O'Neill

Current Controversies in Philosophy of Mind
Edited by Uriah Kriegel

Forthcoming

Current Controversies in Philosophy of Film
Katherine Thomson-Jones

Current Controversies in Metaphysics
Edited by Elizabeth Barnes

Current Controversies in Political Philosophy
Edited by Thom Brooks

Praise for the Series

"This series constitutes a wonderful addition to the literature. The volumes reflect the essentially dialectical nature of philosophy, and are edited by leading figures in the field. They will be an invaluable resource for students and faculty alike."
            Duncan Pritchard, The University of Edinburgh

Current Controversies in Virtue Theory

Edited by
Mark Alfano

NEW YORK AND LONDON

First published 2015
by Routledge
711 Third Avenue, New York, NY 10017

and by Routledge
2 Park Square, Milton Park, Abingdon, Oxon, OX14 4RN

Routledge is an imprint of the Taylor & Francis Group, an informa business

© 2015 Taylor & Francis

The right of the editor to be identified as the author of the editorial material, and of the authors for their individual chapters, has been asserted in accordance with sections 77 and 78 of the Copyright, Designs and Patents Act 1988.

All rights reserved. No part of this book may be reprinted or reproduced or utilised in any form or by any electronic, mechanical, or other means, now known or hereafter invented, including photocopying and recording, or in any information storage or retrieval system, without permission in writing from the publishers.

Trademark notice: Product or corporate names may be trademarks or registered trademarks, and are used only for identification and explanation without intent to infringe.

Library of Congress Cataloging-in-Publication Data
Current controversies in virtue theory / edited by Mark Alfano. — 1st ed.
  pages cm. — (Current controversies in philosophy)
  Includes bibliographical references.
  1. Virtue. I. Alfano, Mark, 1983– editor.
  BJ1521.C88 2015
  179'.9—dc23
  2014031929

ISBN: 978-0-415-65820-1 (hbk)
ISBN: 978-0-415-65821-8 (pbk)
ISBN: 978-1-315-72800-1 (ebk)

Typeset in Minion
by Apex CoVantage, LLC

Printed and bound in the United States of America by
Edwards Brothers Malloy on sustainably sourced paper

for Nori

Contents

Acknowledgments		ix
Contributors		xi
Introduction Mark Alfano		1
1	**What Is a Virtue?**	6
	A Pluralist Theory of Virtue Heather Battaly	7
	Against Radical Pluralism Liezl van Zyl	22
	Study Questions	33
2	**Does Virtue Contribute to Flourishing?**	35
	How Virtue Contributes to Flourishing Robert C. Roberts	36
	Virtue and Oppression Nancy E. Snow	49
	Study Questions	59
3	**How Are Virtue and Knowledge Related?**	61
	Virtue Epistemology: Character Versus Competence Ernest Sosa	62

	Character Virtues, Epistemic Agency, and Reflective Knowledge Jason Baehr	74
	Study Questions	87
4	**How Are Virtues Acquired?**	91
	From Personality to Character to Virtue Daniel C. Russell	92
	Russell on Acquiring Virtue Christian B. Miller	106
	Study Questions	118
5	**Can People Be Virtuous?**	123
	Ramsifying Virtue Theory Mark Alfano	124
	Ramsify (by All Means)—but Do Not 'Dumb Down' the Moral Virtues James Montmarquet	136
	Study Questions	147
6	**A Brief Introduction to Other Virtue Theoretic Controversies**	150

References	154
Index	160

Acknowledgments

Expressing justified gratitude is one of life's greatest joys.

I got the idea for this book after talking with John Turri, the series editor. He seemed interested, so I pursued the idea. Several people warned me against doing an edited volume—that it would be a huge hassle and more trouble than it's worth. And so I'm delighted and a bit surprised to say that, thanks to my conscientious contributors, the terrific staff at Routledge, and my own newfound patience, assembling this particular volume was a breeze. Thanks to John Downes-Angus, Andy Beck, and Laura Briskman for their help with the manuscript. Thanks to John Turri for encouraging me to follow through with this project. And thanks most of all to my contributors: Heather Battaly, Liezl van Zyl, Robert Roberts, Nancy Snow, Ernest Sosa, Jason Baehr, Daniel Russell, Christian Miller, and James Montmarquet. Without their exemplary work, this book would not exist.

I'm especially grateful as well to my uncle, Edward Alfano, who agreed to contribute the art on the front cover.

In addition, I am thankful for the opportunity to work on this project that was afforded by my year as a postdoctoral research associate at the Princeton University Center for Human Values and Center for Health and Wellbeing.

Thanks, finally, to my wife, Veronica, for putting up with my blathering on about this when I should have been making scintillating conversation.

Contributors

Mark Alfano is Assistant Professor of Philosophy at the University of Oregon. He specializes in moral psychology broadly construed, including virtue theory, decision making, ethics, and experimental philosophy. His first book was *Character as Moral Fiction* (2013). He has also participated in a number of interdisciplinary projects, including a grant-funded investigation of the nature, causes of, and consequences of intellectual humility.

Jason Baehr is Associate Professor of Philosophy at Loyola Marymount University in Los Angeles. He works on epistemology and virtue theory. In this capacity, he has published one book, *The Inquiring Mind: On Intellectual Virtues and Virtue Epistemology* (2011), and led a large grant applying virtue epistemology to educational theory and practice.

Heather Battaly is Professor of Philosophy at California State University, Fullerton. Her research interests include epistemology, ethics, and virtue theory. She has published widely in these fields, including two edited volumes: *Perspectives on the Philosophy of William P. Alston* (2005) and *Virtue and Vice, Moral and Epistemic* (2010).

Christian B. Miller is Professor of Philosophy at Wake Forrest University. His work is primarily in contemporary metaethics, moral psychology, theory of action, normative theory, and philosophy of religion. He is the author of *Moral Character: An Empirical Theory* (2013) and *Character and Moral Psychology* (2014), as well as a co-Principle Investigator on a $4,600,000 grant from the John Templeton Foundation on the existence and nature of character.

James Montmarquet is Professor of Philosophy at Tennessee State University. He has written extensively in philosophy of religion, epistemology, and ethics. Among his other work is a notable contribution to virtue theory: *Epistemic Virtue and Doxastic Responsibility* (1993).

Robert C. Roberts is Distinguished Professor of Ethics at Baylor University. His research interests include virtue theory, moral psychology, and philosophy of religion. Among his many publications are *Spiritual Emotions* (2007), *Intellectual Virtues* (2007, coauthored with Jay Wood), *Emotions* (2003), and *Emotions in the Moral Life* (2013).

Daniel C. Russell is Professor of Philosophy at the Center for the Philosophy of Freedom, University of Arizona. He specializes in ancient philosophy and ethics, and his work focuses on ancient philosophy mainly as a source for expanding contemporary options for thinking about how to improve our lives. He has written on Plato's ethics and psychology (*Plato on Pleasure and the Good Life* 2005) as well as contemporary virtue ethics (*Practical Intelligence and the Virtues* 2009). More recently, he has completed a book on happiness and well-being (*Happiness for Humans* 2012).

Nancy E. Snow is Professor of Philosophy at Marquette University, with research interests in moral psychology and virtue ethics. Her most recent book is *Character as Social Intelligence: An Empirical Theory* (2010). She is currently working on two books, one on hope and one on virtue ethics and virtue epistemology.

Ernest Sosa is Board of Governors Professor of Philosophy at Rutgers University. In addition to directing over 50 dissertations, he has published widely in epistemology, including *Knowledge in Perspective* (1991), *Epistemic Justification* (2003), *A Virtue Epistemology* (2007), *Reflective Knowledge* (2009), and *Knowing Full Well* (2011).

Liezl van Zyl is Convenor in Philosophy at the University of Waikato. Her research interests include normative and applied ethics, political theory, and aesthetics. Among her many publications is *Death and Compassion: A Virtue-Based Approach to Euthanasia* (2000).

Introduction

MARK ALFANO

In the *Politics* (1.2), Aristotle says that "he who is unable to live in society, or who has no need because he is sufficient for himself, must be either a beast or a god." With that in mind, and realizing that most contemporary philosophers are neither beasts nor gods, it seems best to conduct our philosophical investigations socially. The aim of the *Current Controversies* series is to articulate areas of philosophical disagreement and to further debates in those areas, with pairs of philosophers engaging in reasoned conversations that will serve as an intellectual wedge for students, teachers, and other researchers. The present volume highlights controversies in virtue ethics and virtue epistemology. Contributors explore areas of agreement and disagreement, along with the substantive and methodological assumptions and premises that give context to the debates.

The theory of virtue is a burgeoning field in both contemporary philosophy and social science, with heated arguments about the conceptual nature and empirical status of virtues, the relations amongst the virtues, and the contribution of virtue to well-being or flourishing. Our contributors face off over five questions:

1. What is a virtue? (Heather Battaly and Liezl van Zyl)
2. Does virtue contribute to flourishing? (Robert C. Roberts and Nancy E. Snow)
3. How are ethical and epistemic virtues related? (Ernest Sosa and Jason Baehr)
4. How are virtues acquired? (Daniel C. Russell and Christian B. Miller)
5. Can people be virtuous? (Mark Alfano and James Montmarquet)

Some of their disagreements are large, some small; some of their disagreements are about first-order claims, some fundamental or methodological.

For instance, Roberts and Snow agree that virtue contributes to flourishing but only as a necessary (not a sufficient) component, that flourishing is a matter of living a meaningful life rather than simply experiencing many episodes of pleasure and few of pain, and that which dispositions contribute in this way depends on what human nature and the rest of the world is like. Snow worries that Roberts—or a facile reading of Roberts—might be taken to suggest that the person whose flourishing is in question cannot be trusted to form an adequate judgment about their own nature and which traits, behaviors, sentiments, and relationships will tend to make it meaningful. In particular, she is concerned by the fact that claims about people's nature have frequently been used to motivate and justify their oppression. For instance, Roberts argues that obedience is a virtue. In Paul's letter to the Ephesians (5:22), we read, "Wives, submit yourselves unto your own husbands, as unto the Lord. For the husband is the head of the wife, even as Christ is the head of the church: and he is the saviour of the body. Therefore as the church is subject unto Christ, so let the wives be to their own husbands in every thing." Verses like this, which make claims about the natures of men and women, have been used for centuries to oppress women. Typically, a woman who dared to challenge such an account of her nature would be ignored—or worse. Roberts doesn't say anything explicit about sex or gender, but his claim that people may not be the best judges of their own natures opens up a space for Snow's concern.

There's a more daylight between Sosa and Baehr, though they themselves seem to disagree about exactly how much. Sosa argues that virtue epistemology should recognize agential competences but not character traits as central intellectual virtues. Baehr questions whether this distinction makes sense, and whether—even if it does—it can be used to do the work that Sosa wants it to.

Russell and Miller disagree even more. Russell argues that the empirical study of psychology reveals that humans are capable of learning to respond to reasons, and capable of learning to respond to them in better, more nuanced, more sophisticated, and more holistic ways. For instance, people acquire skills in a wide variety of domains—from chess to firefighting. This suggests, according to Russell, that we can learn to respond to moral reasons in the same way. If this is right, then an account of virtue puts us on the path from how we are, as psychology describes us, to how we ought to be, as normative ethics prescribes for us. Of course, there's no guarantee that people can, in general, get to the end of the path, but the point is less about being a saint and more about becoming incrementally better. Although Miller is sympathetic to Russell's framework, he argues that the inference from *We can get better at responding to one kind of reason* (skill related) to *We can get better at responding to another kind of reason* (virtue related) is too quick, especially since he doubts that people are, in general, motivated to improve their ability to respond to virtue-related reasons.

The second-largest disagreement, in my estimation, is between Battaly and Van Zyl. Battaly lays out an extremely capacious conception of what a virtue is (Van Zyl dubs it "radical pluralism"), claiming that any disposition that leads to good ends, leads to good effects, or involves good motives should count. On the one hand, this could be seen as a way of disagreeing with no one. Do you think, like Driver and other utilitarian virtue theorists, that only good effects matter, such that the agent's motives are strictly irrelevant to whether she's virtuous? You're right. Do you think, like Kant-influenced virtue theorists, that only good motives matter, such that the effects the agent brings about are strictly irrelevant to whether she's virtuous? You're right too. Against this irenic ecumenicism, Van Zyl argues that the different conceptions of virtue that Battaly tries to allow into her fold are motivated by contrary metaethical, normative, and practical commitments. Driver doesn't just think that producing good effects is virtuous; she thinks it's virtuous because good effects are the only intrinsic values. Kantians don't just think that having good motives is virtuous; they think it's virtuous because good motives are the only intrinsic values. Essentially, Van Zyl is accusing Battaly of being like the rabbi in this classic joke:

> In a small town in Latvia, two men brought their complaints to their rabbi. He listened to one, then said, "You are right." He listened to the other, then said, "You are right." His wife, who had overheard the conversation, interjected, saying, "But they disagree with each other—they can't both be right!" The rabbi responded, "You're right too."

The most fundamental disagreement, though, is between Montmarquet and me. In my contribution, I deploy a method (Ramsification, as developed by David Lewis) from naturalistic philosophy of mind to help resolve an empirical challenge to virtue theory and suggest a relational model of virtue, according to which at least some instances of your being, for example, trustworthy, essentially involve someone else's trusting you. Because Montmarquet disagrees so fundamentally with my naturalism, he devotes his contribution to a sustained defense of anti-naturalism in ethics. This is not the place for me to engage in a full-throated defense of naturalism in ethics, so I will rest content to summarize Montmarquet's arguments.[1] He thinks that character is "not well revealed most of the time," which means that scientific investigation of what happens most of the time is more or less guaranteed to fail to latch onto character. He also thinks that the point of making character-trait ascriptions is not, as naturalists would have it, to help predict, explain, and control behavior, but simply to describe and evaluate it in as nuanced and holistic a way as possible.

It should be evident from these brief, selective summaries of the "controversies" in this volume that, although our authors are officially engaged in pairwise debates, there are important themes or threads that tie the debates together. The three most common are *naturalism, demandingness*, and *human nature*.

To what extent is the demandingness of a conception of virtue relevant to that conception's viability? Should we prefer maximally demanding, ideal theories of virtue? Should we opt for highly demanding but (for all we can tell) achievable conceptions of virtue, constrained only by the truism that *ought* implies *can*?[2] Should we, instead, be more skeptical of a theory of virtue the more demanding it grows (perhaps beyond a certain threshold)? If demandingness is admitted to be at least relevant, is there a way to determine how demanding a conception of virtue is without relying on psychological and other relevant science? How can we hope to figure out what human nature is without relying on science? All of our contributors take a stand on these interrelated questions.

Battaly argues for a fairly undemanding notion of virtue, and though she doesn't say here anything about the relevance of science, she has elsewhere (see Battaly 2014) demonstrated naturalistic commitments that may be connected with her pluralistic account of virtue. Like Battaly, Van Zyl does not take a stand on naturalism, but in her contribution she does argue for a fairly demanding conception of virtue as a disposition not only to produce good effects, not only to have good motives, but to produce good effects because one is acting from good motives. In his contribution, Sosa doesn't address the naturalism question, but he objects to character-based virtue responsibilism because it is too "high-minded." Baehr defends his view by arguing that at least his own conception of intellectual character virtue is not as high-minded as one might think, which suggests that he takes demandingness to be a legitimate objection. Roberts points out that one's conception of human nature to some extent determines what one takes flourishing and virtue to be. He is sympathetic to a supernatural, Christian conception, though it is not clear whether he thinks that science cannot help. According to Snow, "We need to pay attention to empirical studies that inform us of the traits children actually use to function and live well. These traits are their virtues." Claims like this, along with her criticisms of outlandish hope, show that she takes demandingness very seriously and is inclined to determine how demanding a view is by looking to the empirical sciences.[3] Russell claims that "to have a view about the virtues is automatically to commit to some deeper view about the building blocks of personality—what we might call a personality *ontology*. For this reason, states about people's virtues are empirically risky." On the demandingness question, his view is complex. On the one hand, he argues here (and elsewhere, such as Russell 2009) that virtue is a regulative ideal, which may be unattainable. On the other hand, he thinks that this ideal must be such that we can try and sometimes succeed in approximating better in the future than the present. He describes this developmental constraint in terms of path-dependency, since *getting (closer to) there* (the regulative ideal) requires at least a notion of where *here* (human nature as studied by psychology and other relevant sciences) is. In his response, Miller puts considerable weight on the fact that there is "ample empirical evidence to support the claim that there are many Surprising Dispositions,"[4] which can be activated unconsciously by situational triggers and lead to virtue-consonant or virtue-dissonant conduct. I bluntly say, "Virtue-terms have empirical content. Attributions of virtues figure in the description, prediction, explanation, and control of behavior." I then go on to argue that we face a choice between a more demanding but nearly unattainable conception of virtue and a less demanding but clearly attainable conception. (Along the way, I point out that different virtues are themselves more or less demanding; high-fidelity virtues like honesty and chastity are awfully hard to live up to, whereas the standards of low-fidelity virtues like generosity and eco-friendliness are more easily met. Against this chorus of naturalistic voices, Montmarquet claims that if empirical results are disappointing, this is no more a blow to virtue ethics than equally disappointing results in national science and mathematics tests are relative to the importance of these subjects, which he follows up by saying that "we are free, guided only by reason and a sense of the possible, to set the bar as high as we like, whatever empirical evidence indicates."

Notes

1. I do some of this in Alfano (2013a) and Alfano and Loeb (2014).
2. See Flanagan's (1991) Principle of Minimal Psychological Realism for an articulation of this position.
3. See also her recent book, *Virtue as Social Intelligence* (2010).
4. He deals with this ample evidence in *much* more detail in his recent books (Miller 2013, 2014).

CHAPTER 1

What Is a Virtue?

Abstract

In her contribution, Heather Battaly starts from the truism that virtues are dispositions that make us better people, that is, qualities that make one an excellent person. She moves from this idea to a taxonomy of ways in which someone could be excellent, which is thus also a taxonomy of ways in which someone could be virtuous. First, one could be excellent by reliably (if not uniformly) producing good effects or ends. Good effects are to be specified by an axiology—or theory of what makes a state of affairs good. In contrast, good ends are specified relative to the thing that has those ends; for instance, the end of a knife is to cut, of a doctor to heal, and so on. Second, one could be excellent by reliably (if not uniformly) having good motives. If one is sufficiently lucky (or not too unlucky), of course, acting from your good motives will also typically produce good effects. Thus, we have a 2-by-2 distinction, as seen in Table 1.1:

Table 1.1 What Is Necessary for Virtue?

	Good ends or effects	*~Good ends or effects*
Good motives	Aristotle Hursthouse Zagzebski Battaly Van Zyl	Kant Battaly
~Good motives	Driver Sosa Battaly	

Battaly argues that we should recognize a disposition as a virtue if and only if it reliably produces good effects or ends, or reliably makes its bearer have good motives. Her account is thus disjunctive, acknowledging a trait as a virtue unless it neither produces good effects nor involves good motives. Against this, Liezl van Zyl argues that *only* traits that involve *both* good effects or ends *and* good motives deserve to be labeled virtues. She describes this as a mixed account, though we might also call it a conjunctive, in contrast with Battaly's disjunctive view. One way in which this disagreement might be adjudicated is to make a continuous rather than a categorical distinction: instead of insisting on distinguishing between traits that *are* and *are not* virtues, it might be more fruitful to *rank* traits on a scale of virtuousness or desirability. For instance, presumably Battaly and Van Zyl would agree that mixed virtues are morally superior to (though also harder to acquire than) traits that involve only effects or only motives. And presumably they would also agree that traits that involve neither are worse than all of the alternatives. Whether they would agree in ranking motive-only versus effect-only traits I cannot say.

A Pluralist Theory of Virtue

Heather Battaly

Virtue: The Basics

What is a virtue? How are virtues different from vices? Do all virtues share the very same features, or are there different kinds of virtues? Let's begin by considering which qualities might count as virtues. Do qualities like being smart, fair, brave, open-minded, and funny count as virtues? What about enjoying life, caring about others, having empathy, and having good judgment? At one time or another, philosophers have counted all of these qualities as virtues. There is general philosophical consensus that justice (fairness), courage (bravery), temperance (enjoying life), and wisdom (which is connected to having good judgment) are virtues. These four qualities appear on the lists of virtues generated by Plato, Aristotle, David Hume, and much more recently, Rosalind Hursthouse and Linda Zagzebski. But, there are other qualities which appear on some lists of virtues but not others. Wit (being funny), appears on the lists of Aristotle and Hume; being open-minded appears on Zagzebski's list; and being smart (having a reliable memory and logical skills) appears on Sosa's list. Any basic account of virtue—one whose primary job is to distinguish virtue from vice—should be broad enough to include all of the above qualities. There is something that all of these qualities have in common—something that makes them virtues, rather than vices.[1]

We should notice that the qualities above are a diverse lot. Some of them, such as being smart and being open-minded, are primarily intellectual qualities—they are concerned with intellectual goods like truth, knowledge, and understanding. Other qualities, such as being brave, caring about others, and empathy, are moral qualities—they are concerned with a broader set of goods, including the overall welfare of ourselves and others. Cross-cutting the distinction between moral and intellectual is a distinction between hard-wired capacities, acquired skills, and acquired character traits. Some of the qualities above, such as having empathy and being smart, are arguably a combination of acquired skills and hard-wired capacities. Others, such as open-mindedness and courage, are acquired character traits. So, what makes all of these qualities virtues? What do all of these qualities have in common? The rough answer is that they all make us better people. In other words, virtues are qualities that make one an excellent person. Granted, a person can be excellent in a variety of ways. For instance, she can be excellent insofar as she is has a reliable memory; or insofar as she is attuned to the emotions of other people; or insofar as she is open-minded, courageous, or benevolent. But the main point is that whatever diverse features these qualities have, they are all virtues because they are all excellences. In contrast, vices are defects. Vices are qualities that make us worse people. Analogously, there will be a variety of different ways in which one can be a worse person.

These basic accounts of virtue and vice are quite broad. Unlike much work in contemporary virtue theory, which treats virtue ethics and virtue epistemology as separate fields, the basic account above includes *both* moral qualities and intellectual qualities. It also includes qualities like courage and cowardice, over whose acquisition we exercise considerable control, alongside qualities like reliable and unreliable memory, over which we have relatively little control. David Hume famously includes all of these sorts of qualities—intellectual as well as moral, and involuntary as well as voluntary—on his lists of virtues and vices. Hume (1966) argues that attempts to exclude intellectual qualities from the category of virtues will fail. In his words, if we were to "lay hold of the distinction between intellectual and moral endowments, and affirm the last alone to be real and genuine virtues, because they alone [led] to action" then we would quickly discover that "many of those qualities . . . called intellectual virtues, such as prudence, penetration, discernment, discretion, [have] also a considerable influence on conduct" (p. 156). Nor, on Hume's (1978) view, can we exclude involuntary abilities, since some of them are "useful" to the people who have them—some involuntary abilities enable the people who have them to attain good effects (p. 610). For Hume, then, virtues that are intellectual are no less genuine than virtues that are moral; and virtues that are involuntary are no less genuine than virtues that are voluntary. Our basic account of virtue agrees with Hume on both of these points.

But our basic account of virtue and vice is so broad that it is difficult to apply. To apply them, we need to be able to determine whether a quality is an excellence or a defect, and *why* it makes one a better person or a worse person.

Below, I argue for pluralism; roughly, the view that there are different kinds of virtues. In other words, pluralism claims that different qualities can make one a better person in different ways. One way that qualities can make us better people is by enabling us to attain good ends or effects—like true beliefs, or the welfare of others. But this isn't the only way for qualities to make us better people. Qualities that involve good motives—like caring about truths, or about the welfare of others—also make us better people, and do so even if they don't reliably attain good ends or effects. These two kinds of virtue capture two different ways of thinking about virtues—they capture two different concepts of virtue. According to one concept of virtue, which I will call VGE, reliable success in attaining good ends or effects is both necessary and sufficient for a quality's being a virtue. But, according to another concept of virtue, which I will call VGM, being successful at attaining good ends or effects is not enough, and may not even be required, for virtue. What is required, and what makes a quality a virtue, are good motives. These two concepts (and kinds) of virtue are typically pitted against each other—philosophers have often defended one concept (and kind) of virtue over the other. But, I will suggest that pluralism is a better view; we would do well to embrace both of these concepts and kinds of virtue. In short, both of these concepts succeed in identifying qualities that are virtues.

VGE: Virtues Attain Good Ends or Effects

According to the first concept of virtue, VGE, what makes a quality a virtue as opposed to a vice is its reliable success in attaining good ends or effects, like true beliefs or the welfare of others. Many of these good ends and effects will be external to us. Success in producing them need not be perfect, but must be reliable. This means that qualities that rarely, but occasionally, fail to attain good ends or effects can still be virtues; but qualities that *reliably* fail to attain good ends or effects cannot. People who try, but reliably fail, to help others (like the character Mr. Bean) do not have the virtue of benevolence. They may want to help others—they may have good motives—but if they reliably and negligently bungle the job, they are not virtuous. Likewise, people who try, but reliably and negligently fail, to get true beliefs do not have intellectual virtues. They may want to get truths—they may have good motives—but if they reliably botch the job, they are not virtuous either. According to VGE, sheer bad luck that is due to no fault of our own can also prevent us from having virtues. People who have the bad luck of being in a demon-world, in which an all-powerful evil demon ensures that their beliefs turn out to be false, or in an oppressive society, in which all or most of their actions turn out to produce harm, do not have virtues. In short, according to VGE, reliably attaining good ends or effects is necessary for a quality's being a virtue.

VGE also entails that reliably attaining good ends or effects is sufficient for a quality's being a virtue. Philosophers who advocate VGE argue that good ends or effects are what ultimately matter—they are intrinsically valuable. Accordingly, they think that any quality that reliably succeeds in producing good ends or effects will also be valuable—it will be a virtue. This means that any quality—be it a hard-wired capacity, an acquired skill, or an acquired character trait—will count as a virtue as long as it reliably produces good ends or effects. Accordingly, a hedge-fund manager, who consistently succeeds in helping others via charitable donations, will have the virtue of benevolence, even if he does not care about others and is solely motivated by tax write-offs.[2] Likewise, students who reliably arrive at true beliefs as a result of their logical skills will have intellectual virtues, even if they do not care about truth and are solely motivated to get good grades or make money. In short, according to VGE, one need not have good motives to be virtuous; one need only be successful at producing good ends or effects.[3]

Are VGE Virtues Teleological or Non-Teleological?

Advocates of VGE agree that good ends or effects are intrinsically valuable. But some of them focus on ends; others on effects. So, VGE comes in two different varieties: a teleological variety that focuses on ends, and a non-teleological variety that focuses on effects. Roughly, teleology is the view that things and people have built-in *ends* or functions. Plato and Aristotle are among the most famous advocates of teleology. They argue that, for example, eyes, knives, doctors, and people in general all have built-in ends or functions. They think that the function (end) of an eye is to see, of a knife is to cut, and of a doctor is to heal the sick. Determining the function (end) of a person in general is a difficult task, even for Plato and Aristotle.

Now, each of these functions—seeing, healing the sick, etc.—can be performed well or poorly. According to the teleological version of VGE, virtues are whatever qualities enable a thing or person to perform its function well (to attain its end). As Plato puts the point: "anything that has a function performs it well by means of its own ... virtue, and badly by means of its vice" (*Republic*, 353c). So, the sharpness of a knife is one of its virtues since sharpness enables it to cut well (to attain its end). Analogously, the virtues of a person will be whatever qualities are responsible for her performing her function well. This means that to figure out which of our qualities are virtues—which of our qualities make us better as people—we must first figure out the function or end of a person.

Other philosophers reject the teleological variety of VGE. They are suspicious of built-in ends and functions, largely for metaphysical reasons. So, rather than define virtues in terms of ends and functions, they define virtues in terms of *effects*, which do not entail a controversial metaphysics.

In short, advocates of VGE think that virtues are qualities that consistently produce good effects. The challenge for this non-teleological variety of VGE is to figure out which effects are good—which are intrinsically valuable—and why.

Advocates of VGE

Plato is among the most famous advocates of the teleological variety of VGE. In *Republic*, he explicitly defines virtues in terms of functions or ends. He argues that the function of a person consists in deliberating, ruling oneself, and more broadly, living (353d-e). On his view, virtues are qualities that enable us to perform these functions well. They are the qualities that enable us to deliberate well, rule ourselves well, and thereby live well.

Which qualities are these? To identify the virtues, Plato argues that each person has a soul that is divided into three parts—reason, spirit, and appetite. Each of these parts has its own function. Roughly, the function of reason is to rule the soul and to know what is good for the whole person. This will include knowing which things she should fear, and which things she should desire. The function of spirit is to enforce what reason says about which things she should fear; while the function of appetite is to accept what reason says about which things she should desire (*Republic* 442c). Of course, each of these functions can be performed well or poorly. Plato thinks that when one's reason, spirit, and appetite are functioning well, one both knows what is good *and* puts this knowledge into practice—one fears all and only the things one should, and desires all and only the things one should. To use contemporary examples, one fears combat but not social interaction at parties, and one desires sex but not sex with one's best friend's partner. Plato argues that the virtue of wisdom is what enables reason to function well, since the wise person knows what is good and deliberates well. Similarly, courage enables spirit to function well, since the courageous person fears what he should; and temperance enables appetite to function well, since the temperate person desires what he should. Famously, he contends that the virtue of justice is what enables the whole person to function well, and function without internal conflict. On his view, justice enables each part of the soul to do "its own work," in harmony with the other parts (*Republic* 441d-e). So together, wisdom, courage, temperance, and justice enable a person to deliberate well, rule oneself well, and thereby live well—they enable her to attain her ends.

Aristotle inherited VGE from Plato. He employs the teleological variety of VGE in Books I and VI of his *Nicomachean Ethics* (NE), but employs VGM (see below) in much of the rest of NE. In NE.VI, Aristotle explains the intellectual virtues. Like Plato, Aristotle thinks that there is a rational part of the soul and that wisdom is what enables it to function well since wisdom gets us knowledge. But, unlike Plato, Aristotle thinks that there are two types of wisdom and two types of knowledge. On Aristotle's view, the rational part of the soul is itself sub-divided into two further parts—the contemplative part and the calculative part. The function (end) of the contemplative part is to get theoretical knowledge, which for Aristotle, included truths about mathematics and geometry. Whereas, the function (end) of the calculative part is to get practical knowledge, about, for example, which actions one should perform (e.g., I should study for the exam tomorrow instead of going to the party.). Aristotle uses these two different functions to identify two different sets of virtues. On his view, intellectual virtues are qualities that enable us to perform these functions well—they enable us to reliably attain practical or theoretical knowledge, respectively (NE.1139b11–13). Aristotle identifies practical wisdom (*phronesis*) and skill (*techne*) as the virtues of the calculative part—they get us practical truths and knowledge; and philosophical wisdom (*sophia*), intuitive reason (*nous*), and scientific knowledge (*episteme*) as the virtues of the contemplative part—they get us theoretical truths and knowledge.

In Book I of the *Nicomachean Ethics*, Aristotle also defines moral virtues in terms of functions. In NE.I.7, he argues that the function of a human being is, roughly, rational activity. Aristotle's notion of rational activity is broader than it might initially seem. It includes contemplating theories and calculating which actions to perform in the intellectual realm (see above). But it also includes doing what reason tells us to do in the moral realm. Of course, we can perform this function (rational activity) well or poorly. Here, as in NE.VI, Aristotle assumes that to perform any function well one must have the corresponding virtues. Accordingly, he identifies courage, temperance, justice, practical wisdom, and philosophical wisdom as virtues, since they all enable us to excel at rational activity.

Granted, Plato and Aristotle think that we must have good motives in order to be morally virtuous. But this is purely a result of the rich notion of human function that they endorse. If they are correct about our ends as humans— if our ends really include ruling ourselves, rational activity, and living in general—and if they are correct that the virtues are qualities that will enable us to attain these ends, then it is no wonder that the virtues require internal features like good motives. If human function is partly internal, then we can expect the virtues to be partly internal. If we instead endorse more modest ends or effects—like the production of true beliefs or welfare—then we can expect motives to drop out of the picture. Sosa's and Driver's views each illustrate this point. Neither of them thinks that good motives are required for the virtues. In short, there is nothing about VGE itself that forces virtues to require good motives.

Ernest Sosa, a contemporary epistemologist, applies VGE to intellectual virtues, such as reliable memory and reliable vision. Sosa straddles both varieties of VGE. When endorsing the teleological variety, Sosa (1991) argues that "grasping the truth about one's environment" is one of the "proper ends of a human being" (p. 271). So, like Plato and Aristotle, he thinks that one of our main functions is to get true beliefs. Sosa also uses Plato's *Republic* and Book VI of Aristotle's *Nicomachean Ethics* to argue that "there is a ... sense of 'virtue' ... in which anything with a function ... does have virtues" (p. 271). Accordingly, Sosa conceives of the intellectual virtues as qualities that enable a person to excel at her function of getting truths. A person performs this function well when she reliably gets true beliefs—roughly, when she gets more true beliefs than false ones. She performs this function poorly when she is unreliable—when she gets more false beliefs than true ones. On Sosa's view, then, one's vision and memory need not be perfect to count as intellectual virtues; they need only be reliable—they need only produce *more* true beliefs than false ones. In short, Sosa (2003) thinks that intellectual virtues are qualities that reliably get us true beliefs. Elsewhere, Sosa (2007) arrives at the same conclusion, but does so via the non-teleological variety of VGE. Accordingly, he argues that even if teleology fails—even if it is ultimately implausible to ascribe functions to human beings—true beliefs will still be good because they are intrinsically, or fundamentally, valuable.

Whichever variety of VGE Sosa employs, he draws the same conclusions. He thinks that getting good ends or effects—true beliefs—is what matters for intellectual virtue; neither good motives nor good actions are required. Accordingly, hard-wired capacities, like reliable memory and reliable vision, and acquired skills, like successfully doing proofs in logic, count as intellectual virtues. Indeed, for Sosa, reliable memory and reliable vision are paradigmatic intellectual virtues. Though Sosa does not preclude character traits from being intellectual virtues, his focus has clearly been on hard-wired capacities and acquired skills. Sosa's article in this volume indicates a welcome shift toward addressing character traits.

Julia Driver, a contemporary ethicist, applies VGE to moral virtues. Unlike Plato and Aristotle, she advocates the non-teleological variety of VGE. In *Uneasy Virtue*, she argues that virtues are qualities that consistently produce good effects. As Driver (2001) puts the point, moral virtues are "character traits that systematically produce more actual good than not" (p. 68). Like Sosa, Driver thinks that a quality need not be perfect to count as a virtue; reliability in producing good effects is enough. Accordingly, she thinks that justice and benevolence are virtues because they reliably produce good effects, even though they occasionally fail to do so. Driver explicitly contends that good effects are the only things that matter for virtue—good motives are neither necessary nor sufficient. On her view, good motives are not necessary for virtue because if one consistently produces good effects, then one has virtues, even if one also has bad motives. So, the hedge-fund manager who consistently donates to hospitals has the virtue of benevolence, even though his motives are selfish. Good motives are not sufficient for virtue because people who consistently produce bad effects do not have virtues, even if they are well-intentioned.

To illustrate, the bungler who produces more harm than good lacks benevolence, even if he has good motives.[4]

VGM: Virtues Require Good Motives

According to VGE, attaining good ends or effects is the only thing that matters for virtue. As long as one reliably attains good ends or effects, one is virtuous. In contrast, the second concept of virtue, VGM, maintains that attaining good ends or effects is either not enough, or is not even required, for virtue. What (also) matters is *why* one attains, or tries to attain, those goods; that is, good motives (also) matter. After all, one might donate money to charity for entirely selfish reasons—not because one cares about the people who are helped, but because one cares solely about making *oneself* look good or feel better. According to VGM, the hedge-fund manager with selfish motives is not virtuous, even if he consistently succeeds in helping others. The same can be said of the student who reliably arrives at true beliefs, not because she cares about truth, but solely because she wants to get good grades or make money.

Unlike VGE, VGM maintains that good motives are necessary for a quality to be a virtue. Why would good motives be necessary if one was already reliably producing good effects? For two reasons. First, advocates of VGM think that virtues are praiseworthy and that praise and blame should only be attached to things we can control. To illustrate, I shouldn't blame a person for her unreliable vision, or praise her for her reliable vision, since she has no control over the hard-wired capacities she ends up with. To be praiseworthy, virtues must be (sufficiently) under our control. Arguably, we have greater control over our motives and actions than we do over our effects in the world. If our motives are developed over time via practice and effort, then we have considerable control over whether we end up caring about helping others, or only about making ourselves look good. But we have less control over our effects in the world, since our good intentions can be defeated by bad luck. Due to no fault of our own, our donations to charitable organizations can end up in the hands of dictators instead of the people who need help.[5] In short, virtues require good motives and good actions because without them, virtues would not be praiseworthy.

Second, advocates of VGM think that the virtues and vices tell us who we are as individual people; they reveal what we each care about and value. Accordingly, good motives are necessary for virtue because they tell us what we care about, and do so in ways that good actions and hard-wired capacities can't. Good actions are limited in what they can tell us about character. Two people may both consistently donate to charity; but one may donate solely to advance his own reputation (our hedge-fund manager), while the other donates to help those in need. Hard-wired capacities (reliable vision) are even more limited, since children and animals can have these capacities even though they have not yet, and may never, develop any values to speak of. For both of the above reasons, VGM restricts virtues to acquired qualities, whereas VGE allows for hard-wired and acquired qualities.

Are Good Motives Enough for VGM Virtues?

According to VGM, good motives are required for virtue. But are good motives, combined with good actions, enough for virtue? For instance, is consistently caring about the welfare of others and consistently doing what a benevolent person would do enough for the virtue of benevolence; or is something else also needed? Some advocates of VGM argue that we also need to reliably get good ends or effects. Others disagree, claiming that good motives and good actions are sufficient. Consequently, VGM also comes in two varieties: the motives-actions-and-ends variety; and the motives-actions-no-ends variety.

According to the motives-actions-and-ends variety, to be virtuous, one must have good motives, perform good actions, and be reliably successful at producing external goods. To illustrate, to have the virtue of benevolence, one must consistently care about the welfare of others, consistently do what a benevolent person would do, and consistently succeed in improving the welfare of others. If one cares about and tries to help others, but one's efforts go astray due to bad luck, then one does not have the virtue of benevolence. Likewise, if one cares about and tries to get truths, but has the bad luck of being in a deceptive environment, one does not have intellectual virtues. To have virtues, one must be effective.

In contrast, according to the motives-actions-no-ends variety, having good motives and performing good actions is required for being virtuous, but getting external goods is not. All that matters is whether one consistently wants and tries to get external goods. Suppose one consistently tries one's best to get truths but due to no fault of one's own has the bad luck of being in surroundings that are deceptive, or consistently tries one's best to help others but due to no fault of one's own has the bad luck of being surrounded by oppressors who prevent one's actions from hitting the mark. Arguably, this bad luck does not detract from the agent's character, since (presumably) she could not have foreseen it, and cannot be blamed for it. According to this variety of VGM, external success is not required for virtue.

Advocates of VGM

Though **Aristotle** employs VGE in books I and VI of *Nicomachean Ethics*, VGM is clearly the star of NE. In NE.II, he famously argues that a virtue is "a state of character concerned with choice, lying in a mean, the mean relative to us, this being determined by a rational principle and by that principle by which the man of practical wisdom would determine it" (NE.1106b36–1107a2). There are two features that identify this definition as an instance of VGM. First, Aristotle claims that a virtue is a "state of character"—an acquired character trait, rather than a natural faculty. He thinks that we can be praised for our virtues and blamed for our vices, but neither praised nor blamed for natural faculties, since the latter are not sufficiently under our control. Second, Aristotle claims that virtues are "concerned with choice." Specifically, he contends that one cannot have a virtue unless one "choose[s] the [relevant] acts, and choose[s] them for their own sakes" (NE.1105a31–32). In other words, to have the virtue of justice, it is not enough to simply perform just acts—to do what the just person would do. One must perform those acts for the right reasons: because one cares about and values justice, not because one cares about looking good. So, motives matter for virtue.

Does Aristotle think that ends also matter for virtue? To endorse the motives-actions-and-ends variety, he must think that virtue requires getting external goods. Let's look at his account of courage. In NE.III, he claims that "the man . . . who faces and who fears the right things and from the right motive, in the right way and at the right time . . . is brave; for the brave man feels and acts according to the merits of the case and in whatever way the rule directs" (NE.111b18–20). Aristotle clearly thinks that a number of things are required for the virtue of courage: the right motives; the right acts (one must face the right things); and the right emotions (one must fear the right things). Does he think courage also requires producing external goods? On his view, would Malala Yousafzai count as having the virtue of courage if she spoke out about education for girls, feared what she should (violence), and had the right motives (sex equality), *but* was ineffective due to the bad luck of living in a region controlled by the Taliban? Would Yousafzai need to make some actual progress toward her goals in order to count as having Aristotelian virtue? Philosophers disagree. Some think Aristotle's account of virtue does require the successful production of good external effects (Alfano 2013a; Russell 2012, p. 125). Others think Aristotle is confused about this point, and his account may not require the production of good external effects (Annas 2003).

Rosalind Hursthouse is a self-proclaimed "neo-Aristotelian" (1999, 8). She is a contemporary ethicist who bases her views about the moral virtues on Aristotle's views about the moral virtues. Like Aristotle, she endorses VGM. She thinks that moral virtues and vices are acquired character traits for which we can be praised and blamed. She also explicitly argues that moral virtues require choice. According to Hursthouse, "there is more to the possession of a virtue than being disposed to act in certain sorts of ways; at the very least one has to act in those ways for certain sorts of reasons" (1999, 11). This means that to have the virtue of honesty, a person must perform the right acts—she must tell the truth when she should. But she must also have the right motives—she must tell the truth because she thinks it is right to do so, not because she thinks she would get caught lying. Hursthouse and Aristotle agree that virtues require getting one's motives, acts, and emotions right. Does Hursthouse think that virtue also requires getting good ends or effects? Though Hursthouse could fall in the motives-actions-and-ends camp, she leans toward the motives-actions-no-ends camp.[6]

Linda Zagzebski is also a neo-Aristotelian. She is a contemporary epistemologist who bases her views about the *intellectual* virtues on Aristotle's views about the *moral* virtues. Zagzebski argues that, like Aristotle's moral virtues and vices, intellectual virtues and vices are also acquired character traits for which we can be praised and blamed. She thinks that the intellectual virtues are character traits such as open-mindedness, intellectual courage, and intellectual humility; they are not hard-wired capacities such as memory and vision. Zagzebski argues that both moral and intellectual virtues require the right motives; performing the right acts is not enough. For instance, to have the intellectual virtue of open-mindedness, one must do more than perform the right intellectual acts—one must do more than consider alternative ideas. One must also have the right intellectual motives—one must care about truth. So, the politician who considers alternative policies, but does so only to get re-elected, is not open-minded. His actions are those that an open-minded person would perform, but his motives are not those of the open-minded person. He is faking it.

Zagzebski, Hursthouse, and Aristotle agree that virtues require getting one's motives, acts, and emotions right. Zagzebski unambiguously argues that virtues also require reliable success in producing good effects. Having the right motives and emotions, and performing the right acts, is not enough for virtue, if one is ineffective. Accordingly, she argues that open-mindedness requires reliably getting true beliefs. If a person is in a deceptive environment, due to bad luck, and gets more false beliefs than true ones, then he isn't open-minded, even if his motives and actions are unassailable. In sum, Zagzebski (1996) thinks that a virtue is a "deep and enduring acquired excellence of a person, involving a characteristic motivation to produce a certain desired end and *reliable success* in bringing about that end" (p.137, my emphasis). Hence, Zagzebski is unambiguously in the motives-actions-and-ends camp.

Like Zagzebski, **James Montmarquet** is a contemporary epistemologist who bases his views about the intellectual virtues on Aristotle's views about the moral virtues. And, like Zagzebski, he thinks the intellectual virtues are acquired character traits that require getting one's motives, acts, and emotions right. But, unlike Zagzebski, Montmarquet is unambiguously in the motives-actions-no-ends camp. He argues that getting good ends or effects is not required for intellectual virtue. On his view, to have the intellectual virtue of open-mindedness, one must care about getting truths (one must have the right motives) and one must consider alternative ideas (one must do what an open-minded person would do). But one need not actually succeed in getting true beliefs. As Montmarquet (1993) puts the point, "truth-conduciveness cannot . . . be the distinctive mark of the epistemic virtues" (p. 20). On this account, if a person consistently cares about truth and consistently considers alternative ideas, she is open-minded. She need not end up with true beliefs. She will be open-minded even if, due to bad luck, she is in a deceptive environment and ends up with more false beliefs than true ones. In short, Montmarquet thinks that intellectual virtues require the right motives and the right acts, but do not require getting good ends or effects. One can be massively deceived and still be intellectually virtuous.

Michael Slote is a contemporary ethicist who clearly thinks that motives matter for virtue. Slote argues that to have virtues like benevolence and empathy, one must have the right motives. Specifically, one must strike a balance between caring about friends and family, caring about strangers, and caring about oneself. People who only care about themselves, or about their own friends and families, do not have virtuous motives. Slote joins Montmarquet in the motives-actions-no-ends camp. Like Montmarquet, he explicitly argues that virtue does not require producing good external effects. In *Morals from Motives* (2001), Slote envisions a person with "fully benevolent or caring motivation" who is, due to no fault of her own, "foiled in her aims," and ends up hurting the people she intends to help (p. 34). He further argues that this person "cannot be criticized for acting immorally, however badly things turn out" (p. 34). In short, Slote thinks that one can produce bad effects and still be morally virtuous. What matters is one's motive.[7]

Why Defend Pluralism about Virtue?

To recap, virtues are basically qualities that make us excellent people. VGE and VGM are both compatible with this basic account of virtue. VGE maintains that virtues require reliable success in getting good ends or effects, but do not require good motives. Here, virtues make us excellent people because having the virtues means that we will consistently produce goods—like true-beliefs and the welfare of others. In contrast, VGM claims that virtues require good motives, but may or may not require good ends or effects. Here, virtues make us excellent people because having the virtues means that we will consistently care about the welfare of others, about true beliefs, and so on. Though these two concepts are both compatible with our basic account of virtue, they are largely incompatible with each other (at least the motives-actions-no-ends variety of VGM is incompatible with VGE). Does this mean that we must choose between VGE and VGM? Does it mean that one of them is 'the real' concept of virtue, and the other is wrong?

I don't think we need to choose between VGE and VGM. I think both of these concepts are legitimate, and that neither is any more or less real than the other. To see why, let's consider two paradigms of virtue: Dr. Gregory House's open-mindedness, and Alice Paul's courage. Dr. House, the protagonist of the television series *House M.D.* (Fox, 2004–2012), is consistently open-minded. In nearly every episode, House and his team of doctors diagnose patients by considering alternatives. In fact, House is so reliant on this process that when his team abandons him, he asks the hospital's maintenance staff to suggest alternative diagnoses.

In the early twentieth century, Alice Paul risked her health and life to get women the right to vote in the United States. Paul was imprisoned, placed in solitary confinement, and force-fed. But she did not give up. Her courage was a crucial element in securing the 19th amendment, which enfranchised women. When we look at patently clear cases of virtue like these, we find that they have some important features in common. For instance, House's open-mindedness and Paul's courage are (1) acquired character traits that (2) involve performing right actions. They also (3) consistently produce goods, like suffrage and true beliefs about patients' diagnoses; and (4) involve good motives. Neither House nor Paul is motivated by money or fame: House cares about truth for its own sake, and Paul cares about women getting suffrage. Interestingly, theorists as diverse as Montmarquet, Sosa, and Zagzebski will all *agree* that House has virtue. Montmarquet will agree because House has an acquired character trait that involves good motives—he cares about truth for its own sake. Sosa will agree because House reliably gets true beliefs—he solves every case, save one or two. And, Zagzebski will agree for both of these reasons. Likewise, theorists as diverse as Slote, Driver, Plato, Aristotle, and Hursthouse will all *agree* that Paul has virtue. Slote will agree because Paul has an acquired character trait that involves good motives—Paul cares about women getting suffrage. Driver will agree because Paul reliably makes progress toward suffrage—she makes the world a better place for women. Arguably, Plato, Aristotle, and Hursthouse will agree for both of these reasons. What this shows is that when all of (1)–(4) obtain, our philosophers agree about virtue.

They disagree about virtue when some of (1)–(4) are missing. To illustrate, suppose there was a person, call him 'House-lite', who was exactly like House, except he didn't reliably get true beliefs about his patients' diagnoses. Suppose House-lite almost never gets the right diagnoses due to bad luck. Here, (3) is clearly missing. Accordingly, Sosa and Zagzebski would claim that House-lite is not virtuous; but Montmarquet would claim that he is. Alternatively, suppose there was a person, call her 'Paul-lite,' who was exactly like Paul, except she didn't have good motives—she only cared about personal fame and fortune. Here, (4) is missing. Consequently, Slote, Plato, and Aristotle would claim that Paul-lite is not virtuous, but Driver would claim that she is.

This shows that disagreements about virtue do not result from a lack of information. All of our philosophers agree that House and Paul satisfy (1)–(4), that House-lite is unreliable, and that Paul-lite has selfish motives. They aren't disputing the facts. Rather, their dispute is a result of the concept of virtue itself. The concept of virtue itself—recall our basic account of virtue—is vague or thin.[8] It tells us that virtues are excellences, but it does not determine which of conditions (1)–(4) are necessary for something's being an excellence. It allows any combination of (1)–(4) to be necessary. Something similar is true of our concept of sport. We all agree that, football (soccer in the United States), is a sport. After all, it is: (i) competitive; (ii) organized; (iii) entertaining; and involves (iv) teamwork and (v) physical skill. But what about golfing, running with a local club, or chess, each of which lacks some of (i)–(v)? Are they sports? Here, we are likely to disagree, depending on which of conditions (i)–(v) each of us favors. The point is that the concept of sport does not determine which of conditions (i)–(v) are necessary. The same is true of our concept of virtue.

Consequently, Slote's claim that good motives, rather than good effects, are required for virtue is no more legitimate than Driver's claim that it is good effects, rather than good motives, that are required. Slote has thickened the concept of virtue in one way; Driver has thickened it in a different way. Both of these ways of thickening the concept—both of these uses of 'virtue'—are legitimate. There is no single right way to fill in the concept of virtue, just as there is no single right way to fill in a sketch (Lynch 1998, p. 63). After all, one way to be an excellent person is to have good motives—to care about the welfare of others, or about truth. Another way to be an excellent person is to reliably get good ends or effects—to make the world better by producing well-being or true beliefs. Since there is no single right way to fill in the concept of virtue, it would be misguided to argue about which of VGE or VGM is 'the real' concept of virtue. Both concepts are legitimate ways to thicken our basic account of virtue. Both concepts succeed in identifying qualities that are virtues.

Still not convinced that we should be pluralists about virtue—not convinced that we need VGE? Many virtue ethicists would agree. VGM has been widely endorsed by contemporary virtue ethicists, but VGE has not.[9] In contemporary virtue theory, the popularity of VGE is restricted almost entirely to reliabilist accounts of virtue (like Sosa's) in epistemology. So, why *is* it important to recognize the legitimacy of VGE across both branches of virtue theory? What are the advantages of VGE, and why is it valuable? Briefly, VGE is valuable, and arguably a necessary piece of our pluralism, for two related reasons.

First, all of the philosophers above agree that it is good to have true beliefs, and to make the world a better place. All agree that such things matter in epistemology and ethics: they aren't the only things that matter, but they are clearly among the things that matter. VGE has the advantage of recognizing that the *qualities* which enable us to attain these goods are themselves excellent qualities—these qualities also matter; and they matter even if they don't involve good motives. These qualities matter precisely because, and insofar as, they enable us to attain (intrinsically valuable) goods. In short, they make us excellent because they enable us to get truths and knowledge, and to improve the welfare of other people and ourselves. And, since they make us excellent, they are one kind of virtue. To put the point differently, VGE recognizes that there is *something* excellent about any quality that produces such goods—even qualities that are hard-wired. Of course, we can't control which hard-wired capacities we possess, so we can't be praised for them; nor do they tell us anything about who we are as people or about what we value. Hard-wired capacities aren't excellent in these ways. But, they are still excellent insofar as they are instrumentally valuable—they get us things that matter. In this manner, VGE accounts for our intuition that there is, indeed, something excellent about being innately smart or innately pro-social. Though we have no control over whether we end up with these qualities, they are still excellent qualities because they get us important goods. VGE does justice to this intuition; VGM does not.

Second, VGE does justice to our intuition that luck plays an important role in whether we are virtuous or vicious. According to VGE, good luck in the way we are constituted (in which hard-wired capacities we have) and in our environments is enough to make us virtuous. Likewise, bad luck in the way we are constituted and in our environments is enough to render us vicious. In this manner, VGE accounts for our intuition that some people are just better situated for virtue than others, either because of luck in their native constitutions or because of the environments in which they happen to live. Analogously, some people are just better situated for sports than others—or for going to good schools, or for having access to education in the first place—either because of luck in their native constitutions or their environments. In epistemology, compare a person with 20/200 vision to one with 20/20 vision. Or, compare a person in a demon-world with a person in an ordinary world. In ethics, compare a person who is stuck in an oppressive and violent society with a person in a free and peaceful one. There is *something* defective about each of the former cases. Unaided, the person with 20/200 vision is likely to get a preponderance of false beliefs about her surroundings. The demon-victim is stuck in an environment that guarantees false beliefs, whatever her qualities.[10] The actions and intentions of the victim of oppression are perverted to produce harm. None of these people can control any of these factors, nor do these factors reveal anything about who they are as people. But, VGE does justice to the intuition that there is still something defective about these factors, even though they are due entirely to bad luck. They are defective insofar as they prevent us from getting important goods like truth and welfare. By comparison, we would be better off in ordinary and free environments with hard-wired capacities that are reliable and pro-social; we would be better off if we produced true beliefs and made the world a better place.

There is something liberating about this view. It allows for vice without blame. It recognizes that sometimes vice happens because of constitutional or environmental factors, over which we have no control.

We need VGE to account for the intuitions above. But, VGE can't do it alone. VGM is also a necessary piece of our pluralism because it does justice to different intuitions. For instance, we might well worry that being stuck in a demon-world or an oppressive society shouldn't reflect poorly on a person's moral and intellectual worth since it is not her fault. Here, the motives-actions-no-ends variety of VGM has the advantage. In insulating virtue from bad luck, the motives-actions-no-ends view can account for the intuition that producing bad effects, when one has *no* control over the effects produced, should not render one vicious. Relatedly, we might think it counter-intuitive to claim that hard-wired capacities can be vices—that a person with 20/200 vision has a vice. We might think that since such people can't be blamed for these qualities, they don't have vices. They are disabled or impaired, but not vicious. Here, too, VGM has the advantage. It does justice to the intuition that if we can't be praised or blamed for a quality, then it is not a virtue or vice. In sum, we should be pluralists about virtue because together, VGE and VGM do a better job of accounting for our competing intuitions than either would do on its own.[11]

Against Radical Pluralism

Liezl van Zyl

In "A Pluralist Theory of Virtue," Heather Battaly offers the following working definition of virtue: virtues are qualities that make one an excellent person. As it stands, this concept is vague or thin, insofar as it does not determine the necessary (or sufficient) conditions for something's counting as an excellence. In order to provide a more substantive account of what it is that makes a quality a virtue, she distinguishes the following ways in which the working definition can be fleshed out.

The first view, held by philosophers like Ernest Sosa and Julia Driver, is that virtues are qualities that reliably attain good ends or effects (VGE).[12] On this conception, something like good vision can count as a virtue, as it reliably produces true beliefs about one's environment. Likewise, benevolence is a virtue if it reliably enables its possessor to benefit others.

An alternative view is that virtues are character traits that involve acting from good motives (VGM). On this conception, what makes benevolence a virtue is that its possessor is characteristically motivated to aim at the good of others. Some advocates of this view, such as Michael Slote and James Montmarquet, claim that acting from good motives is sufficient for virtue. Against this, neo-Aristotelians such as Linda Zagzebski argue that in addition to good motivation, virtue also requires reliably producing good ends or effects.[13] Battaly refers to this position as the motives-actions-and-ends variety of VGM. For the sake of simplicity I will refer to it as a mixed conception of virtue, while reserving VGM for the view that good motivation is sufficient for virtue.

Battaly rejects all three of these positions and instead defends a pluralistic conception of virtue, according to which a trait is a virtue if and only if, and because, it reliably attains good ends *or* involves good motivation (or both). I will discuss two objections to Battaly's pluralism and argue instead for a more demanding or mixed conception of virtue.

Battaly's Radical Pluralism

Battaly arrives at a pluralistic definition of virtue in the following way. She notes that VGE is supported by two intuitions:

1. Things like true beliefs and well-being matter, and there is something excellent about any quality that produces such goods.
2. Luck in our environment is enough to render us virtuous or vicious. We can have virtue without being praiseworthy, and vice without being blameworthy.

VGM, in turn, is supported by a different set of intuitions:

3. Motives and attitudes are important because they tell us who we are as people and what we care about.
4. Virtues are praiseworthy and must therefore be (to a considerable extent) under our control. If we can't be praised or blamed for a quality, then it is not a virtue or vice.

Although Battaly accepts that VGE and VGM are incompatible, she nevertheless argues that it would be a mistake to choose between them; both are required for they each do justice to a different set of intuitions about what makes a quality a virtue. Accepting pluralism with respect to our concept of virtue is no more problematic, Battaly thinks, than being pluralists about our concept of what makes something a sport. We can agree that football is a sport insofar as it is competitive, organized, entertaining, involves teamwork, and requires physical skill, while disagreeing whether to extend the concept of sport to include, say, darts. Nothing in our thin concept of sport tells us which of the characteristic features of sports are necessary, or sufficient, for sportshood. Similarly, our thin concept of a virtue as an excellence is compatible with the two competing ways of fleshing out the details; one way to be an excellent person is to have good motives, and another is to reliably achieve good ends or effects.

To see what Battaly's pluralism looks like in the case of benevolence, consider the benevolence of a well-motivated and successful giver, John. John's benevolence is a character trait he has acquired (as opposed to being a naturally generous disposition) that involves performing acts of benevolence out of a genuine concern for the welfare of others, and the exercise of which reliably increases the well-being of others. John's benevolence is a clear-cut case of virtue; those with divergent intuitions on what makes a virtue an excellence can all agree that it constitutes a virtue. But what of the case of the selfish benefactor Alex, who is motivated to donate out of a desire to increase her public profile, or the ineffective benefactor Tessa, whose well-intentioned efforts at charity are often thwarted because of her clumsiness. Do we want to say that either, or both, of these people have the virtue of benevolence? According to Battaly's pluralistic account of virtue, both Alex and Tessa have the virtue of benevolence, albeit in different ways. Allowing that Alex is benevolent soothes the intuitions of those who think that effects are what matter most, while allowing that Tessa is benevolent accommodates the intuitions that Tessa's well-motivated acts are praiseworthy (despite their impotence), since they tell us something important about her, about what she truly cares about and values. By contrast, according to a demanding or mixed account of virtue, benevolence is a virtue because it involves good motivation (caring about the welfare of others) and also reliably brings about good results.

Before discussing possible objections to Battaly's position, a few comments are in order. First, I agree with Battaly on a fairly trivial point, namely that the traits that we consider to be *excellences* are a diverse lot, and include hard-wired traits such as good memory and being innately pro-social, as well as acquired character traits such as empathy and open-mindedness. These traits are excellences for different reasons, and it would be a mistake to assume they all have one thing in common. A point that we disagree about is whether all these excellences should be called virtues, where "virtue" is defined as traits that make one an excellent *person*. Battaly thinks that all excellences are virtues. By contrast, I maintain that a virtue is a *character trait*, a disposition to act and feel in certain ways. It is "a deep feature of the person" (Annas 2011, p. 9), "a property of the soul" (Zagzebski 1996, p. 102).[14] In this view, the virtues do not include natural capacities or hard-wired traits such as strength or speed, reliable memory or good vision. But this, again, is a fairly trivial point of disagreement, for I accept that certain hard-wired or natural capacities are valuable. I just don't think we should extend the concept of virtue to include these kinds of excellences. If we are going to include things like good memory and reliable eye-sight in the category of virtues, then there seems no good reason to exclude physical features (like long legs and upper-body strength) and practical skills (like baking or building).[15] And once we do so, we'll no doubt find that they don't share a common feature and hence that pluralism is the way to go.

In what follows, I will restrict my discussion to character traits, and the question I will consider is, "What makes a character trait a virtue?" Here a more interesting point of disagreement emerges, for Battaly's pluralism does not merely amount to the claim that there are different kinds of excellences; she also provides a pluralistic account of which character traits are virtues. For example, she considers Dr. House's open-mindedness and Alice Paul's courage. These are "paradigms of virtue," for they are acquired traits that reliably attain good effects and involve good motives. She then goes on to consider whether House-lite, who is exactly like House but fails to get the correct diagnoses, has the virtue of open-mindedness and whether Paul-lite, who is exactly like Paul but only cares about personal fame, is truly courageous. Battaly writes, "Slote's claim that good motives, rather than good effects, are required for virtue is no more legitimate than Driver's claim that it is good effects, rather than good motives, that are required" (p. 20). Her conclusion, then, is that both House and House-lite have the virtue of open-mindedness, and that both Paul and Paul-lite have the virtue of courage.

A final point to note is that Battaly's pluralism is far more radical than the more familiar version defended by Christine Swanton in *Virtue Ethics: A Pluralistic View*. Like Battaly, Swanton (2003) begins with a definition of virtue that is rather thin: "a good quality of character, more specifically a disposition to respond to, or acknowledge, items within its field or fields in an excellent or good enough way" (p. 19). In response to the question of what is involved in responding well to items in the field of a virtue, Swanton gives a pluralistic account. In the case of some virtues responding in a good enough way involves promoting or producing some kind of (external) benefit or value. In other cases, responding well requires loving someone in ways appropriate to various types of bonds, respecting an individual in virtue of her status as an elder or superior, appreciating the value of an artwork, or being open to using or handling appropriate things in appropriate ways (2003, p. 21). Swanton's account of virtue is pluralistic in the sense that it holds that there is no single feature shared by all virtues; instead, different character traits are virtues for different reasons. This kind of pluralism still allows for a very specific (and demanding) view of what is required in the case of a particular virtue. In the case of benevolence, for example, Swanton rejects the utilitarian view that it merely involves promoting the good of others. Instead, she claims that *as a virtue,* "benevolence requires the promotion of good with love in various manifestations, ranging from parental love to humane concern" (2003, p. 23). In contrast to Battaly, then, Swanton would deny that Alex and Tessa have the virtue of benevolence. She would also deny that House-lite and Paul-lite have the virtues of open-mindedness and courage respectively.

Objections to Radical Pluralism

Does anything important hinge on whether or not we call a specific character trait a virtue? As Battaly points out, there is a significant amount of agreement among different theorists about which traits are virtues. Advocates of VGE and VGM would agree that open-mindedness and courage, as displayed by Dr. House and Alice Paul respectively, are virtues. They disagree when some of the typical features of virtue are missing. For example, according to supporters of VGE Paul-lite, who fights for woman's suffrage for the sake of personal fame, has the virtue of courage, but according to supporters of VGM, she merely possesses a useful trait. And in the case of House-lite, who cares about truth just as much as House but never gets the right diagnoses, VGM theorists claim that he is virtuous whereas supporters of VGE say that although he is well-motivated he doesn't yet have open-mindedness as a virtue. Now, if this is all there is to the disagreement, then it seems reasonable for us to conclude, with Battaly, that there can be more than one legitimate conception of virtue, just as there is more than one legitimate conception of sport.

However, I think this is an over-hasty conclusion. There are at least two good reasons why it matters how we define virtue, and both of these reasons point us away from radical pluralism. The first is a theoretical reason: unlike "sport," the concept of virtue held by different theorists generally fits within, and lends support to, a broader normative (or, in the case of the intellectual virtues, epistemological) theory. Embracing a pluralistic definition of virtue is therefore not as straightforward as Battaly suggests. For example, Driver's instrumentalist account of virtue is part of a consequentialist theory of morality, and in order for her to accept a pluralistic account of virtue (and specifically, that a trait can be a virtue even if it does not characteristically produce good results) she would have to admit that her consequentialism is flawed. Likewise, for Slote to accept that a trait can be a virtue even if it doesn't involve good motivation, he would have to admit that there is something wrong with his agent-based virtue ethics. In effect, then, what Battaly is saying is that both Driver and Slote (as well as all other non-pluralists) are wrong about virtue, and wrong in ways that will have significant implications for their broader normative or epistemological theories.

In the same way, we will have to think very carefully about the kind of normative and epistemological theory that would accommodate Battaly's radical pluralism. One worry for Battaly's conception of virtue is just how it will go about accommodating all four intuitions listed above. Intuitions 1 and 3 express different views about what is important, and it is quite possible for one to hold both views simultaneously (which, as we'll see, is what supporters of the mixed view do). However, Intuitions 2 and 4 are not just different, they contradict each other and hence produce contradictory verdicts about whether a given character trait is a virtue. For example, in the case of the demon-world victim who, while striving for true belief, is stuck in an environment that guarantees false beliefs, Intuitions 1 and 2 support the claim that *there is something defective about such a person*, whereas 3 and 4 support the claim that *the person is not vicious because bad luck should not reflect poorly on one's intellectual worth*. In the case of benevolence the implication of Battaly's acceptance of all four intuitions is that Alex (the selfish benefactor) does have the virtue of benevolence (because she reliably brings about good results) *and also* that she does not have the virtue of benevolence (because she is not well-motivated). Battaly will therefore have to respond to the objection that her account violates the principle of mutual exclusivity.[16]

The second reason why it is important how we define virtue (and why we should be hesitant to accept a radically pluralistic account) is more practical and has to do with the fact that virtue, again unlike sport, is an evaluative concept. Finding a definition of sport is an interesting theoretical exercise, which might well improve our communications. In the end, however, whether chess is a game or a sport is not all that important; it certainly won't affect my decision as to whether to take it up. By contrast, and as Battaly herself points out, a virtue is a quality that makes one an excellent person. It is an evaluative concept, and an important one at that. Our interest in defining virtue is not driven simply by a need to group particular traits under the correct headings. Instead, we are interested in defining virtue for what, at least in part, are practical reasons: we want to know which character traits we should try to acquire for ourselves and instill in our children. We want to know what makes for a good or excellent human being because that is what we (should) want to become.

Defining virtue is therefore not at all like defining sport but a bit more like defining "a great serve" (in tennis). Presumably, serious tennis players are interested in what makes for a great serve because they want to acquire one. In contemplating this question they might start with a thin definition: "a great serve is one that wins points." But what is it about a player's serve that makes it win points? Possible answers include: power or speed, accuracy of placement, and topspin. Now, if we assume that each of these things is indeed important, then the obvious conclusion would be that a great serve must have all three features. A pluralistic view of a great serve seems clearly mistaken: a serve that has speed and spin but lacks accuracy is just not a great serve at all.

When we apply this line of reasoning to the definition of virtue we are led away from a pluralistic account and toward a more demanding conception. If, as Battaly claims, attaining ends or effects is important (Intuition 1) *and* being well-motivated is important (Intuition 3), then it would seem to follow that for a trait to be a virtue—an *excellence*—it must possess both these features, for the absence of either would constitute a defect. For example, Tessa's benevolence, which involves good motivation but a rather consistent failure to do much good, is not a virtue because there is something important missing. She might well be on her way to developing benevolence as a virtue, but she is not there yet; she still needs to acquire the skills needed for actually bringing about the good she aims at. Conversely, a trait that involves reliably achieving good results despite poor motivation is useful, and we should be pleased that some people have it, but the selfishly benevolent person is not an excellent human being—a role model—for there is something important missing: they do not care about the people they benefit.

The challenge for Battaly is therefore to show that each of these features (i.e., acting from good motivation and reliably attaining good ends) is so important as to be sufficient for virtue, but without it being the case that the absence of either of these features constitutes a defect which disqualifies the trait from being considered a virtue.

A Mixed Conception of Virtue

According to a mixed conception, a virtue is a character trait that involves acting from a good motive and reliably producing good effects. As Battaly notes, the paradigm cases of virtue, such as benevolence, courage, honesty, and open-mindedness typically involve both good motivation and reliably producing good effects. This does not necessarily support the mixed view, since advocates of both VGE and VGM can come up with plausible reasons why the paradigm virtues possess both these features. VGE theorists could argue that a poorly motivated agent is unlikely to reliably produce good effects. In the case of the selfish benefactor, for example, we might worry that she will stop giving when it is no longer profitable for her to do so. In this view, good motives (as part of a stable disposition) have instrumental value: they ensure that the benefactor will keep on giving. But good motives are not necessary for virtue because there are other ways to ensure reliability.[17] In turn, supporters of VGM believe that good motivation is what is truly important when judging character, but argue that it is doubtful whether someone who consistently fails to produce good results is truly well-motivated. In the case of the benevolent klutz, for example, one would expect that if she truly cared about the well-being of others, she would make the effort to acquire the knowledge and skills necessary to actually help them.[18] However, they would argue that where the failure to achieve good effects is not due to poor (or sufficiently good) motivation, it does not detract from a person's virtue.

What distinguishes the mixed conception from VGE and VGM is that it holds that good effects (or ends) and good motives are independent sources of value. Both are important in their own right. In this regard, it agrees with Battaly's pluralism. What distinguishes the mixed conception from Battaly's pluralism is that it holds that the absence of either of these features is always a defect that prevents a trait from being a virtue.

The mixed conception deals with the two sets of intuitions in the following way. First, concerning Intuition 1, it agrees that things like true beliefs and well-being matter, and therefore makes the production of good effects a requirement for virtue. However, it stops short of saying that producing good effects is sufficient for virtue status. It therefore rejects Intuition 2, namely that good or bad luck is enough to render us virtuous or vicious. The mixed conception accepts Intuition 3 and claims that good motives are necessary for virtue because the well-motivated person has a correct understanding or at least an appropriate attitude toward things. However, when it comes to Intuition 4, an important difficulty arises for the mixed conception. Given the rejection of Intuition 2, it would seem that the mixed conception will have to support Intuition 4, namely that a quality that is not under our control to a considerable extent cannot be a virtue or a vice. However, if the mixed conception claims that both good motivation and good effects are required for virtue, then it seems that whether or not a trait is a virtue can be entirely a matter of luck. To illustrate, consider Battaly's example of the person who lives in an oppressive society so that her kind-hearted acts fail to bring about good ends. In this case it is sheer bad luck that prevents her from having the virtue of benevolence.

The difficulty in making reliably producing good effects a requirement for virtue seems to be that it makes the account vulnerable to the problem of luck. Surely, we want to say that someone like Malala Yousafzai is genuinely courageous and generous without first waiting to see whether her campaign for girls' education is successful. Intuition 4 therefore appears to be correct: bad luck in the effects produced by a particular trait shouldn't reflect poorly on a person's virtue. Does this show that the mixed conception is flawed? Not necessarily. It is tempting to assume, as Battaly does, that Intuition 4 goes *against* making good effects a requirement for virtue. This, I believe, is a mistake, for one can consistently claim that what makes a given trait a virtue is that it produces good effects *in the typical case*, while accepting that a *particular* individual may possess that virtue even though, through sheer bad luck, she usually fails to attain her virtuous ends.

To see how the mixed view can deal with the problem of luck in consequences it is necessary to distinguish two reasons why we might be interested in formulating a conception of virtue. The first is a more general enquiry about types of character traits, namely that of deciding which traits to include on our list of virtues. Benevolence, courage, and wisdom clearly belong on the list, but it is more controversial whether competitiveness, obedience, humility, wit, and charm should be added to the list, and so it is thought that answering the question, "What is a virtue?"—or "What makes a trait a virtue?"—will help us with that. The second reason forms part of the more specific project, namely of deciding whether a specific individual is virtuous or has a given virtue. Does Tessa have the virtue of benevolence, given that her well-motivated actions usually fail to help others? Is Alex benevolent, given that she helps others for selfish reasons?

Now, the mixed conception of virtue is a response to the more general question, and it holds that for a trait to be a virtue it must involve good motivation and also reliably produce good ends and effects. Hence, what makes openmindedness a virtue is that it involves a certain motivational and attitudinal state and reliably produces true beliefs in typical cases. However, one can hold this view and still accept the intuition that luck is not enough to render a person virtuous or vicious. Intuition 4, which we want to support, pertains to the more specific question. An individual can appropriately be said to have the virtue of open-mindedness, even if through bad luck in her environment she fails to secure true beliefs. In such a case, we could say that she has the virtue, and is praiseworthy in this respect, but that it is unfortunate that she finds herself in circumstances where exercise of the virtue does not attain good ends.

Linda Zagzebski, whose conception of virtue Battaly discusses as an example of the mixed view, comes very close to accepting that bad luck in consequences does not affect a person's virtue. As Battaly notes, Zagzebski (1996) defines virtue as "a deep and enduring acquired excellence of a person, involving a characteristic motivation to produce a certain desired end and reliable success in bringing about that end" (p. 137). This definition is clearly an answer to the more general question of what makes a trait a virtue. She writes:

> [W]e would normally say that if the world as a whole were not better off for the presence of a given trait in individual persons in typical cases, we would simply not consider such a trait a virtue. We may assume, then, that nothing is a virtue unless it benefits both the possessor and others in the typical case. (p. 100)

However, when it comes to the specific question, Zagzebski claims that a trait can be considered a virtue in a *particular* case even if it is not beneficial to others. She uses the example of a compassionate but biased judge whose compassion for the victims of crime makes him even more unfair than he would have been without the compassion. Zagzebski maintains that compassion is still a virtue in the unfair judge, even though the world is worse off because he is compassionate than it would be if he lacked compassion, and the reason she gives for this is that his compassion makes his character closer to an admirable one and the world closer to a desirable one than either would be without the compassion. Hence Zagzebski (1996) claims that "virtue is related to good, not by invariably increasing ... goodness for the world, but by invariably making ... the world closer to a high level of desirability" (p. 101).

Zagzebski is also sympathetic to the view that bad luck should not detract from a person's virtue. For instance, she considers Montmarquet's claim that attaining good ends is not required for intellectual virtue. Montmarquet (1993) supports this view by pointing out that intellectual giants like Aristotle, Ptolemy, Galileo, and Einstein probably did not differ significantly in intellectual virtue, even though they differed in the truth of their ideas (p. 21). Zagzebski responds to this by accepting that these thinkers were equal in intellectual virtue, but she argues that it doesn't present a problem for the general claim that intellectual virtue is knowledge conducive. Rather, what this shows, she says, is that an individual needs both intellectual virtue and luck to obtain knowledge. Although traits such as open-mindedness and intellectual courage are virtues because they are knowledge conducive in typical cases, there may be specific cases in which bad luck prevents an intellectually virtuous person from obtaining knowledge (Zagzebski 1996, pp. 190–191).

It is clear, then, that Zagzebski allows that bad luck can sometimes prevent a virtuous person from attaining his virtuous ends. But is it possible (or appropriate) to say that an individual has the virtue of open-mindedness even if the trait is not truth conducive *in the long run* (or over the course of his life time)? Zagzebski considers the case of Joe, whose open-mindedness is not truth conducive due to simple bad luck. She argues that even if Joe's open-mindedness is not truth conducive *for him*, it is still a virtue and it is still a good thing for Joe to have that trait. However, she thinks that in the long run, and if we look at a large number of Joe's beliefs formed over time, "open-mindedness will be ultimately truth conducive, even for him." She concludes: "[I]t is true that an agent does not possess an intellectual virtue unless the trait as possessed by him is truth conducive in the long run, but there may be a period of time during which it is not truth conducive" (1996, p. 186).

In short, then, Zagzebski's conception of virtue is an example of the mixed view. Her response to the general question is that a virtue is a character trait that involves good motives and reliably attaining good ends in typical cases. Her response to the specific question echoes this response: for an *individual* to possess a virtue, he must have virtuous motivation and be reliably successful in achieving his virtuous end. However, it should be clear by now that there is a second version of the mixed view, which gives the same response to the general question, but when it comes to the specific question gives a slightly different response, namely that it is possible for an individual to possess a virtue and yet to fail to attain his virtuous end in the long run. This, I believe, is the view put forward by Rosalind Hursthouse.

Hursthouse responds to the specific question, whether a given individual is virtuous, in Part II of *On Virtue Ethics* (1999). Here she argues that possessing a virtue involves being a certain sort of person with a certain complex mindset, the most important aspect of which is the wholehearted acceptance of a certain range of considerations as reasons for action. Hursthouse also argues that a truly virtuous person will have the wisdom and skills required for effectively securing real benefits, but she accepts that a failure to achieve external effects because of bad luck in the environment does not detract from an individual's virtue. Presumably, this is why Battaly puts Hursthouse's view in the 'motives-actions-no-ends' camp.[19] I think this is a mistake. When it comes to the more general question of which character traits are virtues, Hursthouse gives a teleological account: a virtue is a character trait that benefits its possessor by enabling him or her to flourish or live well. In her view, cultivating the virtues is the only reliable bet for living well, but she accepts that a virtuous person might be unlucky and end up not achieving this end. Bad luck does not prevent such a person from being virtuous (1999, Chapter 8). Like Zagzebski's, Hursthouse's conception of virtue is an example of the mixed view: a virtue is a disposition to act, feel, and reason in certain ways, and what makes such a disposition a virtue rather than a vice is that it typically or characteristically (though not invariably) allows its possessor to attain good ends or effects. What Zagzebski and Hursthouse disagree about is whether a person's ultimate failure to achieve his virtuous end prevents us from saying that he has the virtue in question.

In summary, then, the advantage of adopting a mixed conception of virtue is that it takes seriously both of our intuitions about what is important when it comes to character. Intuition 1 states that things like true beliefs and happiness matter, and we value the traits that produce such goods. Intuition 3 states that motives and attitudes are important because they tell us who we are as people and what we care about. If good ends and good motives are both important, then it follows that the absence of either constitutes a defect, such that the character trait in question cannot be considered a virtue. A trait such as selfish benevolence, which involves producing good effects for entirely selfish reasons, should not be included on our list of virtues, and neither should a trait that does not reliably produce good effects in typical cases. However, it is possible to support a mixed conception while accepting Intuition 4, namely that bad luck in one's environment does not detract from one's virtue.

We are now in a position to see what kind of example might present a problem for the mixed view. It cannot simply be a case where one person's exercise of a trait, even over a lifetime, fails to achieve good ends or effects. Instead, it would have to be an example of a virtue (or a trait widely considered to be a virtue) that lacks either of these features but lacks it in such a way that the absence does not constitute a defect. One possible example is given by Julia Driver: the virtue of modesty. In Driver's view, modesty is a character trait that reliably produces good effects but does not involve a characteristic set of good motives, beliefs, or attitudes. Instead, the modest person suffers from a certain kind of ignorance; he underestimates his self-worth. Yet according to Driver, this ignorance or lack of good motivation does not constitute a defect because it is exactly through his ignorance that the modest person manages to produce the good effects. A person who tries to act modestly necessarily fails at it (Driver 2001, pp. 16–28).

I cannot here consider whether Driver's modesty presents a successful challenge for the mixed view. Suffice it to say, however, that even if we accept that modesty is a virtue (on the grounds that it typically produces good consequences and it lacks good motivation in such a way that the absence does not constitute a defect), and that we should therefore reject the mixed conception, it will still not lead us to embrace the kind of radical pluralism that

Battaly proposes. That is, we won't have to accept that reliably producing good effects is *always* sufficient for virtue. Instead, we would be led to the kind of pluralism proposed by Swanton, namely that some traits are virtues because they reliably produce good effects and involve good motivation, whereas other traits are virtues because they reliably produce good effects (and the absence of good motivation is not a defect) or because they involve good motivation (and the absence of good effects is not a defect). For example, we can still claim, as Swanton does, that what makes benevolence a virtue is that it possesses both features, and hence that the kind of benevolence that lacks either of these features is not true benevolence and therefore not a virtue (or at least, it remains to be shown that it is a virtue). This is quite different from Battaly's radical pluralism, according to which both selfish and ineffective benevolence are virtues.[20]

Study Questions

1. Do virtues require good motivations? Do they require producing good effects in the world? Do they require both good motivations and producing good effects in the world?
2. Is there more than one kind of virtue?
3. What are the advantages of pluralism (the view that there is more than one kind of virtue)? What are the disadvantages of pluralism?
4. What are the advantages of the mixed view of virtue? What are the disadvantages of the mixed view of virtue?
5. What criteria should we use to decide whether pluralism is right or wrong?
6. Does it make sense to rank-order alleged virtues rather than drawing a categorical distinction between them?

Notes

1. This paper is based on Chapter 1 of Battaly (forthcoming), which explores the concepts and views below in greater depth.
2. See Slote (2001, p. 26).
3. One need not have good motives *unless* the good ends or effects are themselves defined so as to require good motives. See the remarks on Plato and Aristotle below.
4. For further exploration of this concept of virtue, see Battaly (forthcoming, Chapter 2).
5. See Slote (2010, p. 134).
6. Hursthouse (1999, pp. 94–99).
7. For further exploration of this concept of virtue, see (Battaly forthcoming, Chapter 3).
8. Battaly (2001).
9. Driver's view is an outlier.
10. Sosa thinks that demon-victims have intellectual virtues relative to the ordinary world, but not relative to their demon-world.
11. I am grateful to Mark Alfano for comments on an earlier draft. I am deeply grateful to Liezl van Zyl for her response, and for helping me think through these matters.

12. As Battaly shows, there are important differences between the teleological and non-teleological versions of VGE. For the sake of simplicity, I will follow Battaly by grouping together all those theorists who believe that what makes a trait a virtue has to do with the fact that the world is somehow better off for the presence of this trait in individuals.
13. The demandingness of this view is what, according to Alfano (2012, 2013a), opens it up to empirical critique.
14. Julia Driver, who claims that what makes a trait a virtue is that it "systematically produces a preponderance of good", similarly accepts that "a virtue is a character trait" (2001, xvii).
15. See Zagzebski (1996, pp. 102–115) for a discussion of the distinction between virtues and natural capacities, as well as virtues and skills.
16. Battaly's pluralism is very similar to a position that Luke Russell defends, and which he refers to as "disjunctive minimalism." Russell notes that a possible objection to this view is that it violates the principle of mutual exclusivity. He uses the example of blind charity, which (we are to suppose) is intrinsically good (for it involves good motivation) but lowers overall happiness. Russell accepts that disjunctive minimalism implies that a single trait can be both a virtue and a vice, but he rejects—controversially—the principle of mutual exclusivity. See Russell (2007, pp. 482–483).
17. See Driver (2001, pp. 53–54).
18. See Slote (2001, p. 18).
19. See also Battaly (forthcoming, Chapter 3).
20. I am grateful to Heather Battaly and Paul Flood for their comments on earlier drafts, and to audience members at the Australasian Workshop in Moral Philosophy at the ANU Kioloa Coastal Campus where I presented an earlier version.

CHAPTER 2
Does Virtue Contribute to Flourishing?

Abstract

In his contribution, Robert Roberts starts by interrogating the question itself. Whose flourishing are we talking about here? Which virtues are we talking about (catalogues across time and place vary pretty widely)? What does it mean to flourish in the first place? From here, he argues that an account of flourishing depends on an account of human nature. If humans are one sort of thing, then "positive affective time-slice happiness" (basically, feeling as good as possible in as many moments of one's life as possible) constitutes flourishing. Some traits—those that tend to make their bearers or other people feel good—would then contribute causally to flourishing, and we might call them virtues. But if, as Roberts thinks, humans are instead entities with built-in purposes and a sense of meaning, then other, quite different traits—those that make their bearers' lives and those of others meaningful—would contribute not just causally but constitutively to flourishing, and we might call them instead virtues. (Battaly, above, would say that such virtues involve reliably attaining good ends.) Roberts points out that, regardless of the account of human nature one finds attractive, virtue will be only necessary and not sufficient for flourishing, since one can experience all kinds of terrible luck. He also admits that the correct account of human nature is a deeply contested notion, a point he illustrates by showing how a Christian perspective makes humility, compassion, and obedience virtues, whereas at least some secular perspectives make them all either neutral or vices. In her response, Nancy Snow largely agrees with Roberts's picture, but she worries that it's all-too-easy to mistake or misconstrue human nature—especially the natures of other humans over whom one has or might take power. For one thing, she shows that the species level hasn't always been the one at which the relevant distinctions were drawn. Historically, gender and race—intra-species distinctions—were highly relevant. She then points out that obedience and humility were prized in women and black slaves, and that this valuation was given intellectual and moral support by a (mistaken) conception of the nature of women and blacks. Rather than contributing causally or constitutively to their flourishing, this conception of their natures and the virtues that allegedly flowed from their natures undermined their material, psychological, and social well-being. She concludes by asking whether we similarly mistake the nature of children when we think that the virtues appropriate to them are outlandish hope (you can do anything if you try hard enough!), trustingness, and innocence that verges on ignorance.

How Virtue Contributes to Flourishing

Robert C. Roberts[1]

The question of our title raises several further questions. *Whose* flourishing is in view—that of the person who possesses the virtue, or that of people whose lives are affected by the person with the virtue? And the answer to that question might depend on *which* virtues are in question—temperance might be thought primarily to benefit its possessor (she's slim and healthy, and her marriage is intact), while justice benefits those who receive just treatment (her friends and associates can trust her to treat them right). But more fundamental than either of these questions is this one: what *is* flourishing, anyway? Is it just a preponderance of pleasure over discomfort? Is it the same as happiness? Is it reliably measured by sincere self-report, or can a person be flourishing more or less than she thinks she is? And if this is possible, *how* can a person be ignorant about her own flourishing? Is the concept of human flourishing tied to the concept of human nature, so that what we take flourishing to be will depend on what we think human beings are? And if what flourishing is depends on what human nature is, might this be a key to the relation between virtues and flourishing, so that to live virtuously just *is*, in some sense, to flourish, since virtues are a fundamental *way* of flourishing? This essay will attempt to answer the question of the title by proposing answers to these other questions. I begin with a discussion of flourishing.

Human Flourishing

Thinkers disagree about human flourishing, and that in two ways. First, they may have different conceptions of what *kind* of thing human flourishing is.

And second, even if they agree on what general kind of thing it is, the kind of thing they agree it to be may have rather starkly variant subspecies.

One answer to the question, "what is human flourishing?" that comes to mind is, "a human being is flourishing when, and only when, he or she is *happy*." But 'happiness' has more than one meaning. Consider *positive affective time-slice happiness*. We say, for example, "the Baylor students were very happy when the Lady Bears won the NCAA women's basketball championship, but were much less so when they returned, later in the evening, to preparing for tomorrow's history exam." Here, happiness is feeling good. Daniel Gilbert (2007) says,

> Emotional happiness ... is the feeling common to the feelings we have when we see our new granddaughter smile for the first time, receive word of a promotion, help a wayward tourist find the art museum, taste Belgian chocolate toward the back of our tongue, inhale the scent of our lover's shampoo, hear that song we used to like so much in high school but haven't heard in years, touch our cheek to kitten fur, cure cancer, or get a really good snootful of cocaine. (p. 30)

In this usage, 'happiness' refers to some particular time-slice: you can be happy one minute and unhappy the next. Gilbert's book offers an explanation why we human beings are so poor at foreseeing what will make us happy in this sense.

He also argues that positive affective time-slice is the primary sense of 'happiness.' He takes on a long and deep tradition in philosophy when he denies the legitimacy of a conception of happiness that ties it closely to virtue:

> For two thousand years philosophers have felt compelled to identify happiness with virtue because that is the sort of happiness they think we ought to want.... But if living one's life virtuously is a cause of happiness, it is not happiness itself, and it does us no good to obfuscate a discussion by calling both the cause and the consequence by the same name.... Happiness is a word that we generally use to indicate an experience and not the actions that give rise to it. Does it make any sense to say, 'After a day spent killing his parents, Frank was happy'? Indeed it does. We hope there never was such a person, but the sentence is grammatical, well formed, and easily understood. Frank is a sick puppy, but if he says he is happy and he looks happy, is there a principled reason to doubt him? ... Happiness refers to feelings, virtue refers to actions, and those actions can cause those feelings. (pp. 34–35)

Gilbert is off-target when he says that virtue refers to actions. Virtues are primarily attributes of persons, and only derivatively of actions. Emily performs generous actions because *she* is generous. And to say that she is generous is to say that you can depend on her, day in and day out, year in and year out, to tend to have generous thoughts, generous motives, generous emotions, and, yes, to perform generous actions. Her record may not be perfect, but a strong tendency is there if she has the virtue.

On a positive affective time-slice conception of happiness, Frank is happy if he feels good, and it's not inconceivable that he's in a state of euphoria now that he's killed his parents. So Frank is in a happy moment. But is he a happy *person*? And here, on this rather different concept of happiness—as an attribute of persons rather than moments in a person's experience—I think we'll find it very hard to conceive Frank as happy. So, using these two different concepts of happiness, it makes good grammatical sense to say, "Frank's happy to have killed his parents, but he is decidedly a very unhappy person." It would be silly to say that virtue is necessary for ever feeling good at all, but it seems quite possible that virtue is required for being a happy person. So this is the sense in which it might make sense to say that virtue is necessary to happiness.

To rule out the happiness of persons in favor of the happiness of moments (person-time-slices) is to adopt a controversial (to say the least) and revisionary concept of a person. Adult human persons have a strong bent to think of themselves and their fellow human beings as having a narrative in which they are a continuous (though no doubt changing) character. A person does not just live; he or she lives *a life*.

That life can be good or bad (good or bad *for the person himself*, as well as for his friends, family, and colleagues, and even the world—consider Gandhi and Hitler). When a person has a life that is good for himself as well as those around him, we may call that person happy. He is a happy person even if, at the moment, he's going through a hard time (let's say he's just been wrongly dismissed from a job that he really enjoyed, and is now unclear about what to do next). He's feeling "down." This is not a happy moment in his life, but that doesn't mean his life is not a happy one.

So what does it mean to have a happy life? Someone who thinks about happiness in the way Gilbert does might admit that lives can be happy as well as moments, but insist that a happy life is just one that has a preponderance of happy moments and is short on very *un*happy (distressed, painful) moments. In that case, he would still be right about positive affect time-slice happiness being the basic kind; it is the kind of happiness that a happy life is made of.

If a happy life is happy because and only because of its happy moments, then a person who sought to have a happy life would want to make maximal use of a machine that I will now imagine. (The following is a modification of Robert Nozick's thought experiment in Nozick 1974, pp. 42–45.) This machine stimulates pleasure centers in one's brain in such a way as to give one pleasure reminiscent of a cocaine high, but so that it does no damage and the experience is always utterly "fresh": you never get tired of it. You can be in ecstasy during your whole waking day, and continue (at a lower voltage) with ecstatic dreams through the night. When you're on the machine, you can't do anything else (work, write, play the piano, interact with other humans), and further, you don't want to; you're completely satisfied. You'll have to get off the machine every now and then to eat, get some exercise, and perform necessary bodily functions, but having once experienced it, you'll always be in a big hurry to get back on it. With such a routine, and given the bodily harmlessness of the machine's action, a person who was wealthy enough not to have to work could spend seventy, eighty, ninety, or a hundred years on the machine, thus having the "happiest" possible life of any human being in history. If you think that positive affective time-slice happiness is all that personal happiness is made of, you will choose life on the machine in preference to a life of meaningful work, worship, play, inquiry, adventure, good friendships, marriage and children and grandchildren.... Even if such activities are on balance affectively positive, they all carry their moments of frustration and discomfort. And, after all, on the affective time-slice view, what makes all of them attractive is just the degree to which they issue in positive feelings.

If you were a utilitarian confronted with the machine, you would wish *everybody* to spend their lives on the machine. The fulfillment of your wish would bring human life as we know it to a complete stop; and a compromise, in which we allow that maximum utility in the world would require almost everybody to spend most of their time *off* the machine, would be a regrettable practical fact. An Aristotelian—someone who thinks that life is fulfilled in characteristically human activities—will think that such regret is foolish. That is, it's based on an unwise conception of human life and well-being.

I propose that wise people would not choose to live their lives on such a machine, nor regret the practical impossibility of doing so, despite its vast superiority in terms of positive affective time-slice happiness. They would not regard it as a good human life, not even as assessed solely from the point of view of the one living the life. What might the wise say in favor of resisting the machine's allure? "Pleasure without meaning is empty" (they don't deny that it can be intense, and very attractive, even overwhelmingly so). "A life on the machine would be a selfish life." "It would not be a worthy life." Worthy of what?—"Worthy of a human being." These are some of the intuitions that a wise person is likely to feel, on contemplating a human life lived for the momentary pleasures of the happiness machine.

Let's try to go deeper into these intuitions. What do these wise people mean by 'meaning'? Why should a life be meaningful? Why isn't it enough that it be pleasant? And what does this talk of 'worthiness' come to? Why should a life be worthy? Again, isn't it enough that it be pleasant? Don't people who want worthiness want it just for the pleasure they derive from it? They have a taste for "worthiness," others have a taste for cocaine. Doesn't it all come down to pleasure in the end? People who think like Gilbert will say yes.

In my first quotation, Gilbert proposes nine examples of positive affective time-slice happiness:

1. Seeing our new granddaughter smile for the first time
2. Receiving word of a promotion
3. Helping a wayward tourist find the art museum
4. Tasting Belgian chocolate toward the back of our tongue
5. Inhaling the scent of our lover's shampoo
6. Hearing that song we used to like so much in high school but haven't heard in years
7. Touching our cheek to kitten fur
8. Curing cancer
9. Getting a really good snootful of cocaine

These are all pleasurable experiences for at least some people (interestingly, probably *not* for *all* people). Gilbert's point is that we speak of them all as "happy" experiences. But notice the diversity among these pleasures that comes out when we apply the words 'worthy' and 'meaningful' to them. The pleasure of seeing our new granddaughter smile for the first time is redolent of family life: an early sign of personality in this little one whose birth was so momentous and so difficult for our daughter, the loveliness of seeing a new generation emerge from our aging loins, or as my mother once said upon hearing of one of her children's pregnancies, "Oh, another child to love!" Compare this for meaning and worthiness with getting a really good snootful of cocaine. The snootful will be more intensely pleasurable, no doubt; but it's at the bottom of the chart for meaningfulness and human worth. Tasting Belgian chocolate toward the back of our tongue and touching our cheek to kitten fur belong on the more sensory and less personal end of the spectrum, in the direction of the snootful of cocaine, but both experiences may be "loaded" with the essentially historical pleasures of nostalgia, their associations with episodes of our distinctively human living. The taste of Belgian chocolate might carry us back to the junior year abroad that we spent in Brussels, where we had some hard experiences and did so much maturing and decided on our career in linguistics. Helping a wayward tourist and curing cancer are both heavy with the associations of our social life, our common threats and concerns, and our solidarity in a context of friends and neighbors and fellow human beings. And the person who takes special pleasure in helping another, or in ridding someone of a life-threatening disease, is a person to whom we attribute virtues like generosity and compassion. Without some such moral disposition, we won't get much of a time-slice buzz out of helping others. But on a positive affect time-slice conception of happiness, pleasure is pleasure, whether it comes from virtuous roots in family life, from the pursuit of deep and interesting questions, from actions of generosity and justice, or a snootful of cocaine.

Gilbert puts down the long classic tradition that associates happiness with virtue by saying that "philosophers have felt compelled to identify happiness with virtue because that is the sort of happiness they think we ought to want." It just wouldn't be right for a moral creep to have genuine human happiness; therefore, when a scumbag seems happy, it can't really be so (says Gilbert say the philosophers). Gilbert is right that the philosophers he has in mind think we *ought* to want a kind of happiness that involves and presupposes our integrity as persons, and our preferring things that are noble and good, rather than merely the joys of our time-slices. But on the deeper conceptions (Plato, Aristotle, Augustine), such person-happiness is not just what we ought to want, but also what we *do* want, even when we don't know we want it. The reason is that these philosophers think we are by nature persons, and thus cannot help but desire happiness as full personal well-being.

Charles Taylor (1985, pp. 15–45) distinguishes two ways that we make evaluations. In *weak evaluation* we express our preferences: for example, in painting our kitchen we might prefer one shade of yellow to another. We might justify our choice "objectively" by reference to how the preferred color looks against the woodwork, but ultimately the choice is just a matter of our tastes or preferences. We don't insist that such an evaluation be objectively "true." It is enough that we like *this* and we dislike *that*. In *strong evaluation*, by contrast, we suppose that there is a truth of the matter. When we talk about people having inherent rights, or about human dignity, or about giving an accused person a fair trial, we are much less inclined to admit that our evaluation is just a matter of taste. (We don't say, "OK, I have a taste for justice, but you prefer injustice. Now can't we just get along?") Here we tend to think that justice being good and injustice bad is not a matter of anybody's preference. It is "written into the very nature of things."

But science might dissuade us from this. It might seem to tell us that even our conceptions of human dignity and fairness and rights are merely products of evolution, and therefore merely "preferences" of our species, with no deeper truth backing them up. In this way, strong evaluation could be eliminated; all evaluation would be weak: just the evolutionarily determined preferences of one species or another. Because of our history, we might have a "hangover" of feeling the force of strong evaluation in some matters (such as justice and rights and our belief in the "nobility" of virtues), but the more deeply we assimilate the scientific thinking, the more comfortable we become with reducing all evaluation to weak evaluation.

Gilbert is typical of mainline contemporary psychology, which fundamentally fails to see a moral order in the *universe*. Instead, whatever "moral order" there is, according to such science, is secondary to gene replication (that is, it originates purely in the service of gene replication and remains just a product of that process) and part of an ultimately non-moral view of human development and functioning. The difficulty with such reduction, from a human point of view, is that it constitutes a debunking of morality that undermines it in anyone who fully appreciates the doctrine (or it creates a kind of schizophrenic doublethink).

By way of concluding this section, I offer two general comments on the positive affect time-slice conception of happiness. First, a time-slice conception of happiness is in tension with the fact that people are historical beings; they live (endure) in time, and identify themselves in terms of the narrative of their lives. If you have a life, you are more than a time-slice, and more than a bunch of time-slices all in a row, one after another. And you may want happiness, not just as a positive affect in the present and in the future, but as the well-being of a life. If happiness is a property of persons insofar as they have lives, then a time-slice conception of happiness is not what mature people are looking for in the way of happiness.

Here's the second comment. Heretofore I've said nothing about the place of negative affect in human happiness. We do tend to associate happiness with pleasant, as opposed to unpleasant, affect. The "positive psychology" movement of Martin Seligman and his colleagues stresses positive affect virtually to the exclusion of negative affect (for example, Seligman 2002; but see pp. 56–57). But if we think (as the positive psychologists do) that being well-formed as persons is a necessary condition for deep happiness, then we must admit that distressing emotions come with the territory. Consider some virtues. To be a *just* person is to care that justice be done, and to care about doing it oneself. But to care about it is to be vulnerable to distress when injustice is rampant or entrenched; it is to be subject to frustrations when one's best efforts are less than successful. *Compassion* involves caring about people who are suffering—wishing that they not suffer. It can lead to rejoicing when one's efforts to relieve suffering are successful, but equally it is characterized by distress at the suffering, and frustration when one's best efforts are blocked. *Self-control* is by nature directed at one's own inclinations and urges that need to be held in check for the sake of some good, and this checking of inclination is often unpleasant. *Love* for another involves rejoicing in the other's blessings and successes, but it will also involve disappointment when the other's projects fail and grief if the loved one is taken away. So if the happy life requires being a fully formed person, and being a fully formed person requires the virtues, then the happy life, almost of necessity, involves negative, as well as positive, affect.

The question of our title is not whether virtue is necessary to happiness, but about the easier question whether virtue is necessary to flourishing. In this first section, I've examined the concept of happiness as a possible explanation of the concept of flourishing. Some people may say that flourishing, for a human being, is just the same thing as being happy. But the notion of flourishing is a more biologically toned concept than happiness. The name of a biological species is usually in the background when we speak of flourishing. Thus flourishing is flourishing as ... where what follows the 'as' is the name of a species. To flourish as a tree is quite different from flourishing as a rabbit, and both are quite different from flourishing as a human being. We've looked at two concepts of happiness as possible explanations of what flourishing is for a human being. One is a subjective time-slice positive affect conception, and it seems pretty obvious that a person could have quite a lot of happiness in this sense and not be flourishing as a human being. One can imagine such a person being vicious and/or mentally ill like Frank who killed his parents, high on drugs or hooked up to our imagined pleasure machine for long periods, and none of these is compatible with human flourishing.

The deeper conception of human happiness, in which happiness depends on virtuous functioning and is compatible with considerable negative affect, is much more promising as a candidate for explaining human flourishing. Indeed, since virtues are classically defined as qualities that make a species-member properly functioning according to its kind, we might think that living virtuously is identical with flourishing. This is not quite right, since the world needs to cooperate for a human being to function properly: you have to have enough food and other physical resources, and some fairly virtuous fellow human beings to interact with. But we can say that virtue is *necessary* for human flourishing, and so we will have answered an even stronger question than our title asks. This answer raises another of our initial questions: *which* virtues promote, or are necessary for, human flourishing?

Human Virtues

Let us suppose that human virtues are qualities of well-being for human beings. They are, as Plato and Aristotle thought, aspects of moral and psychic health. This supposition will not contain much information, however, unless we know which of the possible traits of human beings are the virtues. Any answer to this question is controversial. Moral traditions, and the philosophers and theologians who represent them, have proposed many different lists of virtues. These lists often overlap to some extent, but often, too, they advocate different traits as indicative of psychic health, and give conflicting verdicts on particular traits.

For example, humility is a central virtue in the Christian outlook (see Philippians 2.3–11, John 13.1–20), but is entirely missing from Aristotle's account of virtues, and Aristotle might even regard humility as a vice. Indeed, it is almost absent in Plato as well. At the one point where Plato seems clearly to endorse it (*Laws* 4.716a–b; for a nice discussion, see Pinsent 2012, pp. 248–250), his justification is one that Aristotle is likely to reject: that we all have need of someone to control and lead us, and that humility is necessary for us to be susceptible to such control and leading. In apparent opposition, Aristotle stresses the self-sufficiency of the most fully mature human beings. The stress on self-sufficiency is most evident in Aristotle's account of the virtue of magnanimity or greatness of soul, where he tells us that the great-souled man tries to forget ways in which he is dependent on others, and likes to remember the ways others are dependent on him (Aristotle 1980, 4.3, 1124b10–19; also see 10.7, 1177a27–35; but see his discussion of friendship in Book 8 and 9). Thus he is strongly disinclined to be grateful—another virtue that is prominent in the New Testament (I Thessalonians 5.18, Colossians 3.17).

On the supposition that virtues are traits that make for a properly functioning, flourishing human life, it seems plausible that such differences of opinion about which traits are virtues can be traced to different conceptions of what sort of thing a human being is. As Socrates asks, in defense of leaving other less important or vexing questions to the side, "Am I a beast more complicated and savage than Typhon, or am I a tamer, simpler animal with a share in a divine and gentle nature?" (*Phaedrus* 230a). On the answer to that question will turn the all-important issue about how to live, and how to be an exemplary specimen of our human kind. Now I want to defend the thesis that what flourishing is depends on which virtues you think are the human ones, and that this in turn will depend on what you think a human being is. I will focus on two examples: the virtues of *compassion* and *obedience*. If I am right that difference of opinion about which traits are virtues goes back to differences about what human beings are, and also that virtues are traits of flourishing human beings, it will follow that we can agree on what it is to flourish only if we agree on what human beings are.

Compassion

Martha Nussbaum (2001) comments:

> Compassion is controversial. For about twenty-five hundred years it has found both ardent defenders, who consider it to be the bedrock of the ethical life, and equally determined opponents, who denounce it as 'irrational' and a bad guide to action. (p. 354)

(I am indebted, in this subsection, to Nussbaum's discussion, pp. 354–400, though not everything I say here agrees with her.) What is compassion? Concepts of compassion as a purported virtue will no doubt differ, depending on the particular way that a moral tradition conceives of human beings and of the world in which we live. Some will think it virtuous to feel compassion for a sufferer only if that sufferer is not responsible for his or her suffering (Nussbaum 2001, pp. 311–315; see Aristotle 1926, 2.8, 1385b14), but others will think that compassion can be legitimate even where the sufferer is to blame (Luke 15.11–32, especially 21–22; the heavy stress on forgiveness here and throughout the New Testament seems to account for the lack of the innocence condition that is found in Aristotle and the tragedians). Some will think that compassion always involves construing oneself as vulnerable to the kind of suffering that one laments in the sufferer (see Nussbaum 2001, 315–21; Aristotle 1926, 1385b15), and others that such self-reference is neither necessary nor ideal (see Wolterstorff 2008, p. 218 note). But some marks of compassion will straddle the boundaries between the traditions. For example, the virtue of compassion is a disposition to feel discomfort about the suffering or deficiency of a fellow creature and some motivation to come to his or her aid, to relieve the suffering or alleviate the deficiency.

Aristotle does not include compassion among the virtues he treats in *Nicomachean Ethics*, though he gives no indication of thinking it vicious, either. He makes it a necessary condition of genuine compassion that the one who feels it construe himself as vulnerable to the suffering or weakness that he compassionates in the other, but for Aristotle this self-reference of the attitude does not seem to make it self-serving in the way that Friedrich Nietzsche (1881/1997, section 133) does in the following:

> An accident which happens to another offends us: it would make us aware of our impotence, and perhaps of our cowardice, if we did not go to assist him. Or it brings with it in itself a diminution of our honour in the eyes of others or in our own eyes. Or an accident and suffering incurred by another constitutes a signpost to some danger to us; and it can have painful effect upon us simply as a token of human vulnerability and fragility in general. We repel this kind of pain and offence and requite it through an act of pity; it may contain a subtle self-defense or even a piece of revenge. That at bottom we are thinking very strong of ourselves can be divined from the decision we arrive at in every case in which we *can* avoid the sight of the person suffering, perishing or complain: we decide *not* to do so if we can present ourselves as the more powerful and as a helper, if we are certain of applause, if we want to feel how fortunate we are in contrast, or hope that the sight will relieve our boredom.

As usual, Nietzsche puts his finger on what is of dubious commendation in human conduct. But what he so astutely describes here is not real, virtuous compassion—he himself says in the context that it is what we *erroneously* call compassion—but debased forms of it, false imitations of compassion. A Christian, or someone else who believes that compassion is an aspect of the mature and good human being's character, does not take compassion as a strategy for confirming our power over others. It is not a tactic for getting honor or avoiding dishonor in the eyes of others. It is not a defense against our own vulnerability, or revenge against those self-admiring people who would dominate us and make us feel small. It is not a device for getting applause from observers, or relieving our boredom. Such motivations are no doubt common among us, but they are not what compassion is. It is true that we're usually not entirely absent from a sense of ourselves when feeling genuine compassion. We might, for example, be reminded of a time when we were in similar trouble. While our selves may be dimly in the background of our view of the sufferer, still, when we are really exhibiting compassion we are not at bottom thinking very strongly of ourselves; our mind is on the other and *his* suffering and how to give *him* respite. We are pained at *his* suffering and want it to be alleviated for the sake of *his* comfort. (Even people whose compassion is not very mature will feel a compassion for their own children that cannot be explained in anything like the egoistic terms that Nietzsche proposes.) So in this passage, Nietzsche does not really object to *compassion*, but to a degenerate parody of it. Defenders of compassion will agree with him in deploring the self-deception that he deplores. Yet Nietzsche is, no doubt, an enemy of compassion. So how would the *real* Nietzsche object to *real* compassion?

Compassion is a kind of emotional solidarity or identification with those who are down, with the weak and unglorious. It is a kind of love of those who are in trouble, a caring about them and a wishing them well. But the best and most admirable human beings are for Nietzsche essentially self-sufficient, self-glorifying self-creators. For him, real compassion is a corrupt state of character because it takes seriously human weakness and passivity and need of help. Compassion says, as it were, that such neediness is a normal human state, and in this way its advocates are committed to a provisional pessimism. (I say provisional because whether the outlook is ultimately pessimistic will depend on what other virtues are in the outlook; for example, the outlook might include the virtue of hope.) To the compassionate person such neediness is not demeaning, embarrassing, or shameful, even though it calls out for alleviation—alleviation by *help* from someone. Such neediness is normal for humanity. Nietzsche cannot accept this picture of humanity in its weakness. For him, true humanity is god-like in a way that excludes need, and thus excludes the kind of identification with need that compassionate feeling and action are. Neediness is decadence, and so is taking seriously the neediness of others.

The way compassion "normalizes" need as a general condition of humanity may also explain why Aristotle does not include it among the virtues that he discusses in his ethics, despite giving what looks like a sympathetic view of it in his *Rhetoric*. For, as I have noted, Aristotle, like Nietzsche, makes self-sufficiency a feature of essential (best potential) humanity, though he does so less stridently than Nietzsche. Nussbaum points out that the ancient Stoics also see human beings as god-like in their essential nature, so that, just as self-pity for various temporal set-backs and sufferings is unworthy of human dignity, so too, to feel compassion for others in their supposed troubles is actually an insult to their humanity. Immanuel Kant takes a similar view.

The trait of compassion that some regard as a state of human excellence and spiritual health and maturity and proper functioning, others regard as corruption, disease, and decadence. The difference between these camps derives ultimately from a difference of opinion about what human beings essentially are: are they essentially self-sufficient, so that neediness, and seriousness about neediness, are always deficiency or concession to deficiency? Or is neediness normal for human beings, so that acknowledgment of our own and others' needs is perfectly compatible with the highest human excellence, and indeed must be incorporated into that excellence? On the answers to this question turns the long controversy about the status of compassion as a virtue.

Compassion is a case of a determinate and particular trait that is considered a virtue by some and a vice by others; even where agreement can be reached on what compassion is, one group takes it to be an aspect of human flourishing and the other considers the same trait an aspect of human corruption.

Obedience

The way moral outlooks divide on human nature, and especially on the issue of autonomy versus dependency, is even clearer in the case of the virtue of obedience. As a virtue, obedience is a disposition to respond to the known will of an authoritative other by willing what the other wills because the other wills it by his authority. It does not rule out willing the same thing for other reasons (say, one's insight into the rationality of willing the projected action or state of affairs), though it does not require this, either. That is, the authoritative will of the other may be the sole reason for which the subject wills what he wills and thus performs what the other wills that he perform. It is a responsiveness of a subordinate will to the authoritative one. This responsiveness constitutes a personal relationship with the authoritative other, namely one that we might call "submission"; it is an honoring of the authoritative one, a show of respect for him. As Thomas Aquinas notes, "the virtue of obedience, whereby we contemn our own will for God's sake, is more praiseworthy than the other moral virtues, which contemn other goods for the sake of God" (Aquinas 1947, 2–2, 104 art. 3, *responsio*).

Obedience is a virtue, of course, only if there actually is an authoritative will to respond to in this way. People who think that God does not exist or that God does not have a will for human lives will not think that obedience is a virtue. Also, they may think that human practical rationality is such that any attitude of obedience like the one I have described is a corruption of it or a failure to be mature. It would be the Kantian vice of "heteronomy." (They may admit that obedience is a "virtue" in children, but not a virtue in adults.) On the other hand, if we are, as Christians and other theists think, creatures of a God who has a will for our lives, then obedience will be a central feature of the moral life and a crucial aspect of human flourishing.

Another condition on obedience's being a virtue is that the authority to whom submission is given be genuinely authoritative in the matter at hand (that is, in whatever he or she is commanding, and toward the person of whom she is commanding it). The famous obedience experiments conducted by Stanley Milgram (1974) showed that a surprisingly large number of subjects were willing to obey an apparent order by an "authoritative" experimenter to administer life-threatening electrical shocks to another human being. An adherent of a moral outlook that endorses obedience to genuine authority will think that these experimental subjects showed a deficiency in the *virtue* of obedience, inasmuch as they were insufficiently discriminating about the authority that they obeyed. The virtuously obedient will have the practical wisdom to distinguish a commander who has genuine authority to demand a given kind of action of them from mere pretenders to such authority. In retrospect, it seems quite stupid for someone to think that he ought to administer a dangerous shock to someone, just because an experimenter whom he doesn't know tells him to do so.

Conclusion

I have offered some answers to questions raised by our main question, whether virtue contributes to flourishing. In answer to the question whose flourishing is in view, the distinction between self-regarding and others-regarding virtues is not a helpful one for our question if virtues are all, as *virtues*, fulfillments of our human nature and thus dispositions to function well as human beings, to be psychically healthy and thus to flourish. Temperance, a so-called self-regarding virtue, is no more a fulfillment of our nature than justice, a so-called others-regarding virtue. This seems especially obvious if human beings are essentially social creatures, as most moral outlooks hold. People who are functioning properly as persons benefit both themselves and people whose lives intersect theirs. To the question what flourishing is, after all, I've proposed that it is happiness, but in doing so I have rejected the popular view that happiness comes in time-slices of positive affect. Happiness is a characteristic of a life, and a life has a narrative and is thus more than a collection of time-slices. Furthermore, negative affect can be as indicative of flourishing as positive affect. Happiness involves caring about things that are genuinely important, and given the sometimes frustrating character of the world we inhabit, negative affect will be inevitable for a person who is living well and thus flourishing.

I have argued that, while virtues contribute to flourishing because virtuous living is the most important aspect of human flourishing, this truth is not very informative about what human flourishing is, because it is controversial which traits are virtues. The identity of the virtues depends on what basic human nature is, and what kind of universe we live in. I have argued that what kind of life is normatively characteristic (as contrasted with statistically characteristic) is deeply contested. I don't say, "essentially contested," because I don't want to rule out the possibility of resolution, and I don't say merely, "contested," because I want to suggest that, while resolution of the differences of opinion might be resolvable, there is no historical precedent for a general resolution, so that any possible resolution is somewhere in the (distant) future. I have cited the controversial status of such traits as compassion, obedience, and humility.

So on the account of flourishing and happiness that I have proposed, people are not necessarily the best judges of their own flourishing. For example, if we human beings are creatures of a personal God who has a will for how we live, as Christians think, then a person who exemplifies the utmost in Kantian autonomy will not be flourishing as she might be if atheism is correct. And if atheism is correct, then Christians are wrong about what human happiness is. What flourishing is depends on what human nature is. So happiness is not very well measured by sincere self-report. It is also true that, even if a person has the correct view about human nature and the nature of the universe, he or she may be a poor judge of his or her own functioning: the person may be functioning better or worse, and thus may be flourishing more or less, than he or she thinks. Virtues also govern people's sensitivity to their flourishing; we may deceive ourselves about our true level of happiness, or be ruthlessly honest about it.

Virtue and Oppression

Nancy E. Snow

Does Virtue Contribute to Flourishing?: Yes and No

The premise of this volume is to pit two thinkers against each other so that each offers a different view on a controversial question. Yet there is little with which to disagree in Robert Roberts' elegant and insightful discussion of whether virtue contributes to flourishing. Clearly, virtue does contribute to flourishing in deep and significant ways, as Roberts points out. He begins with a persuasive critique of psychologist Daniel Gilbert's "time-slice" conception of happiness, according to which our long-term happiness consists in aggregated moments of 'feeling good' over time. Roberts argues that this is not what flourishing is. Instead, flourishing requires a life of virtue, and many of those virtues are social in nature. Which traits count as virtues, and what flourishing is, he contends, depends upon what human nature is, and understandings of these concepts differ.

I think all of this is true and important. Yet pitfalls lurk in the story of virtue, flourishing, and human nature. To be sure, Roberts identifies some of them. He is admirably critical of how some philosophers, such as Nietzsche and Aristotle, disdain or exclude some traits, such as compassion and humility, from counting as virtues, and offers diagnoses of why they take the perspectives they do. Nietzsche thinks humanity contains within it god-like elements, and Aristotle prizes self-sufficiency. Thus they see the perfection of human nature as consisting in a certain kind of strength and self-reliant independence, according to which recognition of suffering or weakness has little or no place.

However, there are deeper flaws than Roberts notes in many, if not most, of Western philosophical and theological understandings of human nature, flourishing, and virtue.[2] Starting with the ancient Greeks and continuing throughout most of the Western intellectual tradition, philosophers and theologians have thought that human nature applied most fully and completely only to male citizens or male property-owners. In other words, the conceptions of human nature, virtue, and flourishing to which Roberts refers in his discussion of Western philosophical thought were not universally applied. Today, it is primarily in virtue of his or her rational capacities that a person is thought capable of developing virtue and living a flourishing life. Men and women are regarded as equal in their rational capacities, and thus, as equally capable of having the same virtues and flourishing in roughly the same or similar ways. But this is a relatively recent development. In the historical record, there is robust evidence that women and slaves were thought to be inherently less rational than men, and thus incapable of being virtuous or flourishing in the same fully fledged way as men. Some virtues, such as the ability to command, were thought the exclusive province of men, and neither accessible to nor appropriate for women and slaves.

This has not only been an unfortunate blight in Western intellectual history, but has also had negative practical consequences. Unequal conceptions of the natures of women and men and what constitutes their flourishing have led to the misuse of exhortations and admonitions about virtue to oppress women. Similarly, during the antebellum period of United States history, talk of virtue was used in the American South to oppress black slaves. These examples constitute cases in which women and slaves might have been better judges of their own flourishing than others, especially when those others were people who claimed superiority in the pecking order and were advantaged by maintaining their higher rank.[3] Roberts remarks that "... people are not necessarily the best judges of their own flourishing" (p. 49). The record examined here shows that at times, we have good reason to be cautious about claims that people aren't the best judges.[4]

In the next two sections of this essay, I discuss ways in which conceptions of human nature and flourishing, as well as exhortations to be virtuous, have not been factors in the actual flourishing of women and African-American slaves, but instead, have contributed to their oppression.[5] The theme connecting these sections is that philosophers and others have been mistaken in their views, and have contributed to harm as a result. I end with observations about our conceptions of the nature, flourishing, and virtues of children—a group to which virtue ethicists have as yet paid scant attention.[6] I urge that we examine more closely our assumptions about children, in order not to repeat past errors.

Women

Aristotle's ideas have always been of key importance in the history of philosophy, and his virtue ethics is very much in vogue in philosophy today. Yet parts of his view have had to be jettisoned to ensure gender equality. For example, in the *History of Animals*, he claims, "The fact is, the nature of man is the most rounded off and complete, and consequently in man, the qualities or capacities, ... are found in their perfection" (608b6–8). In the *Generation of Animals*, he asserts that a female is a deformed, infertile male.[7] And in the *Politics*, he contends that "... the slave has no deliberative faculty at all; the woman has, but it is without authority; and the child has it, but it is immature. So it must necessarily be supposed to be with the moral virtues also; all should partake of them, but only in such manner and degree as is required by each for the fulfillment of his duty" (1260a8–17).

It is not immediately obvious why the deliberative faculty of the woman is without authority, but surely this has something to do with her (allegedly) inferior biological nature. The same discussion in the *Generation of Animals* that labels the female as deformed and infertile also associates her with an array of other undesirable qualities: such as being passive, cold, and aligned with privation and matter. The *History of Animals* passage goes on to attribute to women certain negatively valenced emotions and properties: compassion (here not prized by Aristotle), jealousy, hopelessness, tearfulness, despondency, deceptiveness, and the inclination to scold and strike, to name a few (608b8–14). Women's inferior natures are apparently evidenced by their lack of deliberative rationality and proneness to excessive and negative emotions. This theme has resonated through most of Western intellectual history.

One more quote from the *Politics* directly addresses the difference in men's and women's virtues: "... the temperance of a man and of a woman, or the courage and justice of a man and a woman, are not, as Socrates maintained, the same: the courage of a man is shown in commanding: that of a woman in obeying. And this holds of all other virtues" (1260a20–24). In satisfying the desires of men and obeying their commands, women are seen to fulfill their own natures and thereby to flourish. Certain traits, and not others, enable women to do this. Obedience to men, docility, and seeking to please and to cater to men's desires, have often been seen as women's chief virtues.

Aristotle lived and wrote from 384–322 BC. His conception of virtue is complex: a virtue is an entrenched disposition to perceive, feel, and act in certain ways. Virtuous action, according to Aristotle, is guided by excellence in deliberation and appropriate motivation. Women's deficiencies in deliberation relegated them to a sphere of lesser virtue. A much later philosopher, David Hume (1711–1776), had a conception of virtues as dispositions that are useful or agreeable to ourselves or to others. Hume did not extol reason, but thought, to the contrary, that reason should serve the passions. Given the prevailing view of their natures, wouldn't this conception of virtue privilege the position of women? Apparently not. Hume's thoughts on the virtue of chastity are revealing. The nature of copulation makes it the case, he thought, that women more assuredly know who the father of their children are, whereas men are not certain which offspring they sire. Hume asserts, "From this trivial and anatomical observation is deriv'd that vast difference betwixt the education and duties of the two sexes."[8] Women unfaithful in marriage were to be shamed, and the faithful, to be praised. The disapproval of lapses in chastity extends even to women beyond child-bearing age.[9]

It is clear from Hume's discussion that women's virtue of chastity is justified by the need for men to ensure that their children are indeed their own, and thus to keep intact their patrilineal heritages. Hume invokes a broader justification, also—namely, that civil society has an interest in the chastity of both sexes.[10] In other words, civil society has an interest in knowing that family bloodlines are pure and intact (a matter of some importance to the aristocratic classes in the British Isles at the time Hume wrote), and this, in Hume's eyes, justifies more severe restrictions on women's sexual liberty than on men's. The restrictions must extend even to infertile women, an injunction that exceeds the scope of Hume's justification for chastity. Considerations of what is useful or agreeable to women are not mentioned.

Jean-Jacques Rousseau (1712–1780), a French philosopher and contemporary of Hume's, is famous for his inegalitarianism toward men and women in *Emile*. Emile, a natural boy, is to be educated to assume authority and take command, whereas Sophie, his bride-to-be, is educated to be obedient, docile, and pleasing to Emile. Two passages from *Emile* bear witness to this: "To cultivate the masculine virtues in women and to neglect their own is evidently to do them an injury ... do not try to make your daughter a good man in defiance of nature."[11] And, "Nature herself has decreed that woman, both for herself and her children, should be at the mercy of man's judgment."[12]

Rousseau's remark about women and children is suggestive of a view commonly held throughout Western (and seemingly, world) history—that women's place is in the home, tending to the children, the elderly parents, etc., and providing succor and comfort for men, whose lot it is to work to support the household. This sexual division of labor disenfranchises women from participation in public life. Not only were women denied access to paid wages, which would give them a measure of economic independence from men, but they were also denied a voice in the governance of society. For most of history, of course, most men were also denied this voice, but the advent of democracy tragically excluded women's voices. It is true that there have been exceptions. Some queens have reigned, and some women have exerted power through their influence on men. But ordinary women's direct participation in civic life, on a par with that of men, was not to be had until relatively recently in history. The conceptual foundations of such discrimination is found in the writings of philosophers such as Aristotle, Hume, Rousseau, and the many others who uncritically adopted the same or similar views.

A notable bright spot in this bleak history occurred with the publication of Mary Wollstonecraft's book, *A Vindication of the Rights of Woman*. Published in 1792, it was written, at least in part, in response to Rousseau's *Emile*.[13] Wollstonecraft challenged Rousseau's inegalitarian view of men and women, urging that they should be given the same education in order to nurture their rational faculties. Her view, of course, was that women were as rational as men, and could not flourish or have the virtues without the development of their rationality. She writes, "In fact, it is a farce to call any being virtuous whose virtues do not result from the exercise of its own reason" (1975, p. 21).

Wollstonecraft's view began to catch on. In *The Subjection of Women*, written in (1869/2002), the philosopher John Stuart Mill argued in favor of the equality of men and women. He identified the problem so well documented in the history of philosophy:

> All women are brought up from the very earliest years in the belief that their ideal of character is the very opposite to that of men; not self-will, and government by self-control, but submission, and yielding to the control of others. All the moralities tell them that it is the duty of women, and all the current sentimentalities that it is their nature, to live for others; to make complete abnegation of themselves, and to have no life but in their affections. (pp. 137–138)

Mill, though not a virtue ethicist, sums up much of the result of the misinterpretation of women's nature and flourishing and concomitant misidentification of the traits that constitute women's virtues. The result is a deformation of women's characters. Far from being led to flourish and fulfill their natures through the exercise of the virtues mistakenly thought fitting for them, women were stunted and stultified, prevented from developing their reason, talents, and abilities. As with women's activities in public life, there are notable exceptions to this. Novelists such as Jane Austen and George Eliot made places for themselves in the world of letters. But they were exceptions, not the rule. Even today, it is difficult for some women to succeed in certain areas, such as engineering, physics, or philosophy. This is a legacy of a history of oppression to which philosophy, including conceptions of human nature, flourishing, and virtue, contributed.

African-American Slaves

The history of slavery goes well beyond the experience of Africans who were kidnapped and forcibly brought to the New World. Indeed, the history of slavery in the United States goes well beyond the brief remarks given here. As with the case of women, however, there is plentiful evidence in the historical record that African-American slaves were thought to have lesser natures than white men or white women, to be capable of lesser forms of flourishing, and to be capable only of virtues, such as obedience, that were compatible with minimal rational capacities. Historian George Frederickson and biological scientist Joseph L. Graves, Jr., note that the racist ideology of the antebellum south was not settled.[14] There were two main ideologies of slavery. One, allegedly benign, was a form of racist paternalism in which masters saw themselves as benevolent fathers, and slaves, dependent children. The other, called 'polygenesis,' viewed blacks as members of a separate and inferior species.

Racist paternalism is of greater interest here, since it gives ample testimony to the misuse of conceptions of nature, flourishing and virtue. One notable example is the "reactionary seigneuralism" of the proslavery ideologue George Fitzhugh in the 1850s.[15] Fitzhugh, a spokesperson for a view that long predated him, offered the idealized plantation as the preferred model for civil society as a whole. The master took the role of a father or guardian, and the slave, that of a child. Blacks were brought into the family circle of the master by virtue of their dependency on him and on their "common humanity." They were subjected to "family government." Ministers and intellectuals amplified these themes, exhorting slaveowners to be kind to their slaves or "charges," so as to elicit loyalty and obedience from them. Slaveowners were apt to complain of the "duty" and "burden" of slaveowning. But part of the rationale for this was the belief that slaves could not fend for themselves. They were seen as helpless, almost completely dependent on the will of the master.[16]

Two contextualizing social institutions contributed to the scheme whereby the roles and virtues of master and slave were articulated. One, already mentioned, was the plantation. It was seen as an extended "family" in which the master was to act with fatherly kindness, firmness, and forbearance, and the slaves, with obedience, loyalty, gratitude, contentment, industry, humility, shame, submissiveness, and appropriate fear.[17] The second institution, also already adverted to, was religion. Christian ministers—black and white—and church services combatted African "superstition" in order to teach slaves the duty of earthly submission, and the virtues of thrift, industry, and social peace.[18] Indeed, the Biblical curse of Ham was used to justify slavery among whites, and no doubt found its way into many church services.[19] These institutions upheld a social order according to which white masters and their families ruled, and black slaves labored and served, often under appallingly brutal conditions that belied the self-serving veneer provided by talk of Christian virtue. Slavery was built upon the edifice of conceptions of human nature that were inherently flawed—the notions that whites were superior beings, and blacks, inferior. Blacks, deemed incapable of just about anything other than serving as the complete instrument of the master's will, were thought to have their flourishing in exactly that—in serving the master and being cared for in return. Caricatures of happy black slaves, singing in the fields, carefree, docile and submissive, were part of the mythology of slavery that was upheld by admonitions to be loyal, obedient, thrifty, and grateful for the master's "care."

It took a bloody Civil War and years of combatting the "Jim Crow" South to destroy the reality of slavery and some of its legacies. We are still in the process of demolishing the remnants of the mythologies about blacks that hatred and prejudice have generated.[20]

As with our discussion of women, we can end on a brighter note. Samuel K. Roberts (1999) examines the emergence of an African-American virtue tradition dating from the late eighteenth century. He defines the African-American conception of virtue as "a vision of a divinely ordered life in which the disciplined intellect enables persons to struggle against injustice and to forge communities and structures that could ensure the development of the furthest moral and material possibilities of African Americans."[21] He discusses rearticulations of the four cardinal virtues of prudence, fortitude, temperance, and justice, in which each counters a specific aspect of prejudice against blacks.

Prudence, conceived of as a form of discernment that could aid in the achievement of African-Americans' goals, addressed injuries to the intellect and to self-conceptions of blacks.[22] Prudence was a form of intellectual discipline, needed to counter internalized notions of blacks as lazy and stupid, and to perceive the universe as morally ordered toward truth and justice. Only by cultivating this form of prudence could battles against injustice be morally and psychologically sustained.

Fortitude was also key, as it was required in the long-term struggle.[23] Here again, the conception of a divinely ordered cosmos in which truth and justice prevail was central. Fortitude both sustained, and was sustained by, this vision of the moral order. Clearly related to hope, fortitude was the virtue that supported the belief that individuals could change the circumstances that held them back.

Eschewing the notion that temperance is a middle path between desiring too much or too little by way of sex, food, and drink, Samuel Roberts articulates the virtue according to lines suggested by Josef Pieper's view of *temperantia* as the virtue that realizes an inner order within persons.[24] Its usefulness in the struggle against racial prejudice consists in providing protection against the external forces that sought to break down the inner integrity of black people, to instill in them false notions of inferiority, uncleanness, or self-loathing. The inner order of one's life, echoing the notion of the well-ordered soul, indemnifies one against psychological oppression and maintains integrity and consistency of character. Temperance so construed is seen as essential for attaining the goal of racial uplift—for moving black people forward in terms of education and personal and social development.

Finally, justice, in many ways, contextualized and gave point to the virtues of prudence, fortitude, and temperance.[25] The struggle for racial justice was paramount. All virtues of African-Americans were ordered to that end.

The stark difference between the virtues attributed to blacks by proponents of slavery and those that emerged in the African-American virtue tradition are apparent. The difference can be explained by referring to two key concepts that are thematic in this essay. First, each panoply of virtues relies on a different conception of the nature of blacks. Slaveowners and likeminded others assumed that blacks were inferior to whites, and preached virtues that maintained that status quo. The flourishing of slaves who exercised these virtues could amount to little more than a sense of contentedness in having served the master's will. By contrast, the rearticulated virtues of prudence, fortitude, temperance, and justice were grounded in the belief that the nature of blacks is equal to that of whites, that blacks and whites share a common humanity. Beyond this, they address the disadvantaged situation of blacks in the United States. They were conceptualized to enable their possessors to succeed in the struggle for justice and to attain the goal of racial uplift. Flourishing consisted in engaging with the struggle—in moving forward against the forces of oppression.

Children

The moral of the story of the two previous sections is this. Examining the historical record reveals a common flaw: misconceptions of the natures of certain groups—women and African-American slaves—led to mistaken notions of their flourishing and misidentifications of the traits that constitute the virtues of the members of those groups. These mistakes were often not innocent errors, but worked to the advantage of those who made them and to the detriment of women and blacks. Today we face a similar challenge in the case of children. The problem is not that children's natures are thought to be not human, or lesser than human, but that their full nature is still in development. We (adults) often somewhat thoughtlessly assume that children have, or should have, certain traits that we consider to be virtues, such as trustingness, innocence, and hope. In assuming they have or should have such virtues, do we do them an injustice? Do we fail to appreciate their actual circumstances in ways that could cause them harm? Do we thereby advantage ourselves at their expense?

It is worth noting at the outset that sometimes children, especially young children, are placed in situations that are bound to confuse them from the standpoint of their ongoing virtue development. Michael Slote, for example, maintains that " ... trustingness is at best only a desirable characteristic in the young."[26] But is it so desirable? Young children are warned against trusting strangers; in today's society, if they were not so warned, they would be in danger and their parents would be remiss. Trust needs to be appropriate to be a virtue; it needs to be informed by prudence. Depending on their age, children can be incapable of rationally tempering their trust. Very young children do not talk to strangers because their parents admonish them not to. Older children can be lured by deceptive individuals into bad behaviors, such as experimenting with drugs. These kinds of cases bespeak a lack of well-developed discernment—a failing seen in many adults as well. Consider, too, honesty. How many times have young children repeated embarrassing remarks their parents have made in front of them to people not meant to hear? Here, honesty needs to be tempered with prudence and tact.

Challenges in cultivating appropriate trust in children raise especially serious problems. Our societies, that is, societies of early twenty-first century Western democracies, are dangerous for children. This is true for children at any age, but it is especially true for young children. Children at any age face dangers from sexual predators, and the drug culture is now invading grade schools. Tragic killings in schools have broken the hearts of the nation. Scenes of violence, sexual exploitation and degradation, rampant consumerism, and plain bad behavior flood television and the internet. YouTube posts videos of rape. Social media such as Facebook are rife with bullying posts. Parents who seek to control what their children see and hear are faced with obstacles at every turn. Those who judiciously monitor their children's exposure to media at home often deal with problems brought home from school. Bullying in schools is especially problematic.[27] In this climate, how can the virtues of children survive? Would we want to encourage children to be trusting? Can we expect or desire them to maintain child-like innocence? How can they have hope?

An interesting study of childhood hope by geography professor Peter Kraftl (2008) sheds light on these issues.[28] Using statements from foundation websites as well as the United Nations Convention on the Rights of the Child, Kraftl sketches a complex conception that he calls 'childhood' hope.[29] Childhood hope is associated with idealizations of childhood innocence as well as with the idea that children are our future. If they are not properly cared for, our future will be in jeopardy. This conception, he maintains, is an abstraction and an idealization. To get a flavor of the kind of hope childhood-hope is, consider that "Childhood-hope turns 'on hope where there is an obstacle, where the one who hopes cares a great deal, and when there is a great deal at stake.'"[30] Childhood hope here becomes associated with the desire to lift children out of poverty, to provide them with resources for better lives than their parents had, to ensure them with adequate opportunities for education, health, and nutrition. These are worthy hopes, but often they do not correspond well with the actual realities of children. According to the idealized conception, children should have correspondingly grandiose hopes, such as the hope to live better lives than their parents, the hope to have a career as a physician, or the hope to represent their country at the Olympics, and the role of well-intentioned foundations and policy-makers is to help children fulfill them. Yet, juxtaposed with such large-scale hopes, Kraftl presents a series of interviews with young people in which he discovers "everyday" forms of modest hopefulness.[31] These inklings of hope emerge from young people's reflections on themselves, and correlate with self-esteem. The hope actually to be found in the young, he argues, is to be discovered in their everyday routines and practices, not in the idealized conception of childhood hope that often obscures from view the more mundane hopes of young people. Examples of children's more modest hopes include the hope to pass the exam tomorrow, or to have a bullying-free bus ride home from school today. Perhaps at some inchoate level, children do have the larger-scale hopes assumed by the idealized conception. But in their actual lives, their hopes are more modest, more circumstance-based, and more immediate.

The pattern found in this study has interesting implications. Perhaps we do an injustice to children by urging them to have idealized virtues such as trustingness, innocence, and hope. Is our desire that they have and cultivate these idealizations based on our own desires and hopes for the future, and on the delight we take in their apparent innocence, and not in the grim realities they often face? Are we concerned with their flourishing or our own misconceptions? In today's world it is dangerous for children to be too trusting, and they lose their innocence fast. Classroom and social milieus rife with bullying and degradation can cause hopelessness. In wanting them to have idealized conceptions of trustingness, innocence, and hope, we do not seem to be caring for their actual well-being.

The case of hope is especially telling. If children's circumstances are such that they live better with more modest hopes, it damages them if we urge a more idealized view of hope upon them. We misunderstand their lives and their worlds if we fail to take seriously an important finding of Kraftl's study, namely, that modest hopes, and not the grandiose conception, correlate with children's self-esteem. We should be supporting their modest hopes, helping them to achieve them, and thereby building their self-esteem.

The moral of the story is this. In order not to damage our children, we must forego the temptation to encourage them to cultivate idealized traits. Before we extol child-like trustingness, innocence, and hope, we need to ask ourselves whether, given present realities, having these traits will actually help our children to survive and flourish. We also need to pay attention to empirical studies that inform us of the traits children actually use to function and live well. These traits are their virtues.[32] We should encourage and support their development because doing so is in the best interest of our children.

In order to do all of this, we need to have a virtue ourselves—that of open-mindedness. Arguably, those who oppressed women and African-American slaves were lacking in this virtue, as well as in many others. Today, we hope that past is past. Moreover, we hope that our views of children are not infected with ill will. Even if these views are only benignly mistaken, however, we do well to examine our assumptions and revise them in accordance with empirical evidence.

Study Questions

1. Do we need to know something's nature before we can tell what it means for that thing to flourish?
2. When we think about the nature and flourishing of an animal, is the best or only level of analysis the species level? In other words, are intra-species distinctions ever appropriate? Which ones?
3. Nancy Snow claims that there might be virtues distinctive of childhood, though perhaps not the ones that people think. Might there also be virtues distinctive of old age? What would they be?
4. What do you think flourishing is?
5. Are there virtues that any reasonable conception of flourishing, whether religious or secular, would endorse? Which?

Notes

1. I am grateful to Mark Alfano for very helpful suggestions in the revision of this paper.
2. I do not consider non-Western conceptions of human nature, flourishing, and virtue because Roberts does not consider them, and space does not permit it.
3. Care is needed here. I say that women and slaves *might have been* better judges of their own flourishing, and not that they *were*, because of the very real possibility that they accepted the truth of false claims about their nature, virtues, and flourishing. People who believed these falsehoods, whether oppressed or oppressors, were suffering from "false consciousness."
4. I doubt that Roberts would disagree.
5. I draw on two of my previous essays: Snow (2002) and Snow (2004). For an excellent account of virtues under oppression, see Tessman (2005).
6. Exceptions include Slote (1983, pp. 45–52), Kristjánson (2004), and Putnam (1995).
7. For these references, see Warren (1980, pp. 38–39).
8. Hume (1978, p. 571).
9. Ibid.
10. Ibid., pp. 571–572.
11. Rousseau (1911, p. 327).
12. Ibid., p. 328.
13. Though it was also written in response to the French Revolution. Thanks to Mark Alfano for calling this point to my attention.
14. See Frederickson (1971, Chapter 3) and Graves (2001, Chapter 3).

15. See Frederickson (1971, pp. 56–61).
16. See Berlin (2003, pp. 204–205) and Genovese (1974, pp. 75–80).
17. See Genovese (1974, pp. 94–95, 104).
18. Ibid., pp. 170–171.
19. See Ibid., p. 245; Frederickson (1971, pp. 60–61); and Graves (2001, p. 16). Though I did not mention this in my discussion of the use of virtue to oppress women, Old and New Testament texts have also been used to justify women's subordination and subservience to men. See *Genesis* 3:16; *Proverbs* 31:1–9; *Colossians* 3: 18–23; I *Corinthians* 7: 1–3; I *Corinthians* 11: 3–4; I *Corinthians* 11: 9. But see *Galatians* 3: 27–28.
20. For an engaging overview, see Ta-Nehesi Coates's (2014) article on reparations.
21. Ibid., p. 41.
22. Ibid., p. 42.
23. Ibid., pp. 61–62, 66.
24. Ibid., pp. 73ff.
25. Ibid., pp. 62–63.
26. See Slote (1983, p. 49).
27. See Emily Bazelon's (2013) sobering book.
28. This paragraph draws on ideas from my unpublished manuscript, *Landscapes of Hope: The 'What,' 'Why,' and 'How' of Hope.*
29. Ibid., pp. 82–85.
30. Joseph Godfrey, *A Philosophy of Human Hope* (Dordrecht, The Netherlands: Martinus Nijhoff), p. 14, quoted at Kraftl (2008, p. 85).
31. Ibid., pp. 85ff.
32. Alfano (2013a, Chapter 7) does this for children's intellectual virtues.

CHAPTER 3
How Are Virtue and Knowledge Related?

Abstract

In his contribution, Ernest Sosa tries to integrate responsibilist elements into the heart of his reliabilist virtue epistemology. He distinguishes between character virtues, which he deems peripheral or auxiliary, and agential competences, which he deems necessary for high-grade reflective knowledge. In doing so, Sosa distinguishes between dispositions whose exercise *enables* knowledge (e.g., Baehr's responsibilist virtues) and those whose exercise *constitutes* knowledge. The latter are in "the charmed inner circle for traditional epistemology" because their manifestation in the correctness of a belief "*constitutes a bit of knowledge*," whereas the former are beyond the pale of this charmed inner circle because their manifestation merely helps to "*put you in a position to know*" (emphasis in original). Sosa's agential virtues are more than mere capacities like memory and eyesight, but less than the personal-worth-enhancing virtues championed by Zagzebski and Baehr because they don't essentially involve motivation. In his response, Jason Baehr argues that, while the agential competences that Sosa lionizes may indeed contribute to or constitute knowledge, character virtues such as open-mindedness and intellectual courage do as well. In other words, the distinction between character virtues and agential competences does not divide dispositions that don't from dispositions that do belong in the "charmed inner circle." He identifies two ways of arguing for this. First, he tries to show that character virtues straightforwardly satisfy reliabilist criteria for being epistemic virtues. Second, he tries to show that there is little to no substantive difference between Sosa's agential competences and his own character virtues. Baehr concludes by arguing that virtues of intellectual character fall in the intersection of epistemology and ethics, not—as Sosa might be taken to suggest—solely on the ethical side of the divide.

Virtue Epistemology: Character Versus Competence

Ernest Sosa

Having been invited to debate with Jason Baehr the question of how moral and intellectual virtues are related, I will open the debate by discussing his recent book, *The Inquiring Mind* (2011). An outstanding contribution to virtue theory, the book can be viewed as an insightful treatise on that question.

For several decades now, it has been received wisdom that there are two quite distinct forms of virtue epistemology. One of these finds in epistemology important correlates of Aristotle's moral virtues. Such responsibilist character epistemology builds its account of epistemic normativity on the subject's responsible manifestation of epistemic character. The other form of virtue epistemology cleaves closer to Aristotelian intellectual virtues, while recognizing a broader set of competences still restricted to basic faculties of perception, introspection, and the like. This orthodox dichotomy of our field is deeply misleading and will be challenged in this chapter.

In his book, Baehr argues for a distinctive approach, while presupposing the dichotomy and offering detailed critiques of rival approaches. Against my own virtue reliabilism, he charges that it deplorably neglects responsibilist, agential intellectual virtues. Against other responsibilists, he argues that character epistemology can have only very limited success with the issues of traditional epistemology, such as skepticism and the nature of knowledge. Given that there is more to epistemology than those perennial issues, he proposes a focus on his preferred character, responsibilist, agential virtue epistemology. This in his view is how we can best locate epistemological character traits within epistemology, thus bringing epistemology and ethics closer together than in the past. What is more, not only have virtue reliabilists neglected responsibilist, agential intellectual virtues, which are so important for issues beyond those of traditional epistemology. They have even overlooked how important responsibilist virtues are in dealing with those traditional issues once we consider levels of human knowledge more sophisticated than those attainable through simple mechanisms such as sensory perception.

Given how thoroughly and how well Baehr has discussed those issues in his book, that is an excellent place to start our own discussion. In particular, I will discuss his critique of my own alternative approach and offer a defense.

In its discussion of my views the book misfires, or so I will argue. But I hope to rise above polemics to an overview of virtue epistemology, one that reveals more fully the current state of the field, and the options now available at its cutting edge.

Baehr contends "... that the concept of intellectual virtue does merit a secondary or supporting role" (p. 47) in traditional epistemological inquiry into the nature, conditions, and extent of human knowledge. By intellectual virtues, moreover, he means *responsibilist*, agential, character intellectual virtues, not reliabilist faculties. He concludes Chapter 4 as follows:

> We have seen that virtue reliabilists ... must expand their focus to include, not just the more mechanical or faculty-based dimension of human cognition, but also the more active, volitional, or character-based dimension.... The cost of *not* doing so, we have seen, is that reliabilists are unable to account for the sort of reliability involved with ... much of the knowledge that we as humans care most about. (p. 67)

I will defend four claims in response.

> First, from its inception, virtue reliabilism has *always* had that expanded focus.
> Second, responsibilists *have* advocated a *distinctive* conception of responsibilist, character-based intellectual virtue, but it is partial and inadequate.[1]
> Third, and ironically, we should recognize a sort of active, volitional intellectual virtue that will be a special case of reliable-competence intellectual virtue.
> Fourth and finally, we can best understand the responsibilist, character-based intellectual virtues highlighted by responsibilists as *auxiliary* to the virtues that are a special case of reliable-competence intellectual virtue.

A true epistemology will indeed assign to such responsibilist-cum-reliabilist intellectual virtue the *main* role in addressing concerns at the center of the tradition. To anticipate, here is why that is so: because the *sort* of knowledge at the center of traditional epistemology, from the Pyrrhonians through Descartes, is high-level *reflective* knowledge. This is a knowledge requiring free, volitional endorsement by the subject who judges, or the corresponding disposition. Ironically, our reliabilist framework did always potentially, and does increasingly (actually and explicitly) give the place of honor to the agential, volitional approach, a central place that responsibilists either emphatically deny to it (Baehr), or do not successfully provide for it (Zagzebski).

So, my main thesis will be that reliabilist, competence-based virtue epistemology must be understood broadly, in a more positively ecumenical way, with responsibilist agential intellectual virtues at its core.[2]

Before we turn to that, however, here follows a defense against the specific critique offered by Baehr in his book.

Character Theory versus Competence Theory

We begin with quotations showing responsibilist competences to have been present in virtue reliabilism from its inception. Here are two relevant passages (from among many).

1. First an early passage:

> Note that no human blessed with reason has merely animal knowledge of the sort attainable by beasts. For even when perceptual belief derives as directly as it ever does from sensory stimuli, it is still relevant that one has *not* perceived the signs of contrary testimony.... [E]ven when response to stimuli is most direct, *if* one were also to hear or see the signs of credible contrary testimony, that would change one's response. The beliefs of a *rational* animal hence would seem never to issue from *unaided* introspection, memory, or perception. For reason is always at least a silent partner on the watch for other relevant data, a silent partner whose very *silence* is a contributing cause of the belief outcome. (Sosa 1991, p. 240)

That same view stays in place over the many succeeding years until we reach the following:

> I speak of "mechanisms" or processes of belief formation, and sometimes of "input/output mechanisms," but I want to disavow explicitly any implication that these are simple or modular.... [A] mechanism can be something close to a reflex, or it can be a very high-level, central-processing ability of the sort that enables a sensitive critic to "decide" how to assess a work, based on complex and able pondering.[3]

Of course the intention was always to explain knowledge of all sorts, including sorts where the competences involved are those of a skilled art critic, scientist, mathematician, or detective, and not just the sorting competence of a chicken sexer.

2. Those quoted passages should already lay to rest the notion that virtue reliabilism is *restricted* to peripheral or modular or automatic mechanisms of belief formation. What then can possibly have suggested that virtue reliabilism

does exclude the more sophisticated, actively volitional dimensions of our cognitive lives? Consider this from Baehr's (2011) book:

> The tight logical connection between character virtues and faculty virtues is also evident in the fact that when epistemologists offer detailed characterizations of the latter, they have a hard time avoiding talk of the former. Sosa, for instance, in a discussion regarding the fallibility of faculty virtues, notes that the reliability of one's cognitive faculties can be affected by one's intellectual *conduct*. Interestingly, the conduct he proceeds to describe is precisely that of certain intellectual character virtues and vices...
> ... Again, an exercise of character virtues is often manifested in and partly constituted by the operation of certain faculty virtues. Moreover, as the passages from Sosa indicate, the reliability of faculty virtues often implicates one or more character virtues. Therefore the attempt to make a principled exclusion of character virtues from the reliabilist repertoire of intellectual virtues on the grounds that faculty virtues but not character virtues are "sources" of belief seems bound to fail.[4]

The *restrictive* view attributed to me may well need correction, but it never has been my view. The attribution is based on no supportive reference, but only on what is "suggested" by the simplicity of the examples that I use as clear cases of simple knowledge to be explained. It is assumed that the view is *restricted* to the sorts of competences in examples of simple perceptual, introspective, or mnemonic knowledge. But no such explicit restriction can be found in my published work. Passages *are* cited (as Baehr indicates above) where I show clear signs of making *no such restriction*, but those passages are used (surprisingly) to demonstrate the *inadequacy* of my view, for imposing such a restriction. Nevertheless, what has never been *excluded* from my virtue reliabilism is *agential competences*.

On the contrary, the right conclusion is that the restrictive view is *not* my view. I restrict not the competences but only the examples. I focus on those simple enough to reveal more starkly certain basic problems that any theory of knowledge must solve. Further problems may of course arise when less simple instances of knowledge are highlighted. But first things first, and frankly it has been challenging enough to try to deal with the simpler examples first.[5] Although I have always recognized *both* an animal and a reflective level of knowledge, as it happens, my current project is to develop the more agential and reflective side of my virtue epistemology.

3. What could have led to the misunderstanding of my position? *In part,* the reason may perhaps emerge in the following note of Baehr's:

> As I note below, an additional requirement for what Sosa calls "reflective" or "human" knowledge is that the person in question have an "epistemic

perspective" on the known belief, which consists of an additional set of coherent beliefs about the source and reliability of the original belief (see 1991: ch. 11). *Our concern here, however, lies with the virtue component of Sosa's analysis.* [Italics added. The reference is to my (KIP) *Knowledge in Perspective* (Cambridge University Press, 1991).][6]

Here Baehr restricts his discussion of my views to their *animal* component, leaving aside the *reflective* component. Is it any wonder that virtue reliabilism is thought to neglect the active, agential, responsibilist side of epistemology, *when its attempt to do so is arbitrarily left out of account?*

Does virtue reliabilism leave out agency? Does it at least leave out the conscious, intentional, volitional agency that is involved in deliberation and in conscious pondering, or weighing of reasons? Not at all; *at most,* the animal side of virtue reliabilism would be guilty of such negligence if it aspired to be an account of *all* human knowledge.[7] But it has no such ambition. Rather, it has always been joined to an account of the more distinctively human sort of knowledge, the *reflective* sort.

4. Baehr lays out what he takes to be the formal conditions that must be satisfied by any intellectual virtue, *according to Competence Virtue Epistemology* (CVE):

> *WIVA What Intellectual Virtues Are According to CVE* (according to Baehr)
> [Intellectual virtues are] personal qualities that, under certain conditions and with respect to certain propositions, are a reliable means to reaching the truth and avoiding error.

And he attributes to John Greco the idea that intellectual virtues would need to play a critical or salient role in explaining why a person reaches the truth.

Baehr focuses on agential virtues. These virtues have, in his view, certain distinctive features:

a. They are virtues exercised in intentional agency.
b. They are developed through repeated agency.
c. They bear on the personal worth of the possessor.
d. They aid agential success.
e. In epistemology, they concern intentionally conducted inquiry.[8]

Because of its focus on traditional faculties such as perception, memory, and inference, virtue reliabilism is said to *overlook character traits,* such as open-mindedness and intellectual courage. These traits are said to possess the five features of agential virtues listed, and to satisfy the formal conditions accepted by competence virtue epistemology (spelled out in *WIVA* above). Such overlooked character traits are indeed, under certain conditions and with respect to certain propositions, a reliable means to reaching the truth and avoiding error, and their exercise can most saliently explain why the subject gets it right in believing as they do.

Does competence virtue epistemology (virtue reliabilism) plead guilty?

5. Reliabilist intellectual virtues, according to Baehr's *WIVA*, are to be understood simply, by definition, as traits (a) whose manifestations reliably yield true belief, and (b) that play a salient role in explaining why one reaches the truth in cases where one does so. That is indeed an account in the literature, an account of epistemically relevant belief-yielding sources. And there are early passages of mine, such as the following, which might misleadingly suggest that I subscribe to that account:

"We have reached the view that knowledge is true belief out of intellectual virtue, belief that turns out right by reason of the virtue and not just by coincidence."[9]

Although I later retain that view of knowledge,[10] my account of intellectual virtues still differs from *WIVA* in a way that matters for how we should understand virtue reliabilism, or so I will now argue.

6. CVE aims to solve two Platonic problems: the *Theaetetus* problem as to the nature of knowledge, and the *Meno* problem as to its distinctive value. In connection with the definitional problem, CVE proposes that knowledge is belief whose correctness manifests the believer's pertinent competence. So, the pertinent competence (the pertinent reliabilist intellectual virtue) must be one whose exercise can *constitute* knowledge. That is what I claim knowledge *to be*: belief that is correct, that thus succeeds, through the exercise of competence. However, it is crucial to restrict the "through" appropriately. When the correctness of a belief is due to competence in a way that *constitutes* knowledge, it is not enough that the competence reliably puts one *in a position to know*, in a position where one can now exercise one's knowledge-constitutive competences, those whose exercise *does* constitute knowledge.

It may be thought that a virtue such as open-mindedness or intellectual courage could be such a directly knowledge-constitutive virtue. Accordingly, Baehr alleges, the reliabilist, competence-based view neglects responsibilist virtues that it should welcome within its fold, since they too can be important in explaining how a subject gets it right. And it must indeed be granted that, in certain instances, a responsibilist virtue can provide the salient explanation, especially where the truth must be won through complex and competent effort. Courageous and open-minded pursuit of truth—by a scientist, or journalist, or detective—might well enable someone to uncover a truth that escapes all others. Baehr has a telling objection to any form of reliabilist virtue epistemology that requires for knowledge only that the correctness of the knowing subject's belief must derive somehow, perhaps at a great remove, from the exercise of a certain intellectual virtue that is normally a reliable aid to reaching the truth. Such a form of virtue epistemology *would* be negligent if it ignored, or declared irrelevant, any responsibilist virtues that did help one attain truth, including open-mindedness and intellectual courage.

However, Baehr's objection is not relevant to my own form of virtue reliabilism, since the intellectual virtues or competences that matter for my view are not simply those whose exercise through inquiry can reliably help one reach the truth. Rather, they are competences whose exercise can *constitute* knowledge. And a competence whose exercise reliably aids our search for truth—*even* so as to be the salient explanation of why truth is then attained—might easily be one whose exercise would *not* constitute knowledge. It may just fail to be of the right sort to be thus constitutive.

For example, a scientist may follow a healthy regimen with great discipline, and her good health may help explain why she makes her discoveries, by contrast with her wan, depressed rivals; and may even be the salient explanation.

Or, it might work the other way around. It might be that someone's obsessive pursuit of truth, even at the cost of malnourishment and depression, puts them in a position to attain truths that are denied to their healthy rivals. Even if such obsession to the point of ill health does reliably lead to truth on certain matters inaccessible otherwise (even *if*, I say), the exercise of such personal qualities (obsessiveness) would hardly *constitute* knowledge. The long hours, the intense concentration, the single-minded avoidance of distractions, may put the inquirer in a situation, or enable her to attain a frame of mind, or certain skills, through all of which she can have and exercise the competences more directly relevant to the attainment of knowledge. She might acquire important data through a perilous voyage to distant lands, or through observations of the night sky, none of which she could have done without persistent dedication over many years with enormous care.

7. But the point does not require reference to the heroics of a Darwin or a Brahe. A simple example from everyday life should suffice. Suppose a mysterious closed box lies before us, and we wonder what it contains. How can we find out? We might of course just open the lid. In pursuit of this objective we will then exercise certain competences, perhaps even character traits (if the box is locked, or the lid stuck), such as persistence and resourcefulness. And perhaps these qualities (in certain contexts, and in certain combinations) do lead us reliably to the truth. Nevertheless, the exercise of *such* intellectual virtues need not and normally will not *constitute* knowledge, not even when that exercise does indirectly lead us to the truth.

Contrast what happens when we manage to open the lid and look inside. Now we may immediately know the answer to our question, with a perceptual belief—say, *that there is a necklace in the box*—which manifests certain cognitive competences for gaining visual experience and belief. Perhaps this complex, knowledge-constitutive competence first leads to things seeming perceptually a certain way, and eventually to the belief that things are indeed that way, absent contrary indications. A belief manifesting *such* a competence, and crucially, one whose *correctness* manifests such a competence, *does* constitute knowledge, at a minimum animal knowledge, perhaps even full-fledged knowledge (including a reflective component).

It is such knowledge-constitutive competences that are of main interest to a CVE aiming to explain human knowledge. Other epistemically important traits—such as open-mindedness, intellectual courage, persistence, and even single-minded obsessiveness—are indeed of interest to a broader epistemology. They are of course worthy of serious study. But they are not in the charmed inner circle for traditional epistemology. They are only "auxiliary" intellectual virtues, by contrast with the "constitutive" intellectual virtues of central interest to virtue reliabilism.

My distinction has on one side intellectual virtues whose manifestation helps to *put you in a position to know*, and on the other intellectual virtues whose manifestation in the correctness of a belief thereby *constitutes a bit of knowledge*. In my view, a competence can constitute knowledge only if it is a disposition to believe correctly, one that can then be manifest in the correctness of a belief. A competence in general is a disposition to succeed when one aims to attain certain objectives, and a competence to believe correctly is a special case of that.

Responsibilist Virtue Epistemology: Baehr versus Zagzebski

Here is the internecine disagreement in brief.

1. Baehr and Zagzebski share a high-minded conception of intellectual virtues. For them these are character traits that bear on the personal worth of the *person*. They are inherently motivational. Such virtuous character traits are manifest in actions that must be motivated by a virtuous pursuit of the truth. In their view, a belief that derives (at least in important part) from such a virtue must derive from actions that express the subject's love of truth.

2. Zagzebski believes that such character-based responsibilist epistemology can help with the traditional problematic of epistemology, at the core of which is the project of defining knowledge. Indeed, for Zagzebski it is emphatically *this* motivational component that explains the distinctive value of knowledge above whatever value might be found in the corresponding merely true belief. So, she proposes that knowledge is best understood as belief that gets it right through such responsibilist intellectual virtue.[11]

3. For Baehr, however, that approach is blocked by simple counterexamples, such as a pang of pain, or a strike of lightning out of the blue, which one

knowingly discerns with no delay. These one *can't help knowing*, sans deliberation and *unmotivated* by love of truth.

4. Zagzebski responds:

> [My definition] ... does not rule out easy knowledge by sense perception. A person who believes that she sees an easily identifiable object typically knows that she sees the object, provided that there are no indications in her environment that she should not trust her visual sense or understanding of the concept under which the object falls.[12]

And she extends the point to testimony, and presumably would go further.

5. But Baehr insists as follows:[13]

> [If as I work late at night there is a power outage] ... I am, as it were, *overcome* by knowledge that the lighting in the room has changed.... Nor is it plausible to think that I am "trusting my senses" in the relevant, motivational sense.... Again, knowledge of this sort seems not to involve or implicate the knower's agency at all.

And this line of criticism seems right at least to the following extent. We cannot explain the appropriateness of the belief that the room has gone dark as a matter of *non-negligent agency*, if that belief is *not at all* a product of intentional agency, which is the sort of agency important to character epistemology. Surely *motivation* relates to agency, not to passive reactions.[14]

It might be replied that one can take a kind of agential credit for a locomotive's staying on a certain track, despite one's having actively intervened *not at all*. One might still deserve credit even so, *if* there have been junctures where as conductor one could have intervened, where one was free to intervene and, without negligence, freely opted not to do so. Unfortunately, this will not do. The problem is that in the cases urged by the critics, there is no freedom to intervene in what seems clearly to be a belief, and even an instance of knowledge, as with the knowledge that the room has gone dark.

6. Here is the upshot. If we restrict responsibilist virtues to those that are *both* agential *and* bear on the personal worth of the agent, in virtue of their motivational component, then Baehr is right to think that we cannot build a traditional epistemology on such virtues, and Zagzebski wrong to think otherwise. Not even knowledge can be accounted for in those terms. However, in my view Zagzebski is right to think that a traditional epistemology *can* be built on responsibilist virtues, and Baehr wrong to think otherwise. Where they both go wrong is in supposing that responsibilist virtues must involve the personal worth of the agent, must be virtues of *that* sort, involving motivation that passes muster.

Moreover, my point here cannot be dismissed as *merely* terminological. Understood in a metaphysically interesting way, my claim is that the relevant natural kinds for building a responsibilist virtue epistemology are not just the following two: (a) non-agential faculties, and (b) personal-worth-involving, motivationally appropriate agential virtuous competences. We may or may not consider the latter to be a category or kind worth emphasizing. We may or may not consider it worth emphasizing in a responsibilism that aspires to solve traditional epistemological problems. Regardless of all that, there is at a minimum *also or instead* the following epistemic kind: (c) agential virtues. *These obviously go beyond non-agential faculties. So, they go beyond a reliabilism restricted to such faculties.* And so I submit that they can reasonably be considered "responsibilist" intellectual virtues, in the sense that agents would be epistemically, agentially responsible in exercising them, and irresponsible through their neglect, and even vicious through exercise of conflicting dispositions. In other words, they are traits or competences of agents as agents. And among these are the traits or competences of conscious, intentional agents as such.

Virtue Epistemology: Responsibilism as a Kind of Reliabilism

1. In order to circumvent the impasse within responsibilism, we must first be clear that epistemology is not a department of ethics. An extremely high epistemic status, certain knowledge, can be attained with a deplorable state that represents a sad waste of time, as when someone spends a morning determining with certitude how many beans are left in their coffee bag.

Moreover, that is quite compatible with there being special instances of knowledge that *are* outstanding accomplishments, which require an admirable love of truth (on a certain matter) and willingness to pursue it with persistent toil and sacrifice. And it is also compatible with the fact that *possessing knowledge of a certain sort*, for various sorts, is an indispensable part of any flourishing life. Moreover, having sufficient knowledge of a certain sort may be indispensable without *any* particular bits of knowledge of that sort being indispensable, or even much desirable.

Independently of all that, it remains that there is a distinctive dimension of epistemic assessment isolated from all such broadly ethical (or prudential) concerns. Moreover, within this epistemic dimension, love of truth plays a negligible role *at most*, if any at all. Hedge fund managers, waste disposal engineers, dentists, and their receptionists, can all attain much knowledge in the course of an ordinary workday despite the fact that they seek the truths relevant to their work only for their instrumental value. That is why they want them, not because they *love* truth. That seems indeed to be true of service professionals generally, including medical doctors and lawyers. It is not love of truth that routinely drives them in their professional activities, by contrast with desire for professional standing, wanting to help someone, or trying to make a living.

Disinterested, high-minded motivation must be distinguished from intentional, volitional agency. Dispositions to succeed when one tries need not be closely allied with, and much less do they need to be constituted by, a high-minded motivation, one that can bear on the personal worth of the agent, on how fine a person they are. Professionals *are* indeed routinely engaged in intentional, volitional truth-seeking in their work lives, even when they do not disinterestedly, lovingly seek the truth. An assassin may even have *no desire whatever* for the truth on the location of his victim *except only* for the fact that it will make his crime possible. Indeed, if he thought a false belief would at that juncture get him more efficiently to his objective he would heartily approve of his so believing, and would be glad he did so, with no regrets whatever. His search for truth, since agential, is subject to the full range of responsibilist assessment nonetheless. And his knowing the location of the victim in believing as he does about that location, is still better *epistemically* than his merely believing correctly, and of course better epistemically than his believing incorrectly. Similarly, his shot may be an excellently apt shot, and thereby better than an inapt shot (whether successful or not), despite the murderous motivating intention. (That is to say, it is better *as a shot*; it is *a better shot*. It need not be a better entity, or a better thing to happen, nonetheless.)

In conclusion, once we distinguish the *sort* of comparative evaluation (epistemic *performance* evaluation) that is involved in our taking knowledge to surpass merely true belief in (the relevant sort of) value, this removes any temptation to take personally laudable motivation to be the key, even if *in a broad sense* one's cognitive prowess may be a component of one's personal worth, as might be the shooting prowess of our assassin. *Broad* "personal worth" is not what responsibilist, character epistemologists have in mind, at least not Baehr. The assassin is not a better person for being such a good shot. A more accomplished person, yes, but not a better person, in any sense closely related to ethical assessment.

Let us turn now to a second distinction that will help accommodate responsibilism properly in epistemology.

2. At a certain level of abstraction, we can distinguish two sorts of "belief," one implicit and functional, the other explicitly, consciously intentional. It is the latter that needs to be explored in giving *responsibilism* its proper place in epistemology. This is because it is consciously reasoned choice and judgment that most fully manifests our rational nature. It is with such choice and judgment that we reach the level of human functioning that most fully manifests our philosophical attainment. Accordingly, it is such consciously, rationally endorsed judgment that is at the focus of the epistemological tradition from the Pyrrhonians through Descartes. It is not only the *act* of conscious, intentional judgment that is at the core, however, since by extension, there is also the correlated *disposition* to judge upon consideration.

Still, although we do not here focus on functional, implicit belief, what we learn about conscious, intentional belief should carry over to belief generally, whether intentional or functional. The key to the carryover would be a conception of functional belief as still aimed at truth, or at representing accurately and reliably enough. Functional belief might aim at truth functionally: for example, through psychological or biological teleology. This would enable thinking of functional belief also as a kind of action, even when it is only implicit, and not *consciously* intentional. Anyhow, I distinguish such functional belief only to put it aside, so as to focus on the sort of belief that does turn out to be a form of intentional action.

What is intentional belief? How is it structured? We focus on affirmation, and the corresponding disposition to affirm, in the endeavor to answer a given question correctly. Consider the great importance of these for a collaborative social species. They seem essentially required for collaborative deliberation and for information sharing. Take *collaborative deliberation*, right up to the most complex, as in a nation's governance; also, *information sharing*, crucial as it is in a great many contexts, prominently in scientific inquiry.

Such affirmation is largely conscious and intentional. If you add a column of figures in your head, for example, you may seemingly obtain a certain result. But if the problem is complex enough, you may still hesitate to affirm accordingly. You may first take out pencil and paper, or a calculator. Eventually, coincidence of results may provide strong enough evidence, which leads you to assent (perhaps properly so). You *decide* when to assent, you wait until the evidence is strong enough.[15]

We focus on such intentional, judgmental belief. How is it structured? Judgmental belief is definable as a certain sort of disposition to affirm. What sort of disposition? For a start, let us take *judgment* that p to be a certain sort of affirmation *in the endeavor to get it right on whether p*. Judgmental *belief* can then be understood as a certain sort of *disposition to judge* in the endeavor to get it right on whether p, if one so endeavors.

Compare pragmatic affirmation, whether as a means *to reduce cognitive/affective dissonance*, or *to instill confidence that will enhance performance*, or the like. On our conception, the latter is not proper belief. It is rather a sort of "make-belief" or mock belief.[16]

3. What distinguishes real belief from make-belief? The difference involves the subject's intentions. In make-belief one affirms in pursuit of some non-epistemic, practical aim. By contrast, in judgment and judgmental belief one constitutively aims at *getting it right* on the question addressed. Perhaps that is all there is to the difference?

Before us so far is a partial account of judgment as *a certain sort* of affirmation *in the endeavor to get it right on whether p*. Judgmental belief could then be understood as a corresponding disposition: to judge in the endeavor *thus* to get it right on whether p, if one so endeavors.

4. Suppose that reflective knowledge is knowledge properly so-called, and that the highest level of reflective knowledge, of distinctive interest to the philosopher, is the knowledge that gains conscious, agential, judgmental

endorsement. This is the knowledge at the center of the epistemological tradition from the Pyrrhonians to Descartes and beyond. It is not the knowledge that is acquired implicitly with the normal automatic processing that standardly occurs in the normal course of a day. Rather, it is the knowledge that does or at least can stand up to conscious reflective scrutiny, no holds barred. Included here in the knowledge that falls short is not only the implicit belief acquired automatically, but even the explicit and conscious judgment that merely reflects unexamined assumptions absorbed through the force of the culture's hidden persuaders. These judgments can be willingly rendered, explicitly and consciously, while they may still fall short because unendorsed *and not properly endorsable* by that subject, who lacks the rational wherewithal even dispositionally.

Envoi

Finally, an irenic parting. Again, we should gladly recognize the many important intellectual virtues beyond the knowledge-constitutive. And we should welcome the philosophical study of such virtues.[17] There are non-constitutive *auxiliary* virtues whose virtue must be understood within the framework of virtue reliabilism. The reason for this is that what makes them auxiliary virtues is mostly that their exercise enables us to acquire or sustain the complete competence—the Skill, Shape, and Situation, SSS complete knowledge-constitutive competence—in virtue of whose manifestations we know answers to questions in a given domain. (Recall how the competence to drive safely on a certain road would be constituted by the innermost Skill that the driver retains even asleep, by the Shape that requires his being awake and sober, and by the Situation involving a road that is dry enough and not covered by a thick layer of oil.) We are helped to understand why those auxiliary competences count as auxiliary *epistemic* virtues (and not just as general moral or other practical virtues), then, if we understand the structure of knowledge-*constitutive* competences, and can better see which and how auxiliary virtues might enable us to attain and exercise our knowledge-*constitutive* virtues.

Character Virtues, Epistemic Agency, and Reflective Knowledge

Jason Baehr

Ernest Sosa was the first philosopher to deploy the concept of intellectual virtue in the service of contemporary epistemology.[18] His contributions to what has since become a leading approach to epistemology are second to none in volume, quality, and impact. For these and other reasons, it is an honor to have

Sosa carefully address some of my own work in virtue epistemology and to engage with him on several matters central to the field.

Per the debate format, I will take aim at what I take to be a couple of the central claims of Sosa's discussion in this chapter. However, my criticisms are intended to be constructive and illuminating. Rather than try to uncover any deep flaws in Sosa's brand of virtue epistemology, my aim is to push him further along what appears to be his present trajectory, that is, toward an even wider embrace of intellectual character virtues like open-mindedness, attentiveness, intellectual carefulness, intellectual thoroughness, and intellectual courage. I argue that Sosa should conceive of intellectual character virtues, not merely as "auxiliary virtues" or as what I shall refer to here as "epistemic enablers," but also as constitutive elements of knowledge or as "epistemic contributors."

I begin by addressing some interpretive issues concerning the discussion of mine to which Sosa is responding. Next I argue that while intellectual character virtues sometimes function in the merely auxiliary way Sosa describes, they also regularly manifest in knowledge-constitutive epistemic performances. After also considering the relationship between intellectual character virtues and epistemic agency, I conclude, contra Sosa, that intellectual character virtues like open-mindedness, attentiveness, and intellectual carefulness are a part of the "charmed inner circle for traditional epistemology."[19] I close with a discussion of whether a concern with the dimensions of intellectual character that do not partly constitute knowledge is best understood as proper to epistemology, ethics, or both.

A quick note about terminology. Throughout the chapter, I will refer to the traits in question simply as "character virtues" (dropping "intellectual" for simplicity). Also, I will use the term "intellectual virtue" in a quasi-technical way to refer to whatever personal qualities or abilities contribute to knowledge understood within a virtue reliabilist framework.

Interpretive Issues

Sosa argues that contrary to what I suggest in my book, something like character virtues have always been a part of the reliabilist repertoire of intellectual virtues: "responsibilist competences ... have been present in virtue reliabilism from its inception" (p. 64). This claim strikes me as partly right and partly wrong. In some sense, the idea that character virtues have always been present in reliabilism is precisely what I was attempting to defend in my book (2011). A "central claim" of the relevant chapter is that "character virtues satisfy virtue reliablists' formal requirements for an intellectual virtue" (pp. 47–48). In other words, by reliabilists' own lights, character virtues are intellectual virtues. A trickier question concerns the extent to which this point has been recognized or accepted by reliabilists. In his discussion in this chapter, Sosa makes clear that he has always thought of epistemic reliability as involving a volitional and characterological dimension. And he cites some passages from his earlier work that suggest as much. Sosa is correct that I interpreted him as failing to fully recognize or accept that character virtues satisfy the conditions for an intellectual virtue. While this interpretation was at least somewhat tentative (I argued merely that "there is reason to think" that Sosa does not regard character virtues as intellectual virtues and that he "apparently believes" as much), and while I did offer several reasons in support of this interpretation (including its endorsement by fellow reliabilist John Greco), I now see that it was both mistaken and hasty. I am grateful to Sosa for this correction.

It would also be a mistake, however, to conclude that reliabilists in general have been or are committed to including character virtues in their repertoire of intellectual virtues. In the chapter Sosa criticizes, I also look closely at the views of Greco and Alvin Goldman (pp. 49–50). Unlike Sosa, these authors are more explicit about their exclusion of character virtues. Goldman (1992), for instance, says:

> In the moral sphere ordinary language is rich in virtues terminology. By contrast there are few common labels for intellectual virtues, and those that do exist—'perceptiveness,' 'thoroughness,' 'insightfulness,' and so forth—are of limited value in the present context. I propose to identify the relevant intellectual virtues ... with the belief-forming capacities, faculties, or processes that would be accepted as answers to the question 'How does X know?' In answer to this form of question, it is common to reply, 'He saw it,' 'He heard it,' 'He remembers it,' 'He infers it from such-and-such evidence,' and so forth. Thus, basing belief on seeing, hearing, memory, and (good) inference are in the collection of what the folk regard as intellectual virtues. (p. 162)

I conclude that while Sosa has always thought of certain instances or types of knowledge as requiring something like an exercise of character virtues, the same cannot be said of virtue reliabilists or of virtue reliabilism in general.

Character Virtues: Epistemic Contributors or Mere Enablers?

The foregoing, largely irenic picture is not entirely accurate. When Sosa says that "responsibilist competences ... have been present in virtue reliabilism from its inception," he apparently is not talking about familiar responsibilist traits like open-mindedness and intellectual courage. Rather, he seems to be referring to a different set of agential or character-based abilities that fall somewhere between "non-agential faculty virtues" and responsibilist character virtues (see especially the discussion on pp. 64–9). This is strongly suggested by Sosa's description of responsibilist character virtues as "auxiliary virtues" that put a person "in a position to know" but do not constitute knowledge and therefore are not intellectual virtues in the strict sense (p. 67).

To state Sosa's position more simply, it will be helpful to have at our disposal a distinction between "epistemic enablers" and "epistemic contributors." Epistemic enablers are qualities that, in Sosa's words, put one *"in a position to know*, in a position where one can now exercise one's knowledge-constitutive competences"* (p. 67) and epistemic contributors are qualities of the latter sort—qualities *in virtue of which* one knows. Accordingly, Sosa appears to be committed to the following claims:

1. Character virtues function merely as epistemic enablers.
2. There is, however, a related but distinct set of characterological or agential virtues—call them "reliabilist agential virtues"—that are epistemic contributors.
3. Thus reliabilist agential virtues but not character virtues belong in the reliabilist repertoire of intellectual virtues.

This interpretation of Sosa's position is borne out by several passages in his discussion above, including the following:

> ... we can best understand the responsibilist, character-based intellectual virtues highlighted by responsibilists as *auxiliary* to the virtues that are a special case of reliable-competence intellectual virtue. (p. 63)
>
> ... open-mindedness, intellectual courage, persistence ... are not in the charmed inner circle for traditional epistemology. They are only "auxiliary" intellectual virtues, by contrast with the "constitutive" intellectual virtues of central interest to virtue reliabilism. (p. 69)

While these and related passages seem clearly to support (1)–(3), there is some textual evidence for thinking that in fact Sosa wants to leave the door open to the possibility that character virtues can be epistemic contributors. Specifically, at one point he says of persistence and resourcefulness (two clear examples of character virtues) that the "the exercise of *such* intellectual virtues need not and normally will not constitute knowledge, not even when that exercise does indirectly lead us to the truth" (p. 68). "Need" and "normally" suggest the possibility that at least in certain cases character virtues do function as epistemic contributors.

How, then, should we understand Sosa's position here? I think the total evidence of his discussion above favors the stronger interpretation according to which character virtues are not epistemic contributors.[20] Again, this impression is difficult to escape given his straightforward claim that character virtues "are not in the charmed inner circle for traditional epistemology." And it seems especially clear in his remark that character virtues "are *only* 'auxiliary' intellectual virtues, by *contrast* with the 'constitutive' intellectual virtues of central interest to virtue reliabilism" (emphasis added). I will, at any rate, assume this stronger interpretation in the remainder of the chapter. However, even if this interpretation is mistaken, there remains plenty of notable distance between Sosa's view and my own. At most, Sosa appears open to the possibility that character virtues are epistemic contributors only in rare or non-standard cases. Against this claim, I turn now to argue that it is not in fact rare or unusual for an exercise of character virtues to partly constitute an item of knowledge.

We may begin by considering Sosa's case for the claim that character virtues do not function as epistemic contributors. His discussion suggests two main arguments for this claim. The first is that character virtues—at least as understood by some responsibilists—are too normatively demanding. Sosa correctly notes that for both Zagzebski and me, to possess a character virtue, one must be disposed to engage in a certain kind of intellectual activity characteristic of this virtue out of something like a "love" of truth or other epistemic goods. Now, as Zagzebski and I think of it, the "love" in question need not be understood in strongly desiderative terms (hence the scare quotes). I claim, for instance, that "the positive orientation central to personal intellectual worth is not necessarily desiderative in nature . . . it can also take a purely volitional form" (p. 109). In other words, one's personal intellectual worth can be enhanced on account of a volitional commitment to reaching the truth even if this commitment is not rooted in a strong desiderative or affective attachment to truth. A more accurate way of understanding what Zagzebski and I are getting at here is in terms of the notion of *intrinsic epistemic motivation*. We maintain that virtue-manifesting intellectual activity must be motivated at least partly by an intrinsic concern with epistemic goods like truth and knowledge—a concern or desire for these goods *as such* or *considered in their own right*, not merely for the sake of some additional (potentially non-epistemic) good that might result from their acquisition.[21]

Thus the motivational requirement on intellectual virtue that Zagzebski and I subscribe to may not be quite as "high minded" or demanding as Sosa suggests. This clarification notwithstanding, Sosa rehearses a convincing case for the claim that even a weaker motivational requirement of the sort just sketched is problematic vis-à-vis an attempt to give a virtue-based account of knowledge. The problem is that a great deal of knowledge evidently can be acquired in the absence of virtuous epistemic motivation. My knowledge, at the onset of a sudden and unexpected power outage, that the room has suddenly gone dark need not manifest any intrinsic concern with getting to the truth. Such knowledge might come to me entirely unbidden. In fact, if it is sufficiently important to some other purpose of mine that the room remains lit (e.g., if I am struggling to meet an imminent writing deadline), I might even will that the proposition in question be false, while nevertheless still knowing it to be true.

While Sosa is correct that we should not think of intrinsic epistemic motivation as a requirement for knowledge, this does not warrant a dismissal—even from a reliabilist standpoint—of traits like open-mindedness, intellectual carefulness, intellectual thoroughness, intellectual honesty, or intellectual rigor. As Sosa's own discussion suggests, a person can have a settled disposition to think and reason in ways that are open, careful, thorough, honest, and rigorous, while having little or no intrinsic concern with any epistemic goods:

> Hedge fund managers, waste disposal engineers, dentists, and their receptionists, can all attain much knowledge in the course of an ordinary workday despite the fact that they seek the truths relevant to their work only for their instrumental value. That is why they want them, not because they *love* truth. That seems indeed to be true of service professionals generally, including medical doctors and lawyers. It is not love of truth that routinely drives them in their professional activities, by contrast with desire for professional standing, wanting to help someone, or trying to make a living. (p. 71)

While Sosa does not put the point quite this way, if the people he describes are habitually and intelligently attentive to important details, careful and thorough in their research, if they are regularly open to expert advice, listen fairly to alternative standpoints, and persist in their attempts to acquire knowledge, then surely it will make sense to think of them as having the *traits* of attentiveness, intellectual carefulness and thoroughness, openmindedness, fair-mindedness, and intellectual persistence. Further, given the plausible assumption that these traits are epistemically reliable, it will also make sense to think of them as *virtues* in some legitimate and familiar sense.[22]

As this suggests, it is at least open to Sosa to treat *broadly motivated* attentiveness, intellectual carefulness, and so on as epistemic contributors, where such motivation includes either intrinsic epistemic motivation or the sort of instrumental motivation just described. Again, he could treat these traits as such because of their contribution to their possessor's epistemic reliability. In fact, a similar view has already been defended by Julia Driver (2000), who claims that a trait like attentiveness or intellectual carefulness is an intellectual virtue if and only if "it systematically (reliably) produces true belief" (p. 126). While, in my own work, I have defended an account of intellectual virtue whereby intrinsic epistemic motivation is a necessary feature of an intellectual virtue, I have also taken pains to endorse pluralism about kinds or concepts of intellectual virtue that leaves room for a conception of precisely this sort:

> I think a single trait of character can be intellectually excellent and thus an 'intellectual virtue' in more than one way . . . a character trait's being epistemically reliable or truth-conducive is both necessary and sufficient for its counting as an intellectual virtue according to a certain viable 'externalist' model of intellectual virtue. (2011, p.105)

Finally, for reasons noted above, I maintain that this is the right conception to adopt where the objective is to offer a philosophical account of knowledge anchored in the concept of intellectual virtue.

To summarize: given Sosa's theoretical aims, he is right to deny a motivational requirement on intellectual virtue; however, this does not warrant banishing character virtues from the "charmed inner circle" in traditional epistemology. For, again, a person can possess the trait of open-mindedness, intellectual carefulness, or intellectual courage without being motivated by a concern with epistemic goods as such. Further, these traits can be viewed as epistemic contributors on non-motivational grounds. Indeed, reliabilists in particular are in a good position to view them as such, for the traits in question contribute importantly to epistemic reliability.

While the latter move is open to Sosa, he seems unlikely to make it. For he also gives a second reason for thinking that character virtues are not epistemic contributors. A central thesis of Sosa's discussion is that while character virtues can put us *in a position* to know, they are not the sort of cognitive competence *in virtue of which* we acquire knowledge—they are not knowledge-constitutive. Referring to character virtues, he comments:

> When the correctness of a belief is due to competence in a way that *constitutes* knowledge, it is not enough that the competence reliably puts one *in a position to know*, in a position where one can now exercise one's knowledge-constitutive competences, those whose exercise *does* constitute knowledge. (p. 67)

In what sense do character virtues put us in a position to know? Sosa explains:

> The long hours, the intense concentration, the single-minded avoidance of distractions, may put the inquirer in a situation, or enable her to attain a frame of mind, or certain skills, through all of which she can have and exercise the competences more directly relevant to the attainment of

knowledge. She might acquire important data through a perilous voyage to distant lands, or through observations of the night sky, none of which she could have done without persistent dedication over many years with enormous care. (p. 68)

Again, for Sosa, while cognitive activity of the sort just described can facilitate knowledge, it is not constitutive of knowledge. He illustrates this point with the following example:

Suppose a mysterious closed box lies before us, and we wonder what it contains. How can we find out? We might of course just open the lid. In pursuit of this objective we will then exercise certain competences, perhaps even character traits (if the box is locked, or the lid stuck), such as persistence and resourcefulness. And perhaps these qualities (in certain contexts, and in certain combinations) do lead us reliably to the truth. Nevertheless, the exercise of *such* intellectual virtues need not and normally will not *constitute* knowledge, not even when that exercise does indirectly lead us to the truth. (p. 68)

What does constitute knowledge in such a case? The fairly obvious answer is visual perception. While character virtues may put one in a position to know by helping one figure out how to open the box, one knows what is in the box on account of *seeing* it.

A slightly different way of putting this point is that while intellectual virtues are manifested in the process of inquiry, which often leads to or terminates in the formation of a belief, they do not manifest in belief-formation itself.[23] Understood in this way, I concur with much of what Sosa has to say. I agree, for instance, that character virtues do bear frequently and centrally on the process of inquiry and therefore often leave their possessor in a good position to acquire knowledge. I also agree that character virtues do not (typically) manifest in the automatic or agency-independent formation of beliefs.[24] However, Sosa himself makes a good case for thinking that belief formation is not always passive or automatic—as in cases of what he calls "intentional, judgmental belief" (p. 73). The question, then, is whether character virtues can manifest in knowledge-constitutive cognitive performances of this sort. Sosa seems to think not. I disagree.

I maintain that character virtues regularly manifest in cognitive acts like judging, perceiving, noticing, and grasping and that such acts often enough are knowledge-constitutive in Sosa's sense. Consider, for instance, a case in which a person notices an important visual clue or detail on account of his focused attention or attentive observation. As I am conceiving of the case, it is not as if the person exercises attentiveness and then, only subsequently, sees the relevant detail. Rather, attentiveness is manifested in the act of visual perception itself. It is *in* or *through* focused or attentive looking that the detail is perceived. To come at this from another angle, consider how we might answer the following question: on account of which cognitive competence does the person acquire knowledge? One answer might be: good vision. But this is an underdescription. For it could be that most people with perfectly good vision would fail to see the relevant detail. A better answer would be something like: *attentive* and *careful* visual perception. This puts the spotlight back on character virtues. It suggests that the person acquires knowledge on account of his intellectual attentiveness and carefulness, that is, on an account of a manifestation of these traits in the operation of his visual faculty.

Alternatively, consider a case in which, through an act of *honest* introspection, a person becomes aware of the fact that she doubts a certain claim that she has long taken herself to firmly believe. Again, it would be misguided to say that this person manifests intellectual honesty and then, in a separate cognitive act, becomes aware of the relevant fact. Instead, it is thorough or in virtue of her introspective honesty that she grasps her doubt. Her intellectual honesty manifests in an act of introspection. Or, consider a similar case in which a person is presented with counterevidence that defeats the justification of one of her beliefs. The defeating relation is subtle enough that it could easily be missed, even by people whose cognitive faculties are operating normally. The person in question, however, is habitually thorough and open-minded. In an exercise of these traits, she grasps and accepts the fact that her belief is unjustified. Again, by all appearances, her knowledge of this fact is partly constituted by her thorough and open-minded use of reason.

These examples underscore a critical point: namely, that the exercise or manifestation of character virtues cannot be divorced from the operation of perceptual or other cognitive faculties like introspection and reason. It may be tempting to think that the operation of character virtues somehow precedes and thus is distinct from the operation of cognitive faculties. However, this is a mistaken view. Intellectual character virtues manifest in the operation or exercise of cognitive faculties. They harness and regulate these faculties in rational and reliable ways. Indeed, what would it be for a person to exercise open-mindedness, attentiveness, or intellectual carefulness *without* making use of one or more cognitive faculties? Could we even begin to describe the operation of a character virtue without reference to the operation of a cognitive faculty?

The emerging picture is one according to which character virtues are both epistemic enablers and epistemic contributors. In some situations, character virtues may—in precisely in the way Sosa describes—put one in a position to acquire knowledge without partially constituting that knowledge. In other situations, however, they may be manifested in cognitive performances—in judging, perceiving, noticing, grasping, etc.—that do contribute to knowledge.

Character Virtues and Epistemic Agency

One way to put the conclusion just reached is that the class of character virtues intersects with the class of reliabilist agential virtues. Alternatively: character virtues sometimes function as reliabilist agential virtues. Now I want to look more closely at this relationship. How exactly do character virtues stand relative to the agential virtues described by Sosa?

To answer this question, we will need to get further clarity on what exactly the latter virtues amount to. This is not an easy task. Sosa makes the following claims about reliabilist agential virtues: (a) they aim at truth; (b) agents are responsible for their exercise and irresponsible for neglecting their exercise; (c) they involve intentional, volitional agency; and (d) they are manifested in the conscious, reflective scrutiny and "conscious, agential, judgmental endorsement" (p. 73) of first-order beliefs. While this characterization is suggestive, Sosa does not provide any specific examples or concrete cases of agential virtues. This raises the question of how, more precisely, we might think of them. That is, how might we understand the volitional, truth-oriented competences in virtue of which a person with reflective knowledge responsibly scrutinizes or endorses her first-order judgments?

We can begin by noting how such scrutiny or endorsement might go *wrong*, for example, how it might be *irresponsible*. As Sosa suggests elsewhere (2011), one might engage in second-order reflection on a first-order judgment in ways that are *biased* (p. 16). Similarly, such reflection can be *hasty, shallow, superficial, provincial, cowardly*, or the like.[25] Indeed, it is difficult to imagine other sorts of ways in which such reflection might go wrong that are at once volitional and a matter of personal responsibility. In any case, given this understanding of what it is for reflective scrutiny and endorsement to go wrong, a certain conception of *responsible* doxastic reflection immediately presents itself. Specifically, responsible scrutiny and endorsement of a first-order belief is scrutiny and endorsement that is *honest, fair, careful, thorough, open, courageous*, and so on. Put in agential terms, the claim is that responsible doxastic reflection requires an exercise of character virtues like intellectual honesty, fair-mindedness, intellectual carefulness, intellectual thoroughness, open-mindedness, and intellectual courage.

A more controversial question is whether the class of reliabilist agential virtues is *reducible* to the class of character virtues. I am not sufficiently confident about how Sosa is conceiving of reliabilist agential virtues to defend an affirmative reply to this question. Thus I leave open the possibility that some reliabilist agential virtues are not character virtues. However, the point remains that it is difficult to say much about the way in which the kind of "conscious, agential, judgmental endorsement" in question might be good or responsible without invoking the language of character virtues. For this reason the difference between character virtues and reliabilist agential virtues is at best unclear

This leads to a further point. Consider how moral virtues are sometimes thought to stand relative to practical reason or moral agency. Aristotle, for instance, thinks of moral or ethical virtue as (largely) constituted by a disposition to choose in accordance with a mean—to choose the right actions, at the right time, in the right amount, toward the right person, and so on.[26] For Aristotle, *individual* moral virtues capture what this looks like from one situation to another: in some contexts, excellence in moral agency looks like giving a certain amount of one's financial resources to a particular cause and in a particular way (generosity), while in other contexts it might look like facing down one's fears confidently and in the service of a worthy end (courage), while in others still it might look like resisting or regulating one's bodily appetites (temperance). One way to put Aristotle's view is that moral virtues constitute the excellences of practical reason or moral agency.

What might a similar view amount to in epistemology? As Sosa makes clear, some knowledge can be acquired independently of epistemic agency. In other cases—and especially in cases of reflective knowledge, which Sosa describes as "at the center of the epistemological tradition from the Pyrrhonians to Descartes and beyond" (p. 74)—knowledge makes significant agential demands. As we have seen, this does not mean merely that agency must be *operative* in the formation of the relevant belief, even operative in a strong and central way. Rather, agency must be involved in ways that are *good or excellent*. We have seen further that the excellence in question is naturally describable in virtues terminology. This suggests the following general picture: just as moral virtues are the excellences of moral agency, intellectual character virtues are the excellences of epistemic agency. On this view, the concept of intellectual character virtue picks out what it is for epistemic agency to function well—or in a responsible, truth-oriented way—from one situation to another. Again, in some contexts, this might amount to exercising caution in the drawing of a conclusion, in others it might look like honestly and courageously confronting a piece of counterevidence, and in others still like carefully and thoroughly probing the evidential basis of a belief. I mention this view as a possibility that merits further consideration. Though I lack the space to explore the view in detail here, to the extent that it is plausible, the distinction between character virtues and reliabilist agential virtues looks fragile indeed.

This has further implications for our understanding of the relationship between character virtues and knowledge. Sosa argues that reliabilist agential virtues are crucial to the possession of knowledge, particularly reflective knowledge. If this is right, and if the difference between reliabilist agential virtues and character virtues is slim (or non-existent), then character virtues also turn out to be critically important to knowledge—not merely in an indirect or instrumental fashion, but constitutively.

Epistemology, Ethics, or Both?

I close with a brief reflection on the boundaries of epistemology and on where a concern with character virtues falls with respect to these boundaries. If we are right to think that character virtues figure centrally into the conditions for reflective knowledge, then it is beyond question that a certain kind of philosophical reflection on these traits is proper to epistemology. But imagine that our concern is with the way in which character virtues bear on the cognitive life more generally, for example, with how they are related to "cognitive flourishing" or a good intellectual life.[27] At a couple of different points in his discussion, Sosa alludes to the view that a concern with the aspects or dimensions of virtuous intellectual character that are *not* knowledge-constitutive, while philosophically legitimate, is proper to *ethics* rather than epistemology. Sosa does not explicitly endorse this claim; nor do I think this is his considered position on the matter.[28] However, it would not be very surprising if no small number of epistemologists were to be tempted by this perspective. This is especially true given that the dimensions in question are personal and normatively robust. Once a concern with these dimensions is divorced from a concern with the nature of knowledge, it might seem than any remaining philosophical work in the vicinity would fall to moral philosophers, not epistemologists.

Where, then, does broader philosophical reflection on intellectual character—reflection on character virtues and their role in the cognitive life, considered apart from their status as epistemic contributors—figure relative to the boundaries of epistemology? In the remainder of this chapter, I argue that such reflection lies at the intersection of epistemology and ethics. It is properly epistemological; however, on a sufficiently broad conception of the field, it also falls within the purview of ethics.[29]

First, despite the fact that intellectual character virtues, especially when conceived of as involving an element of intrinsic epistemic motivation, bear on the personal worth of their possessor in a manner analogous to moral virtues, it is important not to lose sight of the fact that they nevertheless *aim* at and are *reliably productive* of distinctively *epistemic* goods like truth, knowledge, and understanding. Indeed, this is one familiar way of trying to demarcate intellectual character virtues from moral virtues.[30] A related point, also widely acknowledged, is that intellectual character virtues have a unique and central bearing on the process of *inquiry*, which of course is also epistemically oriented.[31] These aspects of character virtues are significant, for epistemologists have long been focused on the personal capacities, cognitive faculties, and epistemic practices that aim at and reliably lead to true belief. Nor has their concern with these things been limited to whether or how they figure into the necessary and sufficient conditions for knowledge.[32] Accordingly, why not think of philosophical reflection on the intentional and causal relations between character virtues and epistemic goods as proper to epistemology?

A reply might be that any kind of philosophical reflection on personal character is proper to ethics. On a sufficiently broad conception of ethics, this may be correct; however, this hardly shows that such reflection is proper *merely* to ethics. Indeed, it seems arbitrary in the extreme to treat the *non-volitional* or *non-characterological* aspects of human psychology that are aimed at and productive of epistemic goods as falling within the purview of epistemology, while treating the volitional and characterological aspects that are similarly aimed and productive as proper only to ethics. A much more plausible position is that reflection on both sets of qualities or capacities is proper to epistemology, even if reflection on the volitional and characterological qualities is also proper to ethics, broadly conceived.

Second, it is significant that epistemic ends can conflict with what we typically think of as moral ends.[33] Consequently the personal qualities aimed at and productive of these ends can conflict as well. Imagine, for instance, a scientist enthralled with his quest for empirical knowledge. He sees explanatory understanding of a certain dimension of scientific reality as an estimable human good, one that is worth pursuing and acquiring at least partly for its own sake. This orientation in turn compels him to inquire in ways that are careful, thorough, tenacious, honest, open, and so on. However, the scientist is so deeply and personally invested in his quest for understanding that he severely neglects his various duties to his spouse, children, friends, and neighbors. At first glance, the scientist would appear to be intellectually virtuous but not morally virtuous. Given this tension between intellectual character virtues and paradigmatic moral virtues, the instinct to classify broad philosophical reflection on the former as proper to ethics but not epistemology seems misplaced.

There are, of course, relatively broad conceptions of morality according to which the type of conflict in question is not really between epistemic ends and moral ends but rather between moral ends of two different types or varieties (viz. epistemic and moral in some more familiar or paradigmatic sense). Take, for example, the view that the moral domain is coextensive with the domain of human flourishing. Presumably the scientist, on account of his virtuous orientation toward and pursuit of epistemic goods, is flourishing in certain respects. (Compare him with a person who is similarly neglectful of his most important relationships but who, unlike the scientist, is also intellectually indifferent, lazy, hasty, biased, narrow-minded, etc. Surely the latter person is flourishing to a lesser extent than the scientist.) This reopens the possibility that a concern with the relevant dimensions of intellectual character is proper only to ethics, broadly construed. However, unless one has a good principled reason for excluding all characterological considerations from epistemology, this response is liable to fall flat. Again, a more plausible conclusion is that the concern in question is proper to both epistemology and ethics, broadly construed.

I conclude that philosophical reflection on the role of character virtues in the cognitive life is proper to epistemology even when such reflection is abstracted from any concern with whether or how character virtues constitute knowledge. But it need not be proper only to epistemology. On a sufficiently broad conception of ethics, such reflection falls within the purview of this field as well. It represents a point of intersection between epistemology and ethics. This underscores the possibility of innovative philosophical work that brings together the best thinking and theoretical resources from epistemology with the best work in areas like virtue ethics, moral psychology, and action theory.[34] The potential result is a deeper philosophical understanding of the personal or characterological dimensions of the life of the mind.

Study Questions

1. Give examples of dispositions that are (a) agential competences but not character virtues, (b) character virtues but not agential competences, and (c) both agential competences and character virtues.
2. Some philosophers have argued that knowledge is more valuable than mere true belief not because it leads to better consequences but because it manifests virtue. How would Sosa respond to this claim? How would Baehr respond?
3. In the previous controversy, Robert Roberts and Nancy Snow agreed that virtue contributes to flourishing. They were focused, however, on moral virtue. Does intellectual virtue of the sort that Sosa or Baehr identify contribute to flourishing? Explain.
4. Should at least some intellectual virtues be conceived of as having an element of intrinsic epistemic motivation? Explain.
5. What is the point of distinguishing between things that fall within the "charmed inner circle" of epistemology and things that don't?

Notes

1. On this, as we shall see, there is dissension in the ranks of responsibilists. Zagzebski hopes and believes that responsibilist virtue theory can solve traditional problems of epistemology, whereas Baehr declares defeat, at least in crucial part. Here I side with Zagzebski's aspirations, but agree with Baehr that they have not been attained so far. Rather than conceding defeat, however, I will offer a better responsibilist account, one that welcomes responsibilism at the core of virtue reliabilism.
2. In what follows I will characterize my view indifferently as "reliabilist" or "competence" virtue epistemology (CVE).
3. Note 9 of Chapter 4, "Epistemic Normativity," of my *A Virtue Epistemology* (2007).
4. These passages are from the concluding paragraphs of Section 4.2 of Baehr's book.

5. What follows will take up problems of epistemic agency as its main focus and will exploit distinctions that deal directly with additional problems that arise once virtue epistemology becomes more explicitly and voluntaristically agential.
6. This is note 4 of Chapter 4 of Baehr's book.
7. In fact, not even animal knowledge is necessarily so exclusive, as should have been clear already in the main text, and will be emphasized in section D3 below.
8. Baehr, *passim*; e.g., Section 2.2.1, pp. 22–25.
9. Sosa (1991, p. 277). This, by the way, is the earliest statement of the *knowledge as apt belief* view of knowledge, so in advocating it, I do not follow suit, contrary to Baehr's footnote 8, on p. 37.
10. This is emphasized in footnote 2 of Chapter 2 of my book *A Virtue Epistemology* (2007). That footnote makes it explicit that the view developed in that later book is essentially that same view, now better formulated, based on an improved conception of aptness, and explicitly amplified to cover performances generally. And the conception of intellectual virtues required for this view differs importantly from the *WIVA* that Baehr attributes to virtue reliabilists.
11. Occasionally, and more recently, she takes the somewhat different view that it is the knowledge that *does* manifest such high-ranking virtues that has relevant distinctive value, even if there is a lower order of knowledge that lacks it. But this will not help with the *Meno* problem, which is not really solved through appeal to such worthy belief motivated by the love of truth. What makes knowledge of the right way to Larissa better than mere true belief need not depend on such knowledge's being an achievement that deserves admiration, nor that it be pregnant with pragmatic value. This is increasingly clear if we switch the example to one of knowing which is the *shortest* road to Larissa. Of the two obvious roads, the shortest may be just infinitesimally shorter, so that its increment of pragmatic value is negligible. Moreover, one's knowledge may have been attained through the most ordinary testimony, by asking a passerby, which would merit little personal credit or admiration. And yet knowing what one believes is in that case still better than merely getting it right by luck. The sense in which it is still better comports with the fact that epistemology is not a department of ethics. Epistemic attainments, like good shots, are not quite generally and inherently valuable in any objective sense. In spite of that, the good ones are still "better" than alternatives even so. Knowledge is in that way a better attainment than belief that does not succeed or does so just by luck. But this *general* superiority is not a quasi-ethical matter of motivation. It is rather a matter of competence, which is often and importantly enough a matter of intentional agency, but can also be just a matter of functional, biological or psychological teleology.
12. Zagzebski (2008, p. 128).
13. *The Inquiring Mind*, p. 44.
14. Though see Alfano (2012; 2013a, Chapters 5–6; 2014b).
15. This is both how it seems (at least to me) and, in the absence of any ostensible defeating reason, this is (I say) how it is. I find that claim no less proper than the following: that sometimes I *decide* to raise my right hand and that sometimes I *know* that I see my right hand (and see it go up); that these things seem to me to be so, and that, in the absence of ostensible defeating reasons, they really are so.
16. I have been asked whether this cuts psychological reality at the joints. Although I am not entirely sure what is at issue in this question, I do think there is such a thing as the act of affirming, and that it can take the form of public assertion or that of private affirmation to oneself. I think that this is an act of crucial importance for a social species that depends as heavily as we do on collective deliberation and on the sharing of information. Moreover, it also seems crucial to distinguish various importantly different objectives that one might have in performing that act. And, for epistemology, there is a particularly important intention that one might have in performing it, namely that of getting it right *thereby* on the relevant "whether" question. So, I submit that we do well to recognize that particular act for special attention: the act of affirming in the endeavor *thereby* to get it right reliably enough,

the act of *judgment*. Closely related to that is of course the corresponding disposition, which one might then label "judgmental belief."
17. And celebrate their insightful study, as in the books of Zagzebski (1996) and Baehr (2011).
18. See his 1980 paper "The Raft and the Pyramid: Coherence versus Foundations in the Theory of Knowledge."
19. At least for traditional epistemology as approached from a reliabilist perspective. For the purposes of this paper, I will, with Sosa, be taking this perspective for granted.
20. Of course, reliabilist agential virtues may be "character virtues" of a sort; but I am here using "character virtues" to refer to those traits of intellectual character of interest to virtue responsibilists—traits like open-mindedness, intellectual courage, intellectual honesty, and so on.
21. Such motivation is important to their status as traits that contribute to personal worth. See my (2011, Ch. 6). For a similar view, see Zagzebski (1996).
22. It is worth bearing in mind that to be reliable, such dispositions presumably will need to be grounded in an *immediate* or *instrumental* concern with truth or accuracy and that this concern will need to be reasonably *stable* and *broad*. While these conditions are plausibly met by the service professionals noted above, it is doubtful that they are met in Sosa's assassin case discussed on p. 72. The underlying disposition guiding the assassin's cognitive activity is evidently quite narrow and unstable.
23. Sosa says: "In my view, a competence can constitute knowledge only if it is a disposition to believe correctly, one that can then be manifest in the correctness of a belief" (p. 69).
24. I say "typically" to allow for the fact that they can be manifested in, for instance, passive "noticings" or similar cognitive events that are the result of virtuous cognitive habits developed over time.
25. See Sosa's discussion on pp. 7, 12, and 21.
26. For Aristotle, virtues have an affective dimension as well; however, this is less immediately relevant to moral agency, which is my primary concern here.
27. This bearing might be logical, causal, intentional, or otherwise; and the states in question might include epistemic goods other than knowledge, for example, understanding, insight, or wisdom.
28. The latter impression is based on personal conversations with Sosa.
29. It might be wondered why we should care about this question in the first place. I briefly note two reasons. First, it is not difficult to imagine that the instinct to punt the relevant kind of reflection on character virtues to ethics might be due in part to a kind of dismissiveness ("I'm interested in the analysis of knowledge, which is a central epistemological project; insofar as character virtues aren't relevant to this project, I'm not interested in them, and they're not important to epistemology"). Such dismissiveness is worth calling out and resisting on principle. Second, given that character virtues aim at epistemic goods, are reliably productive of such goods, and have an important cognitive and epistemic component (Baehr 2013), it would be unfortunate if epistemologists, who are experts on such things, were to leave such reflection entirely to their colleagues in ethics. In other words, epistemologists have theoretical resources and expertise that would substantially benefit the philosophical work that gets done in this area.
30. See Chapter 6 of my 2011 monograph, *Knowing Full Well*, for more on the aim of character virtues and Chapter 4 for a discussion of their reliability. See the appendix of that work, Zagzebski (1996), and Driver (2000) for discussions of the distinction between intellectual virtues and moral virtues.
31. See Hookway (2003) for more on the role of character virtues in the context of inquiry and for a supporting account of the scope of epistemology.
32. From a historical standpoint, one thinks of work by philosophers like Locke and Descartes that is widely regarded as a contribution to the theory of knowledge but the scope of which is much broader than that of recent epistemology. More recently, William Alston (2005) has vigorously defended a broad conception of epistemology. He comments: "[W]hat can be said

on the subject of what does and does not count as epistemology? I think the best we can do is the following. What we call 'epistemology' consists of some selection from the problems, issues, and subject matters dealt with by philosophers that have to do with what we might call the cognitive side of human life: the operation and condition of our cognitive faculties—perception, reasoning, belief formation; the products thereof—beliefs, arguments, theories, explanations, knowledge; and the evaluation of all that. So a very broad conception of epistemology would be *philosophical reflection on the cognitive aspects of human life*" (pp. 2–3). Interestingly, Alston goes on (pp. 3–4) to identify reflection on intellectual character virtues considered apart the analysis of knowledge or justification as a prime example of philosophical work that falls within these boundaries and that merits closer attention among epistemologists.

33. "Typically think of" is significant because, as I get to below, on a broad enough conception of the moral, epistemic ends may be moral ends of a particular sort.
34. For an example of work in this direction, see Miranda Fricker's groundbreaking book, *Epistemic Injustice* (2007).

CHAPTER 4

How Are Virtues Acquired?

Abstract

In his contribution, Daniel Russell considers a challenge to the very idea of the virtues on the grounds that experimental evidence suggests that human behavior has surprisingly little to do with acting for reasons. Russell argues that it must be the case that humans can learn to do better at responding to reasons since this is in fact what people do learn when they acquire skills. More than that, the human potential for skill reveals generally that the basic psychological elements of human personality must be such that humans can train and shape them so as to become more responsive to reasons. Russell argues that that general revelation could help us understand the basic psychology of the virtues as well, and explores developments in social-cognitive theory to illustrate both how a single account of the psychological elements at work in skill might also account for the elements at work in virtue, and how a single account of how people acquire skills might also account for how people learn to be virtuous. In his response, Christian Miller agrees with Russell that our account of virtue has to be tethered to our best scientific understanding of what people are capable of. He also agrees that the social-cognitive approach to personality and character is interesting and promising. However, he worries that Russell has not fully confronted one of the main challenges to acquiring the virtues, namely the presence of beliefs and desires whose impact on conduct typically goes unnoticed but which systematically thwarts the development and expression of virtue. Miller discusses one of Russell's main suggestions for combating such beliefs and desires, namely by educating people about their presence in the first place. He notes that there is very little experimental evidence at the time about the effectiveness of this approach, and also that it may be unrealistic to expect people to be able to keep track of all this additional information about themselves and use it effectively when the time comes.

From Personality to Character to Virtue
Daniel C. Russell

Sometimes when we talk about "virtue," that term is little more than shorthand for observed behaviors; in this sense, "Louise is generous" simply summarizes some things we have seen Louise does. But this is to speak loosely. When we speak *strictly* about virtue, we are attempting to say something about a *person*, and in particular something fairly specific about his or her personality: personality involves certain psychological structures or mechanisms that account for how people behave, and when those structures are excellences we call them virtues. So to have a view about the virtues is automatically to commit to some deeper view about the building blocks of personality—what we might call personality *ontology*.[1]

For this reason, statements about people's virtues are empirically risky since our best understanding of personality might give no reason to believe in such things as virtues in the first place. Any account of the mechanisms by which people *behave well or badly* rests on an underlying account of the mechanisms by which people *behave* in the first place, so philosophical work on virtue is necessarily invested in psychological work on personality.

Here we confront a challenge. On the one hand, our longest philosophical tradition on the virtues, a tradition commonly associated with Aristotle, takes the virtues to involve not merely what one does but also one's reasons for doing it, and for doing it at a certain time, in a certain manner, and so on.[2] In any situation, there are good reasons to act in some ways and not others, and the virtues involve reliably responding to those reasons. But on the other hand, there is extensive experimental evidence suggesting that human behavior has less to do with responding to reasons than we suppose—people are surprisingly wayward. In that case, perhaps thinking of moral action in terms of virtuously responding to reasons is no more viable than thinking of it in terms of the so-called four humors, since the former rests on as defunct an ontology of personality as the latter.[3] People simply do not work that way.

I propose that the way to address this worry is to start by observing that if the very idea of responding to reasons casts doubt on the very idea of virtue, then for exactly the same reason it must cast doubt on the very idea of *skill* as well. Acquiring a skill also involves becoming more responsive to reasons. To build well, to drive a car well, to teach well, to play chess well, to diagnose a patient well—all of these involve grasping and acting on reasons to do some things and not others. Since such skills exist, it must be the case that humans are capable of responding to reasons, their meager and wayward psychological resources notwithstanding. And so there are two questions. One, could a single, empirically plausible account of personality *both* provide an ontology of the virtues *and* account for how we are able to acquire skills, wayward creatures though we are? And two, could the psychological paths by which humans acquire skills, also be available as paths for acquiring virtues?

My answer to both questions is yes, and the personality ontology I shall use to bridge virtue and skill is what psychologists call the "social-cognitive" approach to personality. Social-cognitive theory understands personality as a network of "mediating processes" by which people both interpret their surroundings and adjust their behavior to them. My proposal is that both the virtues and skill could be understood in terms of such mediating processes.

Why focus on social-cognitive theory? Even though social-cognitive theory is generally regarded as an empirically plausible approach to personality,[4] I advert to it here only as a *representative illustration* of how a single personality theory might account for both virtue and skill. My way of thinking of the virtues does not stand or fall with social-cognitive theory. But focusing on social-cognitive theory also has an argumentative advantage, since it has emerged from the very body of evidence that gives rise to our present challenge.[5]

From Personality to Character

Social-Cognitive Personality Theory

What is distinctive of the social-cognitive approach to personality is the idea that personality is an organized suite of reciprocal mediating processes by which people both (1) interpret or construe the situations in which they find themselves and imbue those situations with meaning, and (2) adjust their behaviors to those situations so interpreted.[6] Psychologist Nancy Cantor gave a nice summary of these mediating processes in her 1990 paper, "From Thought to Behavior: 'Having' and 'Doing' in the Study of Personality and Cognition."[7] In particular, she simplified the diverse cognitive and affective mediating processes down to three basic mechanisms. I think of the first two of these mechanisms as mechanisms for *construing our experiences* and the third as a mechanism for *adjusting our behaviors*.

First, people have different sets of beliefs and expectations that filter their perceptions of events and that lead them to attach different meanings to events when they transpire and as they are remembered. These bodies of active information are called *schemas*, and they provide "interpretive knowledge with which to frame experience and to anticipate events."[8] Schemas are organized structures of information that guide us in giving meaning to social situations, serve as the basis of our emotional reactions to events, and shape how we store events in memory. Schemas are also used for inferring other people's intentions, categorizing situations, persons, actions, and events, and anticipating certain outcomes.

Second, people are not passive observers of events but have goals and expectations that lead them to envision different ways of participating in events so as to bring about certain changes. That is, people have *tasks*, or avenues of potential activity that come about as people imagine different futures and adopt some of those imagined futures as personal goals. People's goals imbue their construal of various situations with personal interest.[9]

And third, people also differ in their choices (not necessarily *conscious* choices) for working toward their goals in different situations. In other words, people make progress on their tasks through the use of certain *strategies*, which include "processes of anticipation, monitoring, and retrospection to direct behavior in context."[10] Strategies enable one to regulate and adjust one's behavior within situations so as to bring about certain outcomes, by delaying gratification, controlling impulses, and making and executing plans over time.

In addition to these basic mediating mechanisms, there is also the *activation* of them. For example, everyone remembers embarrassing himself at some point, everyone prefers not to embarrass himself, and everyone has some facility at avoiding embarrassment; but not everyone has the same *propensity* to construe social situations in terms of their potential for embarrassment. In people we might call "shy," schemas for embarrassment are constantly "online"—in technical parlance, they are "chronically accessible"—and construing situations via that schema even becomes automatic.

What accounts for a heightened propensity to activate certain schemas? Psychologist Augusto Blasi argues that individuals have a sense (not necessarily an explicit or articulated sense) of the essential self or identity, a network of assumptions about the background conditions that make oneself, one's life, and one's environment recognizable as one's own.[11] Different dimensions of this identity can vary in terms of their centrality, depth, and importance to one, and psychologists Daniel Lapsley and Darcia Narvaez argue that the more relevant a schema is to interests and concerns of great personal importance, the more likely that schema is to become chronically accessible in daily life and, potentially, automatic.[12]

Social-Cognitive Character Theory

The activation in everyday life of a schema of great personal importance is the crucial point at which social-cognitive theory moves from personality to *character*. Blasi argues that schemas can also involve moral categories, such as honesty, trustworthiness, compassion, and fairness, and that people differ in the depth of these schemas within their personality.[13] Such differences can be understood as differences in character: to have a "moral character" is to act in accordance with a will and a sense of identity that is structured according to moral commitments about which one cares deeply, including a strong desire to act consistently with those commitments and aided by a suite of self-regulatory capabilities.[14]

Following Blasi, Lapsley and Narvaez argue that moral personality can be "understood in terms of the chronic accessibility of moral schemas for construing social events."[15] In particular, Lapsley and Narvaez conjecture that schemas corresponding to deep and central commitments with respect to moral categories would also be "chronically accessible for interpreting the social landscape," and that such accessing would potentially become automatic, just as happens in the case of other personality attributes.[16] One's character, on this view, is a function of how various moral categories are accessible for interpreting social life, making choices, and guiding behavior.

Now, there are a few things to note about this social-cognitive approach to character. For one, it is important to understand that even though this is an account of *character*, it is nonetheless only a *descriptive* account: it is an attempt to say what sort of thing, psychologically speaking, a moral character or a particular moral attribute would be. In other words, it is an account of what it is to have *a* character, but not necessarily an *excellent* character, so we should not mistake it for a theory of the virtues.

Another thing to note is that this approach to character and moral development is still a relatively recent development in the field and so the research in this area is still emerging. As Lapsley and Narvaez put the point, this approach is "a strategic bet."[17] Even so, "strategic" is an apt description of it, since social-cognitive theory is sufficiently mature in personality theory that it might be usefully extended to the field of moral development. Furthermore, focusing on the activation of schemas corresponding to closely held commitments to moral values seems a very natural way to undertake that extension.

Lastly, it is worth noting that such an approach would also offer a natural way to understand the underlying psychology of the virtues. Roughly, to have a virtue would be to have certain deep, standing goals that account for the activation of schemas for interpreting the social landscape, as well as discriminatory skills for defining determinate goal-relevant tasks and strategies for adjusting behavior so as to realize those goals. In fact, we shall see that such an approach would mirror Aristotle's.

From Character to Virtue?

It is at this point that we must ask some tough questions, though. Even if social-cognitive theory offers the best available account of character, it is still true, as I said above, that having *a* character is not the same thing as having a *good* character. As Christian Miller rightly observes, even if the social-cognitive approach can give an account of character, it does not follow that it can give an account of virtue.[18] I will go further: the elusiveness of virtue could prove to be one of the chief lessons of social-cognitive theory itself. The central idea of social-cognitive theory is that personality coherence exists at "the point of transaction between person *and context.*"[19] Would moral improvement be better understood in terms of certain changes within *persons*, or in terms of the careful engineering of *contexts*?[20]

Of course, we should not make the dichotomy too stark. On the one hand, our virtues are surely not independent of the company we keep, the opportunities for temptation we avoid,[21] and the practices, cultures, and institutions of the groups to which we belong.[22] And on the other, the influence of context surely is accompanied by the influence of internal features of persons, such as their moods.[23] Rather, the challenge is that the basic elements of personality and character might offer us so little to work with that our prospects for moral improvement would be better if we focused more of our energy elsewhere than on such "personological" changes as the cultivation of (alleged) virtues.

A very simple version of this challenge is that even if social-cognitive theory can reveal the consistency that *personality* has, it would not be the *kind* of consistency that virtues would have to have. Consistency is always relative to some metric or other, but not all metrics are relevant.[24] For example, if Fred refuses to pocket lost money but cheats on tests, his behaviors may still be consistent: he may regard cheating, unlike pocketing money, as a "victimless crime," and for him "victimlessness" may be the deciding factor. Now, when we *describe* Fred's personality or character—for better or worse—his consistency with respect to his own attitudes is the relevant metric of consistency. But when it comes to *virtue*, the relevant consistency is not consistency with what one *thinks* is right but with what really *is* right. Compare virtue to chess skill: as crucial as consistency is to being a winning chess player, consistency per se is not enough, since a player might be consistently awful.

However, the comparison with chess skill shows why this simple version of the worry is actually too simple. It is not as if good chess players are consistent relative to a metric that is *not* their own. Rather, they have trained in such a way as to make *their own* metric coincident with *the right* metric for winning at chess. Likewise, properly generous people (say) are consistent in behavior, and so there is necessarily some metric of theirs relative to which they are consistent. But what makes them properly generous is that in their case that metric is also coincident with the right one for helping and giving to others.[25]

But a subtler version of the challenge is possible. As I have said, in the case of virtue the relevant kind of consistency is consistency in one's *responsiveness to the genuine reasons there are* to behave generously, fairly, and so on. But perhaps the social-cognitive approach cannot make sense of *that* kind of consistency.[26] To be sure, the social-cognitive approach does suggest that, barring interference, a person's behavior will be the output of his or her cognitive and affective mediating processes. But the same approach also recognizes that interference is an alarmingly pervasive fact of life, and so among the things we consistently do is to respond to variables of context that have nothing to do with good reasons, and may not even have anything to do with *reasons* at all.[27]

The most graphic illustration of the power of context, of course, is Stanley Milgram's famous obedience experiments. In the original experiments, Milgram discovered that roughly two-thirds of his subjects would comply with even nonchalant instructions from an authority figure to administer what they believed were painful and even dangerous electric shocks to other people. In subsequent variations, however, Milgram discovered that he could reduce compliance levels significantly by varying whether the recipient of the shocks was visible, for example, or whether the instructions were given in person or by phone.[28]

The trick, then, is to explain *both* why the original compliance levels were so high *and* why compliance was so variable when conditions changed. An explanation friendly to social-cognitive theory might focus on how subjects construed the situation, along the following lines. In the original experiments, the initial subjects were so baffled by the utter nonchalance of the only person to whom they could look for expert guidance in an alien situation, that they were at a loss as to how to construe the situation in the first place—they could not get a "lock" on it, so to speak. In subsequent variations, by contrast, the situation changed just enough that more subjects could get a sufficiently firmer lock on it.[29]

Now, the reason a hypothesis like that would be friendly to the social-cognitive approach is that it would account for the existence of constant underlying mediating processes even in situations that play havoc with them. But of course, while the havoc that situations play with people's mediating processes can reveal the *causes* of people's behavior, those causes have nothing to do with responding to *reasons*. On the contrary, that havoc reveals how even irrelevant details within a situation can lead people to do exactly what they know too well they have reason *not* to do. In that case, *our behavior just might have less to do with responding to reasons than our hopes of acquiring virtues would require*. If so, then a character-based approach to moral behavior and development would simply put more weight on the elements of our psychology than they can bear. People do not work that way.

So perhaps what we *really* learn from social-cognitive theory is that our psychological mediating processes are so easily thrown off track that they are not the sorts of things that could be consistent in the way that virtue is supposed to be consistent. Perhaps social-cognitive theory gives us no reason to think of moral development in terms of acquiring virtues. On the contrary, perhaps social-cognitive theory actually *undermines* that thought.

I have lingered because I think this is a serious challenge for any attempt to understand moral behavior and development in terms of the virtues. But I now want to argue that we have every hope of meeting this challenge, and not in spite of what social-cognitive theory shows about behavior, but precisely *because of* what it shows. If social-cognitive theory shows us how easily people are thrown off track, it also shows us that our basic psychological mediating processes open up certain paths along which people can train to do better—in particular, to do better at things like building a wall or winning a game or healing a patient. In this respect, I propose that virtue is parallel to skill: a virtue is best understood as the result of exploiting the paths available to creatures with minds like ours for training to do better at things like being a good friend, a generous giver, and a fair-minded arbiter.

Personality, Skill, and Virtue: A Common Ontology

A Social-Cognitive Approach to Skill

When a social-cognitive theorist looks at skill, he or she understands skill in terms of the schemas, tasks, and strategies that experts have as well as how they activate them. First of all, unlike a novice, an expert has superior schemas—a store of knowledge about the target area that is large, is highly organized as a network, and has a rich structure whereby salient items of knowledge are accessed when needed. Experts also have the benefit of an extensive background of practicing that makes these schemas highly accessible. As a result, experts have applicable knowledge that enables them to arrive at very different representations both of situations and of opportunities for goal-directed action (or so-called affordances). On the social-cognitive approach, it is because of the richness of their schemas that experts are able to extract information that is highly relevant to their goals, so that they efficiently identify the most salient options for action.[30]

Second, skill also involves mediating processes by which experts are oriented toward the distinctive goals or *tasks* of the skill.[31] For example, this is how social-cognitive theorists interpret findings such as those of William Chase and Herbert Simon in their groundbreaking study of chess skill.[32] Chase and Simon found that what is distinctive of highly skilled chess players is a developed ability to draw on their knowledge and experience of chess in intensively *goal-directed* ways.[33] Surprisingly, Chase and Simon found that expert chess players excelled not in overall memory for chess[34] but rather in focusing their attention on strategically relevant groupings or "chunks" of pieces, seeing those chunks as parts of episodes of chess play organized in terms of strategic goals. "Memory for moves," Chase and Simon concluded, "is probably segmented into little episodes, each organized around some goal."[35] Or as a social-cognitive theorist would put it, skilled players have rich schemas that are oriented very effectively with respect to their tasks.

Third, experts also have distinctive *strategies* for understanding and solving problems that arise in the target area. For one thing, experts are more skilled at precisely defining the problems that face them and then matching those problems to schemas held in memory. For another, experts are able to employ complex rules, problem-solving heuristics, and automatic procedures to construct sophisticated plans of action, whereas novices tend to be shallower about the problem and less selective about opportunities.[36]

Lastly, a social-cognitive approach to skill also emphasizes the *way* that these basic elements are deployed, because the working of these basic cognitive mediating processes both in personality and in skill is largely automatic.[37] On this approach, one of the chief ways in which people acquire skill is by developing tacit and automatic processes for defining situations and adjusting their behavior to them. In the case of skill, automaticity—or more specifically, what psychologists call "*goal-dependent* automaticity"—is not mindless. It is consistent with control, and actually helps people be much *more* mindful in a couple of ways.[38] One, attention is a scarce resource, and making certain processes automatic allows a skilled person to concentrate attention where it is needed most. And two, in the case of skill automatic behaviors are themselves mindful: they are consciously instigated, consciously guided, and consciously interrupted or terminated, all in accordance with the expert's goals.[39]

So, on a social-cognitive approach, skill is understood as the result of exploiting potentialities available in the basic psychological elements that constitute personality. Skill is a matter of taking our capacity to be consistent in accordance with *some* standard and turning it into consistency in accordance with the *right* standard for the skill. Skill is a matter of being able to intelligently define a goal, perceive affordances with respect to that goal, and be effective in one's use of those affordances, all in a way that allows attention to be allocated efficiently. On this view, skill is how creatures that operate via social-cognitive mediating processes like ours develop not just consistency but consistent *excellence*. Skill is how creatures like that become more responsive to reasons.

A Social-Cognitive Approach to Virtue

Social-cognitive mediating processes can be trained to be responsive to reasons—we see this in the case of skill. In other words, we can identify paths for improvement that are available for humans as social-cognitive theory understands them. I propose that we take a parallel approach to the virtues: *virtues are what come from improving along the various paths for improvement that are actually available*. Skill is the result of exploiting potentialities within the basic psychological elements that constitute personality, and I propose that that is the best way to understand the virtues as well.

We can begin by taking a hint from Aristotle, whose main treatise on the virtues (*Nicomachean Ethics* II) opens with the observation that a virtue is an attribute we acquire through repeated and focused practice, in the same way that we also acquire a skill. For Aristotle, to say that someone has either a virtue or a skill is to say simultaneously that that person is committed to acting for a certain standing goal and that he or she is adept at finding what it would take to realize that goal in concrete, here-and-now circumstances (VI.1, 12). So, on the one hand, to say that a person is generous is to say that that person's standing goal is to help others by sharing resources, in the same way that to describe someone as a physician is to describe him or her in terms of the standing goal of healing by use of medicine. And on the other hand, a generous person, like a physician, has certain practical abilities for defining the problems to be overcome in realizing that standing goal:

- A critical or discriminatory ability to survey the available information so as to formulate an accurate view of just what the case at hand is (VI.10);
- a further discriminatory ability to consider the case at hand from multiple points of view so as to take a more reasonable perspective on it (VI.11); and
- the ability to then specify a determinate course of action to realize one's as-yet indeterminate goal in the case at hand (VI.11).[40]

Taken together, Aristotle calls these abilities practical intelligence (phronesis), and they are a bridge from the *goal* of helping or healing to a grasp of what helping or healing *would actually look like*, here and now.

Like skill, virtue is concerned with interpreting the varying circumstances before us and carefully adjusting our behaviors to the particular circumstances of time and place (*NE* VI.1, 1139a6–11), in much the way that an archer adjusts his or her aim at a target (1138b21–34). Or to take another analogy, practical intelligence is like perception,[41] in the sense that people with practical intelligence are able to see the world in ways that others do not, as also happens in the case of skill. In the terms of social-cognitive theory, people with practical intelligence can be understood as people who have developed rich schemas for defining problems, detecting goal-relevant information, and perceiving relevant affordances.[42]

Paths for Skill and Paths for Moral Development

Can virtue be *acquired* along the sorts of paths that are used in the development of skill? As Aristotle observes, virtue is a capacity for doing, but of a very different sort from the capacity for seeing: we do not acquire the capacity for seeing through practice, training, and developing habits, but that *is* how we acquire the virtues, and in this respect acquiring a virtue is exactly like acquiring a skill (*NE* II.1). That may be correct as far as it goes, but we still have to ask whether the *conditions* under which practice is effective for learning a skill also obtain in the case of developing a virtue.

Daniel Kahneman identifies two main conditions on the acquisition of skills:[43] one is that the target area have sufficiently regular patterns to be learned in the first place; and the other is that we receive clear and prompt feedback about our efforts. For example, both conditions are met when learning to drive a car: braking followed by stopping forms a regular pattern, and pressing the brake pedal yields prompt and unambiguous feedback. But of course, learning to be generous could not possibly be like *that*. I lend a friend money and he is pleased to be out of a jam; but for all that, have I really *helped* my friend, as opposed to (say) merely enabling him to put off dealing with the underlying problem that keeps getting him into jams like this one? Or did I stop to consider whether the money I gave him had already been spoken for—or whether it was even mine in the first place—so that my alleged "generosity" was also unjust? And even if I was genuinely and excellently helpful, is it clear what I should repeat in relevantly similar situations? Is it even clear what would make other situations "relevantly similar" in the first place? We learn to drive a car in a "clean" environment, so to speak, with respect to Kahneman's two conditions; but moral development takes place in "messy" environments, so there is no guarantee that the available paths for learning a skill are also available for developing a virtue.[44]

However, there are two things we should note about messy environments. The first is that, even in the case of skill, messy environments are normal. For example, steering a large ship through a harbor involves turning a wheel and then waiting several minutes for feedback.[45] Even tougher, learning to be a good poet, painter, or even builder involves not just learning *how* to make a good poem, painting, or wall, but also learning *at the very same time* what makes a poem, painting, or wall a good one in the first place. When it comes to very complex skills, messy learning environments are standard issue. Indeed, it is that very messiness that makes it *a matter of skill* to be able to detect and respond to the *relevant* patterns as opposed to the limitless irrelevant patterns that are there in the mess.[46]

And so the second thing to notice is that there are also psychological paths available *for overcoming messy environments themselves*, and they too are among the very paths that people exploit when they acquire skills. In other words, there are skills for acquiring other skills, and a very important part of the study of the psychology of expertise is the study of how experts acquire the skills to manage messy environments.

An illustrative discussion of this research is Robin Hogarth's book *Educating Intuition*.[47] One of the chief ways that people make messy environments more manageable, Hogarth explains, is by seeking the wisdom of others. For instance, surgeons learn more when their formal training is complemented by apprenticeships and by studying transcriptions of experienced surgeons verbalizing their thoughts as they examine and consider a variety of cases.[48] This sort of practice helps students learn where to put their attention in the first place and how to identify the most useful points of feedback. In other sorts of cases, learners may struggle with a new skill because their perceptions in the target area are tainted by bad habits they already have, such as forming stereotypes, trusting clever con artists, or forming preferences based on how options are presented. Fortunately, there are skills for counteracting these habits, such as developing the new habit of seeing one's initial reaction not in the first instance as evidence for a judgment or a reason for action, but as an explanandum to be scrutinized and assessed. In general, messy environments are such that the salient information to learn is hard to find, and so the first skill to learn is how to seek relevant information actively and systematically. Hogarth compares this skill to scientific method, since it involves better habits of observation, considering multiple perspectives, looking for evidence, and appreciating the limits of one's own knowledge.

Are these pathways for managing messy environments similarly available in moral development? I cannot answer that question as fully as it deserves, but I can point to some important parallels between problems that plague moral behavior and problems that skill training puts in its sights. The world daily tests our character, and our greatest struggles stem not so much from ignorance of the answers as from not realizing when the test has begun.[49] This is because attentional resources are scarce, so attention occupied with one or two features of a situation is unavailable for its other features.[50] For example, psychologist Ulric Neisser found that when students were shown a film of two teams passing basketballs and told to count the number of passes made by one of the teams, only about one in five noticed a woman with an umbrella strolling across the court about halfway through the film.[51] Attention can also be co-opted by early impressions and stereotypes that dominate what we subsequently notice and can even stop us noticing disconfirming feedback.[52] So, just as it is now familiar to us that humans have bounded rationality, we must also get used to the fact that humans have "bounded awareness."[53]

The thing to notice at present, though, is that awareness is not just bounded in the moral domain. It is bounded everywhere, and the acquisition of skill is in large part a matter of making efficient use of our awareness precisely because it is bounded.

The key to improving awareness is not to notice more things but to notice more relevance. For example, Marina Myles-Worsley and her colleagues discovered that expert radiologists were better, as one would expect, at recognizing the chest x-rays of unhealthy patients than radiology students were. But what is surprising is that the experts were also somewhat *less* accurate than the students at recognizing *normal* x-rays.[54] The experts did not notice more than the students did—they noticed *less*. The benefit of experience lies in how experts direct their attention, focusing on what is relevant and looking past the rest.[55] Likewise, Hogarth's discussion of stereotyping and credulity is chiefly in the context of hiring, which is extremely difficult to do well both because feedback on decisions is poor (feedback on hires is slow in coming, and of course feedback on non-hires never comes at all) and because perceptions of candidates can be easily co-opted by impressions that are misleading and difficult to correct. Hogarth argues that experts get better by fighting fire with fire, acquiring the habit of automatically scrutinizing the impressions that automatically arise.

Our awareness is bounded in the ethical realm, but only because it is bounded everywhere. At the psychological level, the human limitations that frustrate moral behavior are very the same ones that experts must also learn to manage in acquiring a skill.

I argued above that a social-cognitive ontology can underwrite an account of skill—that is, an account of a practical form of responsiveness to reasons. If a social-cognitive ontology is inadequate for an account of the virtues, this will not be due to the very idea that the virtues are responsive to reasons. And I have argued now, in a preliminary way, that the psychological paths by which we acquire skills are also the sorts of paths by which we could become virtuous. The cognitive and affective barriers to acquiring a virtue are no different from the barriers to learning a complex skill, barriers that we can apparently learn to recognize and overcome, albeit with much focused effort.[56]

Getting Better

A Place for Ideals

On the way of thinking about the virtues that I have sketched here, the central concept is that of *getting better*: knowing where humans have to start, how they ever manage to progress, and in light of those things, where humans can actually aspire to go. But that word "aspire" raises questions about *ideals* of virtue. The obvious way to think about ideals is that they describe the destination we aspire to reach, and the question of moral development is how to get there from here. By contrast, the approach I have sketched focuses on where we can actually go given where we have to start. So, what becomes of ideals and aspirations?

We do need ideals, but not as objects of aspiration. Consider Aristotle's claim that the virtues are such that, to have any virtue, one must have every virtue (*NE* VI.12–13).[57] If this is part of our aspirational ideal, then it seems that our very idea of virtue rests on the possibility of approximating to—and perhaps even achieving—this ideal. But then when we turn and look at the psychological resources we actually have to work with, the answer to the question, "How could we ever get there from here?" is that in all likelihood we couldn't.[58]

But "How could we ever get there from here?" is the wrong question. There is a place for ideals, but ideals can be *regulative* rather than aspirational. Here is what I mean. Getting better is not just changing but *improving*, and so we need to be able to ask in what direction "better" lies. It is at this point that something like Aristotle's idealization—what we nowadays call the unity of the virtues—has a role to play, because it tells us that becoming more generous, say, cannot be understood as merely being more disposed to perform certain stereotypical behaviors, for instance. Merely giving larger amounts or giving more often is the sort of change that could go along with becoming *less* sensitive to considerations of fairness or friendship or human well-being in one's giving—and *that* is not to improve in generosity, because generosity is an excellence. That is what I mean by a regulative ideal: when we are faced with multiple possible directions for developing, we need to know which direction to take in order to get *better*, not merely to get somewhere else. The ideal is not what we aspire to be, but it does helps us see what changes would count as real aspirations.

Putting Feasibility First

A regulative ideal is an abstract model that helps us get some traction on the direction in which "better" lies. It does no less, and it does no more. It is an ideal, but it is an ideal we can live with, because to have an ideal like that is to consider *first* what is psychologically feasible for us, and *then* ask what aspiration would be more than just a daydream.

It turns out that the order matters. In the study of moral development, labor is divided between philosophers and psychologists: philosophers ask what it is for an attribute to be an excellence, and psychologists ask what it is for an excellence to be achievable. But the division of their labor is one thing; the *sequence* in which that labor gets done is another. For much of the twentieth century that sequence was for philosophers to go first and psychologists second. Lawrence Kohlberg's conception of moral maturity owed less to psychological investigation than to reading John Rawls, and so he proposed that moral maturation must be a process of becoming more explicit in deliberation and more focused on universal principles.[59]

Now, Kohlberg's choice to sequence philosophical reflection ahead of psychological investigation is intuitively appealing, like first setting a goal and then finding the means.[60] The problem with that sequence, though, was that everywhere else in psychology the emerging picture of human action was that it was the product not of explicit deliberation but of making more of human thought automatic so that the scarce resources of attention can be directed where they are needed most.[61] Kohlberg told us where moral development should take us, and apparently we cannot get there from here. People do not work that way.

Sequencing the philosophical and the psychological labor in that order is what I call a "path-independent" approach to moral development, since thinking about virtue goes on in advance of investigating the available psychological paths. The general problem with a path-independent approach is that the philosophical work goes on unconstrained by limits of psychological feasibility, so that once the psychological work gets underway, there is every chance of discovering that we are not equipped to go where the philosophers aspired for us to be. Dividing that labor is crucial, but so too is the order in which it is carried out, and the path-independent order is a non-starter.

Fortunately, we can reverse that order: first, psychologists tell us what they can about how people ever manage to get better at all—more skillful, say—and then, second, philosophers look at the available paths for improvement and ask *to what we might hope to aspire given what paths are actually available*. On this approach, the philosophical goal is to determine how we might make the most of our developmental options in order to get better, in exactly the way that *skill* makes the most of those paths, except that in this case the improvement concerns becoming not a better chess player or builder or poet, but a better friend, a more generous giver, a fairer arbiter. This kind of approach to moral development I call a "path-dependent" approach,[62] and its central idea is that our philosophical vision of moral development must be bounded by constraints of psychological feasibility.

A Question of Hope

How much can we hope for given the paths that are available to us for getting better? I think we can have a *modest* hope. We have only messy environments to work in, and anyway, much of doing better is unlearning what we find it natural to do badly.[63] And while we can learn to arrest stereotypes when they arise, for example, there is probably less we can do to stop them arising in the first place.[64] So maybe the most we can hope for is to get a *little* better. But we should remember that a modest hope really is a hope, and getting a little better can do a lot of good. We dream of a world without ugly stereotypes altogether, but imagine how vastly better our world would be than it is now if people became more aware of their stereotyping and better at arresting it before acting or forming judgments. People who are just a little better are people who can change the world. If anything, that is probably the only world-changing there ever is. That is how people work.

Our hope is also a *sober* hope. Getting better is hard; it is almost certainly harder than we realize. Virtue is not just a summary of what someone does. It is a deep feature of the person who does it. That deep feature does not just happen—it really is an achievement. And the study of skill reveals that it is the sort of achievement that takes time, effort, and focused, directed practice. Virtue is like a skill, but it is like the sorts of skills it takes a lifetime to master.

If even then. An excellence is exactly what a virtue is—it excels beyond what we have any right to hope for without going through the hard training.

The approach to moral development I have sketched here cannot even try to promise everything we might have wanted. But what makes an approach good is not how much it tries to promise but how reasonable the hope is that the promise could be kept. Hope that is reasonable, modest, and sober is a very real hope indeed. And it is more than a daydream.[65]

Russell on Acquiring Virtue

Christian B. Miller

It is a great pleasure to be able to engage with Professor Russell's important work on virtue. Russell is one of the leading scholars working on issues about character today, and there is much to learn from his discussion in this chapter and his many other writings.

In what follows, I first summarize what I take to be the main claims made by Russell, above. While I will largely agree with the framework he has set out, I will nevertheless suggest in Section 2 that there is a significant challenge to virtue cultivation that comes in the form of certain widely held unconscious psychological dispositions that are not virtuous. Finally in the last section, I briefly discuss Russell's main suggestion for addressing the challenge posed by such dispositions.

Russell's Main Claims

Russell's section of the chapter has two primary goals as I see it. The first is to articulate, at least in a preliminary way, an account of the psychological structure of the virtues that is informed by our best empirical research. The second goal is to establish, again in a preliminary way, why it is reasonable to hope that we can make at least some progress in becoming more virtuous people, given this understanding of what the virtues are like. My primary focus in this chapter will be on his second goal.

I suspect most people think that his second goal hardly needs any defense. Isn't it just a basic datum of our ordinary moral experience that we can make some progress in becoming virtuous? Yet one of the themes supposedly emerging from the empirical literature, especially in the so-called situationist tradition in social psychology, is that our behavior is rarely responsive to good moral reasons. And responsiveness to good reasons is absolutely central to acquiring the virtues, at least on the picture of virtue that Russell and I (not to mention Aristotle and Aquinas) take seriously. So without such responsiveness, the prospects for becoming virtuous, even to a weak or moderate degree, are thought by some to be dim.[66]

Russell is not the only philosopher today who is discussing virtue cultivation in light of the contemporary psychological evidence. Indeed, others have already appealed to the "social-cognitive" approach, most notably Nancy Snow in her 2010 book *Virtue as Social Intelligence*. Similarly, Ernest Sosa and Julia Annas have independently made much of similarities between virtues and skills.[67] But Russell's novel contribution, as I see it, is to bring these two strands of the literature together in interesting ways.

There are at least two ways to understand Russell's approach to virtue cultivation. The first is what I consider to be the most natural reading of his contribution to this chapter, and it can be set out carefully as what I will call the Analogy Argument:

1. Expertise in a skill can be understood using a social-cognitive approach, and such skills are reasons-responsive.
2. Moral virtues are, in the relevant respects, suitably analogous to skills.
3. Therefore, moral virtues can be understood using a social-cognitive approach, and such virtues are reasons-responsive.
4. The development of virtues is suitably analogous to the development of skills.
5. Therefore, the development of virtues can be understood using a social-cognitive approach, and in a way that is reasons-responsive.
6. Therefore, "the human limitations that frustrate moral behavior are the very same ones that experts must also learn to manage in acquiring a skill."[68]

For instance, clearly some people have acquired the skill of playing chess to a very high degree of expertise, a skill that in the best players is reliably responsive to the reasons there really are to make various chess moves. This skill in turn, "is a matter of being able to intelligently define a goal, perceive affordances with respect to that goal, and be effective in one's use of those affordances, all in a way that allows attention to be allocated efficiently. . . . Skill is how creatures like that become more responsive to reasons."[69]

On this interpretation, then, Russell's idea is that because of the close analogy with skills, moral virtues should work in much the same way. The virtue of compassion, for instance, might centrally involve the goal of helping others for their own sake, combined with various abilities and strategies aimed at trying to realize that goal in concrete situations. And when it comes to acquiring the virtues, given (4) there is a close analogy with skills here as well. So the challenges to becoming virtuous, including those outlined by situationists in psychology, are going to be the same sorts of challenges that there are to acquiring skills. As Russell writes, "The cognitive and affective barriers to acquiring a virtue are no different from the barriers to learning a complex skill, barriers that we can apparently learn to recognize and overcome, albeit with much focused effort."[70] And since we know that people can and often *do* acquire various skills, there is very good reason to be modestly and soberly hopeful that at least some people can make progress in becoming virtuous too.

It turns out, though, that the Analogy Argument is not in fact the argument that Russell himself had in mind, as he has informed me when reading a draft of this discussion. In particular, he did not intend to rest much of his case on the plausibility of the skill analogy. Instead, he describes his own argument this way:

> My thinking is that virtue should be seen in path-dependent ways: we have to understand where we start, what moves are psychologically feasible from there, and which of those moves would constitute improvement. The connection with skill comes in, in asking whether the sorts of developmental paths that are exploited in the case of skill (e.g., habit-forming to optimize attentional resources) might be exploited in moral development too, casting light on psychologically feasible moves.[71]

So on Russell's preferred approach, his main concern is with getting better virtuously, and in order to do, we can look to how we acquire skills in reasons-responsive ways in order to discover similar pathways to managing our own moral improvement. Less is made of the analogy with skills, then, and more of the similar pathways that might be revealed in both cases to getting better at responding to the appropriate reasons.

So if the Analogy Argument is not what Russell had in mind, why include it here? One reason is that it can be used as a tool to more helpfully delineate his actual argument. But another reason is that it is an independently interesting and important argument in its own right, one that I think will tempt many virtue ethicists working on character improvement and one that is deserving of greater attention and discussion. So let me consider both of these arguments going forward.

Magnifying a Challenge to Virtue Cultivation

Let me start with the Analogy Argument. One way to criticize it is to try to show that there are important relevant differences between a virtue and a skill. This was a common move during philosophical discussions of virtue in the 1960s and 1970s, as seen for instance in the work of James Wallace, Philippa Foot, and others.[72] But it turns out that the pendulum seems to have swung in the opposite direction in recent years, with philosophers like Robert Roberts, Hubert Dreyfus, Daniel Jacobson, and Julia Annas offering compelling defenses of the analogy.[73] I find this recent work persuasive and so accept the analogy, at least as it applies in this context.[74]

Another move by a critic would be to object to the social-cognitive approach in psychology on independent grounds, perhaps by searching the research literature for reasons why this approach is problematic. But this line of criticism also does not strike me as promising—the social-cognitive approach is extensively developed and empirically supported, and elsewhere I have even put it to use in developing a theory of moral character myself.[75]

But then if moral virtues are suitably analogous to skills, and if both virtues and skills can be unpacked by the social-cognitive approach, it might seem like there is little that remains for the critic to question about the Analogy Argument. That would be to move too quickly, though. For consider the claim I outlined in (4) to the effect that the *development* of skills and virtues is suitably analogous. And recall that the argument never says that virtues are *identical* to skills or a kind of skill, only that the two are analogous in relevant respects. Two things could be analogous to each other in various ways, but also be formed or created in different manners and face their own unique obstacles.

Indeed, it seems to me that there is a very large obstacle to virtue cultivation whose contours have emerged more clearly in the psychology literature in recent years, and also one that does not arise in any obviously analogous manner for skills like mastering chess or racing cars. As we will see later, even if I am wrong about this claim and it turns out that there is a similar obstacle for those skills too, there would *still* be an important challenge remaining to the Analogy Argument. It is also a challenge that will apply to Russell's argument as well.

To appreciate the obstacle to virtue cultivation, I need to take a quick detour through the psychology literature as it pertains to moral behavior. As I read that literature, one emerging idea over the past fifty years can be stated as follows:

Surprising Dispositions

The behavior of most individuals tends to be influenced by various situational forces that activate certain of our mental dispositions—certain beliefs, desires, emotions, and the like. Furthermore, the functioning of these dispositions and their degree of impact on behavior are underappreciated by both ordinary people and even trained philosophers and psychologists. We can call them 'Surprising Dispositions.'[76]

Here are some examples of these dispositions:

> Beliefs and desires concerned with harming others in order to maintain a positive opinion of myself.[77]

Beliefs and desires concerned with harming others in order to obey instructions from a legitimate authority.[78]

Desires concerned with helping when doing so will contribute toward extending my good mood, and more so than any alternative reasonable means of doing so which is thought to be available.[79]

Desires concerned with helping when doing so will contribute toward alleviating my feelings of embarrassment, and more so than any alternative reasonable means of doing so which is thought to be available.[80]

Desires concerned with not helping when helping is thought to potentially earn the disapproval of those observing me.[81]

Desires concerned with cheating when the benefits of cheating (significantly) outweigh the costs, while also desiring as much as possible to still be thought of as an honest person by oneself and others.[82]

Many other examples could also be given. What is going to be true of all these beliefs and desires is that they often operate unconsciously in most people, and especially in those who do not have a background in psychology. For instance it is well known that ordinary estimates of people's willingness to obey authority figures in doing horrendous actions are much lower than is reflected in actual behavior. Similarly, it is widely accepted by psychologists that fear of earning the disapproval of observers plays a significant role in studies of group helping, and yet notoriously participants in those studies do not cite the role of unresponsive group members in explaining their failures to help.[83]

Now there is no way I can review all the actual studies that support the possession of these dispositions.[84] Instead let me just summarize three studies by way of illustration:

Dime in the Phone Booth. Finding a dime or not in the coin return slot of a phone booth seemed to make a significant difference (88% versus 4%) to whether a participant would subsequently help picked up dropped papers. There were replication problems with this study, but other studies on mood effects found a similar pattern.[85]

Lady in Distress. In Latané and Rodin's classic 1969 "Lady in Distress" experiment, the main dependent variable was whether participants exhibited any helping behavior after hearing a loud crash in the next room and a woman's scream, followed by cries of pain from a bookshelf apparently having fallen on top of her. Participants alone in the next room helped 70% of the time, while a participant in the same room with an unresponsive confederate helped only 7% of the time.[86]

Bathroom. 45% of participants agreed to deliver some documents 40 meters away in the control condition of a study by Cann and

Blackwelder, but 80% of people did so in the experimental condition. The only difference was that participants in the experimental condition had just exited a public bathroom.[87]

We can see how someone might connect these particular studies to the existence and influence of various Surprising Dispositions—studies such as these may reveal the existence and causally significant influence of dispositions to, for instance, maintain a good mood (*Dime in the Phone Booth*), avoid potential disapproval (*Lady in Distress*), or relieve feelings of embarrassment (*Bathroom*).

My view is that, using hundreds of relevant studies, psychologists have indeed provided us with ample empirical evidence to support the claim that there are many Surprising Dispositions that are widely held and that, when activated or triggered, can have a significant impact on our thoughts, motives, and behavior. Suppose this is right. What relevance does it have to Russell's discussion above? Quite a bit.

When we turn to an ethical evaluation of the Surprising Dispositions, it should be readily apparent that they are *not* constituents of the moral virtues, at least as traditionally understood. The first two are incompatible with the virtue of non-malevolence, the next three are incompatible with the virtue of compassion, and the final one is incompatible with the virtue of honesty.[88] In some cases this failure of virtue could be because certain Surprising Dispositions will lead to behavior that is not virtuous—in other words, they will lead the person who has them to not help, or to cheat, or to aggressively hurt others, all at times when those are morally reprehensible things to be doing. Or in other cases the dispositions could lead to appropriate behavior, but not for morally good or praiseworthy reasons. Rather the person might help another in need, for instance, but primarily for egoistic reasons like maintaining a good mood or relieving one's embarrassment. Either way, this is not how a moral virtue is supposed to operate.

Furthermore, as *Surprising* Dispositions, they are causally operative under our conscious radar screen, and so when they influence behavior we will often have no idea that they are doing so until after the fact, if even then. After all, most participants were likely unaware of the effect of the dime or emerging from the bathroom on their subsequent helping, and similarly we already saw that fear of disapproval in front of strangers can lead us to do nothing to help during emergencies, even though that is not what we consciously think is holding us back. Thus because they are (i) widely held, (ii) causally influential in many morally relevant situations, (iii) non-virtuous in their motivational and/or behavioral effects, and (iv) unconscious in their functioning, the Surprising Dispositions are a significant impediment to virtue cultivation.

As a result, any account of virtue cultivation and development will have to come up with the following:

Virtue Cultivation Strategies Focused on Surprising Dispositions: Develop one or more realistic and empirically informed ways for most human beings to avoid falling short of virtue in the course of their upbringing *because of the presence and role of the Surprising Dispositions*, or if they have already fallen short by adulthood, to *overcome their Surprising Dispositions* so that they can still develop a virtuous character over time.

Clearly there is much more to a story about virtue cultivation than just trying to overcoming the Surprising Dispositions. There are all kinds of problematic *conscious* psychological obstacles, such as mistaken moral beliefs, weakness of will, overly strong emotional responses, lethargy, and so forth. But while I cannot argue for this here, it seems clear to me that no matter how much we might improve in these respects, we will inevitably fall short of being even weakly virtuous if, unconsciously, we also have the Surprising Dispositions playing a significant causal role.

My point in taking this detour through some of the psychological research is to highlight one of the major obstacles that exists to carrying out the project of virtue cultivation. With this background in place, let me return to both the Analogy Argument and Russell's argument. Recall that one of the premises of the Analogy Argument was that:

(4) The development of virtues is suitably analogous to the development of skills.

On the surface at least, it is not clear what would correspond to the Surprising Dispositions in the case of leading examples of skills such as playing chess masterfully or successfully engineering a large bridge. But if this is right, then the virtue cultivation strategies that focus on our Surprising Dispositions will not have an analog in the case of skills. And given what a robust obstacle such dispositions are to becoming virtuous, the contribution that the skill analogy would make to understanding virtue development would be significantly diminished.

This is *not* to say that even skilled players or workers do not cheat or exhibit verbal aggression. Furthermore, when they do act this way, this could at times be for motivating reasons of which they are not even aware. But this is all beside the point, because these are *moral* failures, not failures *qua* a skilled player of chess or master chef. The chess player who gloats at the end of each victory and mocks his opponent could be an excellent player even though he is a rotten person. His bad behavior in these respects need not detract at all from his skill at playing chess.

To make the analogy to skill development work, we would instead need to find cases where there are unconscious psychological dispositions that, when activated, routinely lead to poor performance *of that very skill*. And such a task is harder than it might initially seem. For instance, a chess player's impatience or distractibility could clearly undermine his concentration and cost him valuable position on the board, but these would not be relevant examples since the player could easily discern the role of these psychological factors even in the midst of a game.[89]

Suppose I am right about all this. Then (4) can be called into question. But now suppose I am wrong about all this. In other words, suppose that we *can* come up with close analogs to the Surprising Dispositions in the case of chess or car racing or bridge building.[90] Even then, an important gap would still remain. For at this point we know *almost nothing* about what strategies actually work to overcome the Surprising Dispositions in the moral case. And, I suspect, the same would be true in the case of the skillful actions as well (although first we would need to see what the surprising dispositions there actually look like!). So until we can come up with such strategies, it remains uncertain how much hope we can reasonably have in the prospects of gradually becoming more virtuous.

But recall that the Analogy Argument is not Russell's actual argument. Does the above concern apply to his argument as well? It does. But Russell also provides at least one suggestion for how one might begin to address what I am calling our Surprising Dispositions. Let me consider that suggestion in some detail in the final section of this chapter.

A Positive Suggestion

If there are a number of psychological dispositions that (i) often operate unconsciously or outside our conscious awareness, (ii) have important implications for moral behavior, and (iii) can prevent that behavior from having moral worth or can even lead to the performance of morally forbidden actions, then a natural strategy to use in trying to become a more virtuous person is to first become better aware of and familiar with these processes. Once we recognize their presence, the thought is that we can then be more mindful when in situations in which they might be activated, and work to compensate for, correct, or counterbalance them. As Aristotle himself noted long ago, "We must also examine what we ourselves drift into easily. For different people have different natural tendencies toward different goals, and we shall come to know our own tendencies from the pleasure or pain that arises in us. We must drag ourselves off in the contrary direction; for if we pull far away from error, as they do in straightening bent wood, we shall reach the intermediate condition."[91] To take an example of how this might go in practice, if we become aware of the processes responsible for the group effect on helping, for instance, we might become more alert to the negative moral effect that non-responding others can have in emergency situations, and so try to focus more on our conscious moral values and less on the fear, say, of what others might think if we tried to help.[92]

Several philosophers and psychologists have advanced this line of thought in recent years.[93] And Russell seems to have something like it in mind when discussing the research of Robin Hogarth. He stresses in that context the importance of learning "how to seek relevant information actively and systematically" about one's reactions and habits, and of "acquiring the habit of automatically scrutinizing the impressions that automatically arise."[94] And in summarizing his discussion, he concludes in an important passage that I have already quoted, that "[t]he cognitive and affective barriers to acquiring a virtue are no different from the barriers to learning a complex skill, *barriers that we can apparently learn to recognize and overcome, albeit with much focused effort.*"[95]

The hope, then, is that education about the work of our morally relevant unconscious dispositions can help correct for their operation when they lead us in problematic directions. A small group of studies seems to offer a glimmer of hope for this possibility. In two studies Arthur Beaman and his colleagues had college students hear a social psychology lecture explaining the Latané and Darley model of group effects. They were subsequently presented with a staged emergency—a victim of a bicycle accident in the one case, and a man sprawled against a wall in the other. Helping in the presence of a nonresponsive confederate was 67% versus 27% for controls in the first study, and 42.5% versus 25% in the second (even though in this study the helping opportunity was two weeks later than the lecture).[96] In a less rigorous study, Steven Samuels and William Casebeer contacted students from a social psychology class up to two years later, and for the question, "Did learning about helping behaviour lead you to help in any situation in which you believe you would not have otherwise helped?" 72% answered positively.[97]

Perhaps the most serious challenge from the experimental literature to the proposal comes from Pietromonaco and Nisbett's 1982 study using the Darley and Batson (1973) seminary results. Even though they had just read how hurry is a significant situational variable that led to differences in helping of 10% versus 63%, participants in the Pietromonaco and Nisbett study still estimated that 59% of people in a hurry would stop to help in two closely related situations, while 78% of people who are not in a hurry would stop.[98] As Pietromonaco and Nisbett note,

> In view of the perseverance of this error, we cannot assume that students are learning what we want them to learn when evidence presented in class conflicts with their prior assumptions. Social psychologists may face almost unique educational problems: prior beliefs about such subject matter are so strong that ordinary instructional techniques may not be adequate.[99]

However, their study did not involve actually educating the participants about the psychological processes that could explain the Darley and

Batson data. As they note, such a thorough 'process debriefing' may be more effective.[100]

The goal with this educational strategy is *not* to try to avoid all the potentially problematic situations that we might get ourselves into, an approach that would quickly lead to frustration and failure. Rather the goal is to be aware when we are already in those situations, and be more mindful of how we subsequently behave as a result. So when you hear what sounds like an emergency, even though you are with an unresponsive bystander, you might know to discount the bystander and be more careful to check on the person in apparent need. Or when someone drops papers and you do not immediately respond by helping, you could ask yourself whether you had a good reason for not doing so, or perhaps were being influenced by something non-virtuous below your level of awareness. The next time you see someone drop papers, you could then remember this earlier incident and quickly respond by helping, thereby starting a process of gradually counteracting the unconscious influences that were leading you to not help. Or to take one final and more significant example, if an authority figure pressures you to do something that goes against your moral code, you might be reminded of results like Milgram's and self-consciously assess the justification for obeying in this context.

Thus far, this strategy has focused on taking steps to block our Surprising Dispositions from leading us to perform morally wrong actions, such as shocking an innocent person to death or doing nothing while someone seems to need emergency assistance in the next room. But as we noted, our Surprising Dispositions can also lead to either morally obligatory or supererogatory actions in some cases. The drawback, though, is that when this happens, the actions will often be caused by motives that are not morally admirable. Here, for instance, was one of the earlier examples of a Surprising Disposition:

> Desires concerned with helping when doing so will contribute toward extending my good mood, and more so than any alternative reasonable means of doing so which is thought to be available.

When such a disposition influences helping, the action could be an exemplary one considered in its own right, but if it was primarily motivated in this egoistic way, then it is also an action that has little or no moral worth.

The question then becomes how this strategy would not only combat the effects of Surprising Dispositions in leading to morally wrong behavior, but also the effects of such dispositions in leading to morally admirable actions with morally problematic motives.[101] And the answer, it seems to me, would again have to involve educating people about the pervasive presence and influence of dispositions like the desire to help for the particular egoistic reasons in this example, *as well as* providing us with some account of how morally admirable motives can instead take their place. For instance, perhaps when a person recognizes that she is in a situation that is likely going to trigger a desire to help for egoistic reasons, she can self-consciously put herself into an altruistic mindset by actively empathizing with the person in need in the situation.[102]

Stepping back from these details, what should we make of this general strategy for virtue cultivation in light of our Surprising Dispositions? In theory this strategy sounds promising to me—more promising, in fact, than any of the other strategies I have seen outlined in the philosophy literature for addressing the challenge to virtue cultivation posed by our Surprising Dispositions.[103] But let me end with two cautionary notes as a way to appreciate further some of the challenges that still remain for Russell's project and for the implementation of this strategy more generally. First, as we saw above, the amount of experimental evidence on moral behavior that can be cited in support of this approach is noticeably (and surprisingly) scarce. Far more work needs to be done in studying how successful it might be for a wide variety of dispositions and their effects in lots of different circumstances.[104]

And then there is a second worry. It is that this strategy may be asking too much of what can reasonably be expected of ordinary human beings. For in order to implement this strategy properly with respect to all the moral domains of life—helping, harming, lying, cheating, stealing, and so forth—and in order to cultivate all of the virtues—compassion, non-malevolence, honesty, fairness, temperance, and so forth—it seems that a person would have to keep track of an *enormous amount* of information. First, she would need to be educated about the existence and influence of dozens and dozens of unconscious Surprising Dispositions. Then second, she would need to be mindful enough to check to see whether, when behaving a certain way, she might be influenced by one of them in a morally problematic respect. So the information needs to be stored, and then it needs to be available for recall and application in real-life situations. And this all needs to be done quickly enough before the moment—the emergency, the dropped papers, the opportunity to stand up for the right thing—passes by.

Here is a possible response to this worry that I could imagine Russell making. The advocate of this educational strategy should simply concede that there will be practical difficulties in the short run, but insist that over time this process of self-monitoring can become routine and habitual. At first I might not help someone, and only when it is too late recognize that fear of disapproval was holding me back. The next time when a similar opportunity arises, I might find myself again inclined not to do anything, but this time I check my feeling of aversion and wonder whether it has any legitimate basis. Concluding that it does not, I consciously will myself to help in this case. Over time, the opposition to helping might go away entirely and helping in this situation becomes more automatic. Of course a lot of details would have to be filled in, but perhaps there is something promising to be said along these lines.

At this point, I am left wondering about the following questions:

First, will the experimental evidence concerning moral behavior support this educational strategy, since right now we have hardly any evidence with which to test it?

Second, is it too much to expect of ordinary folks who lead busy lives to learn this much information about themselves and their psychological lives, and then habitually keep track of it on a daily basis in order to acquire the moral virtues?

And third and most speculatively, what would the quality of our lives be like if we had to regularly self-monitor our behavior and guard again the possible negative influence of our many unconscious dispositions?

I do not have the answers to these questions, and strongly commend them to Russell and others for future research.

A Final Concern

Suppose, though, that these questions can be answered in such a way as to vindicate this educational strategy. Or suppose that Russell successfully develops some other strategy for addressing our Surprising Dispositions. Or suppose that an approach drawing on a variety of different strategies points us in the right direction (which is likely going to be the most promising of these alternatives). There is another crucial issue that still remains and that has not even been touched in either of our discussions.[105] It is the issue of motivating people to embark on the path of virtue cultivation in the first place.

Perhaps we can get people to understand themselves a lot better and learn about their Surprising Dispositions. And perhaps we can develop a multi-faceted approach to transforming these dispositions slowly over time into virtuous dispositions. But no one is going to *bother* with this endeavor without being significant motivated to do so in the first place. So how do we get people to *care* enough about becoming more virtuous, and derivatively to care about using these strategies as a means to doing so, in a way that is sufficiently strong and long-lasting to see the project through to completion to at least moderate levels of virtue?

Here we might appeal to the analogy with skills again. For people who do not start out with an innate or natural inclination in this direction, how do they come to care about becoming skilled chess players, race car drivers, or bridge builders? If an answer to this question can be discovered in the case of skills, perhaps it will carry over straightforwardly in the case of virtues.

These questions are extremely pressing and at the present time they still remain unanswered.[106]

Study Questions

1. How are skilled people similar to virtuous people? How are they different?
2. Some skills (e.g., passing, shooting, blocking) are components of other skills (being a good soccer player). Are some virtues components of other virtues? Explain.
3. Psychology concerns what people *are* like; the virtues concern what people *ought* to be like. Do you agree that it is important to understand what people are like before we can really understand what they ought to be like?
4. Skilled people, like expert chess players and experienced radiologists, seem to "see" things in their area of expertise differently than novices do. What are those differences like? Do you think very generous or fair-minded people see things differently than others do?
5. How promising does the strategy of educating people about their Surprising Dispositions seem to you as a means to cultivating virtue?
6. Do you think most people today have progressed to the point of being virtuous to some degree? If not, is this an unrealistic goal or is it still worth trying to become virtuous people?

Notes

1. I owe the phrase to Mark Alfano.
2. Aristotle, *Nicomachean Ethics* II.6.
3. For the analogy, see Russell (2009, pp. 239–240).
4. For a compelling statement of social-cognitive theory, see Cervone and Shoda (1999). For skepticism, see Miller (2014, Chapter 5, Sections 3–4).
5. Indeed, some argue that social-cognitive theory should *discourage* us from framing moral development in terms of virtues: Alfano (2013a); Doris (2002); Miller (2014).
6. Mischel and Shoda (1995). The social-cognitive approach is actually a *family* of personality theories, and some of these theories place special emphasis on the linkage between cognitive structures, on the one hand, that both influence and are shaped in return by emotional responses on the other; these theories describe personality as a "cognitive-affective system" (Cervone and Shoda 1999, p. 8; Mischel 1999; Mischel and Shoda 1995).
7. See also Mischel (1973, pp. 265–276); Ross and Nisbett (1991, pp. 164–167); Cervone and Shoda (1999, pp. 19–20); Lapsley and Narvaez (2004, p. 195).
8. Cantor (1990, p. 746).
9. Cantor (1990, p. 736).
10. Cantor (1990, p. 737).
11. Blasi (1984, p. 131); see also Cantor (1990, p. 739).
12. Lapsely and Narvaez (2004, pp. 200–201) and (2005, p. 30).
13. Blasi (1984, p. 132).
14. Blasi (2005).
15. Lapsley and Narvaez (2004, p. 200); see also (2005, p. 30).
16. Lapsley and Narvaez (2004, p. 201).
17. Lapsley and Narvaez (2004, p. 207).
18. Miller (2014, p. 218).

19. Lapsley and Narvaez (2004, p. 194, emphasis added). See also Cervone and Shoda (1999, pp. –11).
20. On the engineering of surroundings: Merritt (2000); on the engineering of interactions: Alfano (2013b and Chapter 4 of 2013a).
21. Russell (2009, pp. 326–328).
22. Bazerman and Tenbrunsel (2011).
23. Alfano (2013a, pp. 79–80).
24. Doris (2002, pp. 76–85).
25. Russell (2009, pp. 328–331).
26. Alfano (2013a, pp. 78–79); Miller (2014, pp. 210, 218).
27. Ross and Nisbett (1991, Chapters 1 and 2); Alfano (2013a, Chapter 2).
28. Milgram (1974).
29. Ross and Nisbett (1991, Chapter 2). Ross and Nisbett's hypothesis actually seems to be *motivated* by social-cognitive theory, as they themselves argue that the best hope for the "personality theory of the future" is to "continue to stress the importance of understanding people's goals, competencies, strategies, construals, and self-conceptions. Research along these lines is likely to turn up a great many interesting facts about the determinants of human behavior and to tell us a great deal about the nature and degree of consistency to be expected of different kinds of people in different kinds of situations" (p. 167).
30. Lapsley and Narvaez (2004, pp. 199–200); Narvaez and Lapsley (2005, pp. 150–152), discussing Sternberg (1998).
31. Narvaez and Lapsley (2005, pp. 151–152).
32. Cantor (1990, p. 738).
33. Chase and Simon (1973a).
34. Chase and Simon (1973b).
35. Chase and Simon (1973a, p. 264).
36. Narvaez and Lapsley (2005, p. 151).
37. Narvaez and Lapsley (2005, pp. 144–148, 152).
38. Bargh (1989, pp. 35–36, 39); Hogarth (2001).
39. Bargh (1989, pp. 19–27); Logan (1989, pp. 52–65); Hogarth (2001, pp. 208–209); Annas (2011, pp. 13–18).
40. Hursthouse (1999); Russell (2009, pp. 20–25); Russell (2014a).
41. *NE* VI.8, 1142a23–30; VI.10, 1143a5-b5; VI.11, 1143b13–14.
42. Narvaez and Lapsley (2005, pp. 150–152).
43. Kahneman (2011, Chapter 22).
44. Russell (2014a); see also Jacobson (2005, pp. 391, 400).
45. Kahneman (2011, pp. 240–242).
46. I thank Mark LeBar for this way of putting the point.
47. Hogarth (2001). I focus on Chapters 6–7.
48. See also Abernathy and Hamm (1994).
49. Bazerman and Tenbrunsel (2011, pp. 4, 30); for the test analogy: Schmidtz (2006, p. 27).
50. Alfano (2013a, pp. 44–49).
51. Neisser (1979). For discussion see Bazerman and Tenbrunsel (2011, pp. 78–79); cp. Alfano (2013, pp. 49–50).
52. Alfano (2013, pp. 56–59). Similar distortions can occur even in our perceptions of ourselves (Miller 2014, Chapter 3, Section 2).
53. Bazerman and Tenbrunsel (2011, p. 7).
54. Myles-Worsley et al. (1988).
55. Narvaez and Lapsley (2005, pp. 150–151).
56. See Hogarth (2001, pp. 235, 241–243).
57. See Russell (2014b) for discussion of this passage. I discuss ideals and aspiration in more detail in Russell (2009, Chapters 4 and 11).

58. Notice that if "How could we get there from here?" is the question, then not even a skill-based approach to the virtues will help answer it, since of course skills are limited by actual human capacities as well, as Olin and Doris (2014) are quick to point out.
59. Kohlberg et al. (1983); see also Lapsley and Narvaez (2005).
60. But even with *goals and means* that sequencing can be perilous (Russell 2014c).
61. Bargh (1989, pp. 10–27). See also Hogarth (2001, pp. 139–141, 190–193); Narvaez and Lapsley (2005, pp. 144–148); Kahneman (2011, Chapter 22).
62. Russell (2014a). See also Narvaez and Lapsley (2004), who distinguish between "moralized psychology" (path-independent) and "psychologized morality" (path-dependent).
63. Fossheim (2014).
64. Hogarth (2001).
65. I thank Mark Alfano for inviting me to contribute to this collection, and for the chance to think through these issues some more. I also thank Mark Alfano, Mark LeBar, and Matt Stichter for their comments on earlier drafts, as well as the School of Philosophy at Monash University where I presented an earlier version.
66. See, e.g., Merritt et al. (2010) and Alfano (2013a).
67. See Sosa (2009) and Annas (2011).
68. Page 16 in manuscript.
69. Page 11 in manuscript.
70. Page 16 in manuscript.
71. Russell, comments on an earlier draft of this chapter.
72. See Wallace (1978) and Foot (1978).
73. See Roberts (1984), Dreyfus and Dreyfus (1990), Jacobson (2005), and Annas (2011, Chapters 2–5).
74. Having said this, one limitation to the analogy is that while all skills seem to be reasons-responsive, not all virtues are. For a compelling discussion of this point in the context of criticizing Russell's own work, see West (in progress). In addition, see the interesting recent objections to the analogy in Battaly (2011).
75. See Miller (2013). In Miller (2014, Chapter 5), I do raise one criticism against a particular version of the social-cognitive approach, but this criticism (even if successful) would not undermine Russell's project in this chapter.
76. For broadly similar sentiments, see Ross and Nisbett (1991, p. 46), Flanagan (1991, p. 292), Doris (2002, p. 63 fn. 5), Vranas (2005, p. 3), Nahmias (2007, p. 4), and D. Russell (2009, pp. 253, 277).
77. See, e.g., Baumeister et al. (1996).
78. See, e.g., Milgram (1974). As Milgram wrote in an earlier paper, "The person brings to the laboratory enduring dispositions toward authority and aggression..." (1965, p. 274).
79. See, e.g., Carlson et al. (1988).
80. See, e.g., Cann and Blackwelder (1984).
81. See, e.g., Latané and Darley (1970).
82. See, e.g., Mazar et al. (2008).
83. Latané and Darley (1970, p. 124).
84. I have done so to some extent in Miller (2013, 2014).
85. Isen and Levin (1972). For more on some of the replication troubles that arose, as well as other mood effect studies, see Miller (2013, Chapter 3).
86. Latané and Rodin (1969, pp. 193–195), Latané and Darley (1970, pp. 60–63).
87. Cann and Blackwelder (1984, p. 224).
88. I hope that this is easy enough to see, but I also argue for this claim at length elsewhere by formulating specific normative criteria for these virtues and then comparing them to the above dispositions to see how well they match up. The short answer is: not well at all. See Miller (2013, 2014, Chapter 3). Note that it does not follow that they are constituents of moral vices either. In the same discussion, I also argue against this interpretation. For related discussion, see also L. Russell (2009).

89. Sosa (2009) makes use of the skill analogy and focuses specifically on the example of driving competence. He points out a number of (at one time) surprising phenomena in the case of driving, and then makes the plausible point that these phenomena do not undermine the attainment of driving competence in many individuals. His examples are brightness of light, cold and wet bridges, cell phone use, blood alcohol level, and oral versus map directions (p. 284). Sosa's point here is quite plausible in its own right, but note that none of these phenomena is a psychological disposition, and so none of them would serve as an analog of a Surprising Disposition in the driving case.
90. In his discussion in this chapter, Russell offers what is probably the closest analogy to a case of skillful action when he briefly mentions Hogarth's discussion of stereotyping in the context of hiring employees (page 16 in the manuscript). There the stereotypes can function as analogs of Surprising Dispositions that can unconsciously diminish the performance of the very skill in question, namely making good hiring decisions. This does strike me as a good example, and as I note above, my main worry stands regardless of whether there are such analogies in the case of skills or not.
91. Aristotle (1985, 1109b2–8).
92. For a similar example, see Mele and Shepherd (2013, p. 80).
93. As Steven Samuels and William Casebeer (2005) argue, "effective deliberation is enhanced by knowing both how human beings tend to react in certain environments and what stimuli reliably activate those dispositions . . . Once they are able to see what environmental factors have the potential to influence, they may be better prepared to make a decision based on their true beliefs and feelings" (p. 77). Similarly Walter Mischel and Yuichi Shoda (1995) claim that "metacognitive knowledge may help the person to recognize some of the key internal or external stimuli that activate or deactivate the problematic affects, cognitions, and behaviors and the dynamics that occur in relation to those stimuli" (p. 261). See also Sabini and Silver (2005, p. 562); Appiah (2008, p. 49); Badhwar (2009, p. 266); Merritt et al. (2010, pp. 388–389); van IJzendoorn et al. (2010, p. 16); and especially Mele and Shepherd (2013).
94. Page 15 in manuscript.
95. Page 16 in manuscript, emphasis mine.
96. Beaman et al. (1978, pp. 407–408, 410).
97. Samuels and Casebeer (2005, p. 80). It is worth noting, though, that even trained psychiatrists badly underestimated rates of disobedience in the standard Milgram setup (Milgram 1974, pp. 30–31), and Bierbrauer (1979) found that observance of a reenactment of full compliance with the experimenter in Milgram's experiment five still led participants to greatly overestimate levels of disobedience. So this might raise some doubt about the effectiveness of the educational strategy. However, note that in neither case had the participants been educated about the psychological processes at work in disposing people to obey seemingly legitimate authority figures. So these studies do not exactly bear on the proposal above.

    See also Kunda and Nisbett (1986) who found that trained psychologists still badly overestimated the correlations between one person being more honest than another in one situation, and the same relation obtaining in the next situation. And this was the case even despite Walter Mischel, "seated prominently in front of the room!" (1986, p. 210). Yet they concluded that, "it would be premature to be pessimistic about the possibility that training might improve people's ability . . ." (p. 222), and offered some suggestions for improvement (pp. 221–222).

    For relevant discussion, see also Doris (2002, pp. 99–100).
98. Pietromonaco and Nisbett (1982, p. 3).
99. Ibid., p. 4.
100. Ibid.
101. Thanks to Erik Helzer for helpful discussion here.
102. For the relationship between empathy and altruistic motivation, see Batson (2011).

103. For a review of these strategies, see Miller (2014, Chapter 9).
104. For related discussion of this strategy, see Staub (1974, p. 337), Flanagan (1991, p. 314), Arjoon (2008, p. 232), Merritt et al. (2010, pp. 388–389), and especially Samuels and Casebeer (2005). For more general discussion of ethics instruction and improved moral behavior especially with respect to cheating, see Bloodgood et al. (2008) and the references cited therein.
105. Thanks to William Fleeson for discussion here.
106. I am grateful to Mark Alfano for inviting me to contribute this chapter, and to Mark Alfano and Daniel Russell for helpful comments. The material in section three draws on Miller (2014, Chapter 9). Work on this chapter was supported by a grant from the Templeton World Charity Foundation. The opinions expressed here are those of the author and do not necessarily reflect the views of the Character Project, Wake Forest University, or the Templeton World Charity Foundation.

CHAPTER 5

Can People Be Virtuous?

Abstract

In his contribution, Mark Alfano lays out a new (to virtue theory) naturalistic way of determining what the virtues are, what it would take for them to be realized, and what it would take for them to be at least possible. This method is derived in large part from David Lewis's development of Frank Ramsey's method of implicit definition. The basic idea is to define a set of terms not individually but in tandem. This is accomplished by assembling all and only the common sense platitudes that involve them (e.g., typically, people want to be virtuous), conjoining those platitudes, and replacing the terms in question by existentially quantified variables. If the resulting sentence is satisfied, then whatever satisfies *are* the virtues. If it isn't satisfied, there are a couple of options. First, one could just admit defeat by saying that people can't be virtuous. More plausibly, one could weaken the conjunction by dropping a small number of the platitudes from it (and potentially adding some others). Alfano suggests that the most attractive way to do this is by dropping the platitudes that deal with cross-situational consistency and replacing them with platitudes that involve social construction: basically, people are virtuous (when they are) at least in part because other people signal their expectations of virtuous conduct, which induces virtuous conduct, which in turn induces further signals of expected virtuous conduct, and so on. In his response, James Montmarquet does not reject Alfano's proposals regarding Ramsification as an analytical device, but does question whether Alfano's own conception of moral character traits—whatever its empirical adequacy from the standpoint of social science—does justice to our conception of moral responsibility. Because assignments of moral responsibility are so important, he suggests, we would like them and our closely related attributions of moral character to be clear, exact, and amenable to scientific treatment. From both the Tolstoyan and Humean perspectives he distinguishes, however, these assignments and attributions are neither exact nor scientific, but more like an art form.

Ramsifying Virtue Theory

Mark Alfano

Can people be virtuous? This is a hard question, both because of its form and because of its content.

In terms of content, the proposition in question is at once normative and descriptive. Virtue-terms have empirical content. Attributions of virtues figure in the description, prediction, explanation, and control of behavior. If you know that someone is temperate, you can predict with some confidence that he won't go on a bender this weekend. Someone's investigating a mysterious phenomenon can be partly explained by (correctly) attributing curiosity to her. Character witnesses are called in trials to help determine how severely a convicted defendant will be punished. Virtue-terms also have normative content. Attributions of virtues are a manifestation of high regard and admiration; they are intrinsically rewarding to their targets; they're a form of praise. The semantics of purely normative terms is hard enough on its own; the semantics of "thick" terms that have both normative and descriptive content is especially difficult.

Formally, the proposition in question ("people are virtuous") is a generic, which adds a further wrinkle to its evaluation. It is notoriously difficult to give truth conditions for generics (Leslie 2008). A generic entails its existentially quantified counterpart, but is not entailed by it. For instance, tigers are four-legged, so some tigers are four-legged; but even though some deformed tigers are three-legged, it doesn't follow that tigers are three-legged. A generic typically is entailed by its universally quantified counterpart, but does not entail it. Furthermore, a generic neither entails nor is entailed by its counterpart "most" statement. Tigers give live birth, but most tigers do not give live birth; after all, only about half of all tigers are female, and not all of them give birth. Most mosquitoes do not carry West Nile virus, but mosquitoes carry West Nile virus. Given the trickiness of generics, it's helpful to clarify them to the extent possible with more precise non-generic statements.

Moreover, the proposition in question is modally qualified, which redoubles the difficulty of confirming or disconfirming it. What's being asked is not simply whether people *are* virtuous, but whether they *can be* virtuous. It could turn out that even though no one is virtuous, it's possible for people to become virtuous. This would, however, be extremely surprising. Unlike other unrealized possibilities, virtue is almost universally sought after, so if it isn't widely actualized despite all that seeking, we have fairly strong evidence that it's not there to be had.

In this chapter, I propose a method for adjudicating the question whether people can be virtuous. This method, if sound, would help to resolve what's come to be known as the situationist challenge to virtue theory, which over the last few decades has threatened both virtue ethics (Alfano 2011, 2013a; Doris 2002; Harman 1999) and virtue epistemology (Alfano 2012 2013a, 2014b; Olin & Doris 2014). The method is an application of David Lewis's (1966, 1970, 1972) development of Frank Ramsey's (1931) approach to the implicit definition of theoretical terms. The method needs to be tweaked in various ways to handle the difficulties canvassed above, but, when it is, an interesting answer to our question emerges: we face a theoretical tradeoff between, on the one hand, insisting that virtue is a robust property of an individual agent that's rarely attained and perhaps even unattainable and, on the other hand, allowing that one person's virtue might inhere partly in other people, making virtue at once more easily attained and more fragile.

The basic principle underlying the Ramsey-Lewis approach to implicit definition (often referred to as 'Ramsification') can be illustrated with a well-known story:

> And the Lord sent Nathan unto David. And he came unto him, and said unto him, "There were two men in one city; the one rich, and the other poor. The rich man had exceeding many flocks and herds: But the poor man had nothing, save one little ewe lamb, which he had bought and nourished up: and it grew up together with him, and with his children; it did eat of his own meat, and drank of his own cup, and lay in his bosom, and was unto him as a daughter. And there came a traveler unto the rich man, and he spared to take of his own flock and of his own herd, to dress for the wayfaring man that was come unto him; but took the poor man's lamb, and dressed it for the man that was come to him." And David's anger was greatly kindled against the man; and he said to Nathan, "As the Lord liveth, the man that hath done this thing shall surely die: And he shall restore the lamb fourfold, because he did this thing, and because he had no pity." And Nathan said to David, "Thou art the man."

Nathan uses Ramsification to drive home a point. He tells a story about an ordered triple of objects (two people and an animal) that are interrelated in various ways. Some of the first object's properties (e.g., wealth) are monadic; some of the second object's properties (e.g., poverty) are monadic; some of the first object's properties are relational (e.g., he steals the third object from the second object); some of the second object's properties are relational (e.g., the third object is stolen from him by the first object); and so on. Even though the first object is not explicitly defined as *the X such that* ... , it is nevertheless implicitly defined as *the first element of the ordered triple such that* ... The big reveal happens when Nathan announces that the first element of the ordered triple, about whom his interlocutor has already made some pretty serious pronouncements, is the very person he's addressing (the other two, for those unfamiliar with the 2nd *Samuel* 12, are Uriah and Bathsheba[1]).

The story is Biblical, but the method is modern. To implicitly define a set of theoretical terms (henceforth 'T-terms'), one formulates a theory T in those terms and any other terms (henceforth 'O-terms') one already understands or has an independent theory of. Next, one writes T as a single sentence, such as a long conjunction, in which the T-terms $t_1, \ldots, t_n$ occur (henceforth '$T[t_1, \ldots, t_n]$' or 'the postulate of T'). The T-terms are replaced by unbound variables $x_1, \ldots, x_n$, and then existentially quantified over to generate the Ramsey sentence of T, $\exists x_1, \ldots, x_n T[x_1, \ldots, x_n]$, which states that T is realized, that is, that there are objects $x_1, \ldots, x_n$ that satisfy the Ramsey sentence. An ordered *n*-tuple that satisfies the Ramsey sentence is then said to be a *realizer* of the theory.

Lewis (1966) famously applied this method to folk psychology to argue for the mind-brain identity theory. Somewhat roughly, he argued that folk psychology can be treated as a theory in which mental-state terms are the T-terms. The postulate of folk psychology is identified as the conjunction of all folk-psychological platitudes (commonsense psychological truths that everyone knows, and everyone knows that everyone knows, and everyone knows that everyone knows that everyone knows, and so on). The Ramsey sentence of folk psychology is formed in the usual way, by replacing all mental-state terms (e.g., 'belief,' 'desire,' 'pain,' etc.) with variables and existentially quantifying over those variables. Finally, one goes on to determine what, in the actual world, satisfies the Ramsey sentence; that is, one investigates what, if anything, is a realizer of the Ramsey sentence. If there is a realizer, then that's what the T-terms refer to; if there is no realizer, then the T-terms do not refer. Lewis claims that brain states are such realizers, and hence that mental states are identical with brain states.

Lewis's Ramsification method is attractive for a number of reasons.[2] First, it ensures that we don't simply change the topic when we try to give a philosophical account of some phenomenon. If your account of the mind is wildly inconsistent with the postulate of folk psychology, then—though you may be giving an account of something interesting—you're not doing what you think you're doing. Second, enables us to distinguish between the *meaning* of the T-terms and *whether they refer*. The T-terms *mean* what they *would* refer to, if there were such a thing. Whether they in fact refer is a distinct question. Third, and perhaps most importantly, Ramsification is holistic. The first half of the twentieth century bore witness to the fact that it's impossible to give an independent account of almost any psychological phenomenon (belief, desire, emotion, perception) because what it means to have one belief is essentially bound up with what it means to have a whole host of other beliefs, as well as (at least potentially) a whole host of desires, emotions, and perceptions. Ramsification gets around this problem by giving an account of *all* of the relevant phenomena *at once*, rather than trying to chip away at them piecemeal.

Virtue theory stands to benefit from the application of Ramsification for all of these reasons. We want an account of virtue, not an account of some other interesting phenomenon (though we might want that too). We want an account that recognizes that talk of virtue is meaningful, even if there aren't virtues. Most importantly, we want an account of virtue that recognizes the complexity of virtue and character—the fact that virtues are interrelated in a whole host of ways with occurrent and dispositional mental states, with other virtues, with character more broadly, and so on.

Whether Lewis is right about brains is irrelevant to our question, but his methodology is crucial. What I want to do now is to show how the same method, suitably modified, can be used to implicitly define virtue-terms, which in turn will help us to answer the question whether people can be virtuous. For reasons that will become clear as we proceed, the T-terms of virtue theory as I construe it here are 'person,' 'virtue,' 'vice,' the names of the various virtues (e.g., 'courage,' 'generosity,' 'curiosity'), the names of their congruent affects (e.g., 'feeling courageous,' 'feeling generous,' 'feeling curious'), the names of the various vices (e.g., 'cowardice,' 'greed,' 'intellectual laziness'), and the names of their congruent affects, (e.g., 'feeling cowardly,' 'feeling greedy,' 'feeling intellectually lazy'). The O-terms are all other terms, importantly including terms that refer to attitudes (e.g., 'belief,' 'desire,' 'anger,' 'resentment,' 'disgust,' 'contempt,' 'respect'), mental processes (e.g., 'deliberation'), perceptions and perceptual sensitivities, behaviors, reasons, situational features (e.g., 'being alone,' 'being in a crowd,' 'being monitored'), and evaluations (e.g., 'praise' and 'blame').

Elsewhere (Alfano 2013a), I have argued for an intuitive distinction between high-fidelity and low-fidelity virtues. High-fidelity virtues, such as honesty, chastity, and loyalty, require near-perfect manifestation in undisrupted conditions. Someone only counts as chaste if he never cheats on his partner when cheating is a temptation. Low-fidelity virtues, such as generosity, tact, and tenacity, are not so demanding. Someone might count as generous if she were more disposed to give than not to give when there was sufficient reason to do so; someone might count as tenacious if she were more disposed to persist than not to persist in the face of adversity. If this is on the right track, the postulate of virtue theory will recognize the distinction. For instance, it seems to me at least that almost everyone would say that helpfulness is a low-fidelity virtue whereas loyalty is a high-fidelity virtue. Here, then, are some families of platitudes about character that are candidates for the postulate of virtue theory:

(A) *The Virtue/Affect Family*
- (a_1) If a person has courage, then she will typically feel courageous when there is sufficient reason to do so.
- (a_2) If a person has generosity, then she will typically feel generous when there is sufficient reason to do so.
- (a_3) If a person has curiosity, then she will typically feel curious when there is sufficient reason to do so.
⋮
- (a_n) ....

(C) *The Virtue/Cognition Family*
- (c_1) If a person has courage, then she will typically want to overcome threats.
- (c_2) If a person has courage, then she will typically deliberate well about how to overcome threats and reliably form beliefs about how to do so.
⋮
- (c_n) ....

(S) *The Virtue/Situation Family*[3]
- (s_1) If a person has courage, then she will typically be unaffected by situational factors that are neither reasons for nor reasons against overcoming a threat.
- (s_2) If a person has generosity, then she will typically be unaffected by situational factors that are neither reasons for nor reasons against giving resources to someone.
- (s_3) If a person has curiosity, then she will typically be unaffected by situational factors that are neither reasons for nor reasons against investigating a problem.
⋮
- (s_n)

(E) *The Virtue/Evaluation Family*
- (e_1) If a person has courage, then she will typically react to threats in ways that merit praise.
- (e_2) If a person has generosity, then she will typically react to others' needs and wants in ways that merit praise.
- (e_3) If a person has curiosity, then she will typically react to intellectual problems in ways that merit praise.
⋮
- (e_n)

(B) *The Virtue/Behavior Family*
- (b_1) If a person has courage, then she will typically act so as to overcome threats when there is sufficient reason to do so.

(b_2) If a person has generosity, then she will typically act so as to benefit another person when there is sufficient reason to do so.
(b_3) If a person has curiosity, then she will typically act so as to solve intellectual problems when there is sufficient reason to do so.
⋮
(b_n)

(P) *The Virtue Prevalence Family*
(p_1) Many people commit acts of courage.
(p_2) Many people commit acts of generosity.
(p_3) Many people commit acts of curiosity.
(p_4) Many people are courageous.
(p_5) Many people are generous.
(p_6) Many people are curious.
⋮
(p_n)

(I) *The Cardinality/Integration Family*
(i_1) Typically, a person who has modesty also has humility.
(i_2) Typically, a person who has magnanimity also has generosity.
(i_3) Typically, a person who has curiosity also has open-mindedness.
⋮
(i_n)

(D) *The Desire/Virtue Family*
(d_1) Typically, a person desires to have courage.
(d_2) Typically, a person desires to have generosity.
(d_3) Typically, a person desires to have curiosity.
⋮
(d_n)

(F) *The Fidelity Family*
(f_1) Chastity is high-fidelity.
(f_2) Honesty is high-fidelity.
(f_3) Creativity is low-fidelity.
⋮
(d_n)

Each platitude in each family is meant to be merely illustrative. Presumably they could all be improved somewhat, and there are many more such platitudes. Moreover, each family is itself just an example. There are many further families describing the relations among vice, affect, cognition, situation, evaluation, and behavior, as well as families that make three-way rather than two-way connections (e.g., "If a person is courageous, then she will typically act so as to overcome threats when there is sufficient reason to do so and because she feels courageous."). For the sake of simplicity, though, let's assume that the families identified above contain all and only the platitudes relevant to the implicit definition of virtues. Ramsification can now be performed in the usual way. First, create a big conjunction

$$a_1 \wedge a_2 \wedge ... \wedge a_n \wedge$$
$$c_1 \wedge c_2 \wedge ... \wedge c_n \wedge$$
$$s_1 \wedge s_2 \wedge ... \wedge s_n \wedge$$
$$e_1 \wedge e_2 \wedge ... \wedge e_n \wedge$$
$$b_1 \wedge b_2 \wedge ... \wedge b_n \wedge$$
$$p_1 \wedge p_2 \wedge ... \wedge p_n \wedge$$
$$i_1 \wedge i_2 \wedge ... \wedge i_n \wedge$$
$$d_1 \wedge d_2 \wedge ... \wedge d_n \wedge$$
$$f_1 \wedge f_2 \wedge ... \wedge f_n$$

(henceforth, simply the 'postulate of virtue theory'). Next, replace each of the T-terms in the postulate of virtue theory with an unbound variable, then existentially quantifies over those variables to generate the Ramsey sentence of virtue theory. Finally, check whether the Ramsey sentence of virtue theory is true and—if it is—what its realizers are.

After this preliminary work has been done, we're in a position to see more clearly the problem raised by the situationist challenge to virtue theory. Situationists argue that there is no realizer of the Ramsey sentence of virtue theory. Moreover, this is not for lack of effort. Indeed, one family of platitudes in the Ramsey sentence specifically states that, typically, people desire to be virtuous; it's not as if no one has yet tried to be or become courageous, generous, or curious.[4] In this chapter, I don't have space to canvass the relevant empirical evidence; interested readers should see my (2013a and 2013b). Nevertheless, the crucial claim—that the Ramsey sentence of virtue theory is not realized—is not an object of serious dispute in the philosophical literature.

One very common response to the situationist challenge from defenders of virtue theory (and virtue ethics in particular) is to claim that virtues are actually quite rare, directly contradicting the statements in the virtue prevalence family. I do not think this is the best response to the problem, as I explain below, but the point remains that all serious disputants agree that the Ramsey sentence is not realized.

As described above, Ramsification looks like a simple, formal exercise. Collect the platitudes, put them into a big conjunction, perform the appropriate substitutions, existentially quantify, and check the truth-value of the resulting Ramsey sentence (and the referents of its bound variables, if any). But there are several opportunities for a critic to object as the exercise unfolds.

One difficulty that arises for some families, such as the desire/virtue family, is that they involve T-terms within the scope of intentional attitude verbs.[5] Since existential quantification into such contexts is blocked by opacity, such families cannot be relied on to define the T-terms, though they can be used to double-check the validity of the implicit definition once the T-terms are defined.[6]

Another difficulty is that this methodology presupposes that we have an adequate understanding of the O-terms, which in this case include terms that refer to attitudes, mental processes, perceptions and perceptual sensitivities, behaviors, reasons, situational features, and evaluations. One might be dubious about this presupposition. I certainly am. However, the fact that philosophy of mind and metaethics are works-in-progress should not be interpreted as a problem specifically for my approach to virtue theory. Any normative theory that relies on other branches of philosophy to figure out what mental states and processes are, and what reasons are, can be criticized in the same way.

A third worry is that the list of platitudes contains gaps (e.g., a virtue acquisition family about how various traits are acquired). Conversely, one might think that it has gluts (e.g., unmotivated commitment to virtue prevalence). To overcome this pair of worries, we need a way of determining what the platitudes are. Perhaps surprisingly, there is no precedent for this in the philosophy of mind, despite the fact that Ramsification is often invoked as a framework there.[7] This may be because it's supposed to be obvious what the platitudes are. Here's Frank Jackson's flippant response to the worry:

> I am sometimes asked—in a tone that suggests that the question is a major objection—why, if conceptual analysis is concerned to elucidate what governs our classificatory practice, don't I advocate doing serious opinion polls on people's responses to various cases? My answer is that I do—when it is necessary. Everyone who presents the Gettier cases to a class of students is doing their own bit of fieldwork, and we all know the answer they get in the vast majority of cases. (1998, pp. 36–37)

After all, according to Lewis, everyone knows the platitudes, and everyone knows that everyone knows them, and everyone knows that everyone knows that everyone knows them, and so on. Sometimes, however, the most obvious things are the hardest to spot. It thus behooves us to at least sketch a method for carrying out the first step of Ramsification: identifying the platitudes. Call this *pre-Ramsification*.

Here's an attempt at spelling out how pre-Ramsification should work: start by listing off a large number of candidate platitudes. These can be all of the statements one would, in a less-responsible, Jacksonian mood, have merely asserted were platitudes. It can also include statements that seem highly likely but perhaps not quite platitudes. Add to the pool of statements some that seem, intuitively, to be controversial, as well as some that seem obviously false; these serve as anchors in the ensuing investigation. Next, collect people's responses to these statements. Several sorts of responses would be useful, including subjective agreement, social agreement, and reaction time. For instance, prompt people with the statement, "Many people are honest," and ask to what extent they agree and to what extent they think others would agree. Measure their reaction times as they answer both questions. High subjective and social agreement, paired with fast reaction times, is strong but defeasible evidence that a statement is a platitude. This is a bit vague, since I haven't specified what counts as "high" agreement or "fast" reaction times, but there are precedents in psychology for setting these thresholds. Moreover, this kind of pre-Ramsification wouldn't establish dispositively what the platitudes are, but then, dispositive proof only happens in mathematics.

It's far beyond the scope of this short chapter to show that pre-Ramsification works in the way I suggest, or that it verifies all and only the families identified above. For now, let's suppose that it does, that is, that all of the families proposed above were validated by pre-Ramsification. Let's also suppose that we have strong evidence that the Ramsey sentence of virtue theory is not realized (a point that, as I mentioned above, is not seriously contested). How should we then proceed?

Lewis foresaw that, in some cases, the Ramsey sentence for a given field would be unrealized, so he built in a way of fudging things: instead of generating the postulate by taking the conjunction of all of the platitudes, one can generate a weaker postulate by taking the disjunction of each of the conjunctions of *most* of the platitudes. For example, if there were only five platitudes, p, q, r, s, and t, then instead of the postulate's being $p \wedge q \wedge r \wedge s \wedge t$, it would be $(p \wedge q \wedge r \wedge s) \vee (p \wedge q \wedge r \wedge t) \vee \ldots \vee (q \wedge r \wedge s \wedge t)$. In the case of virtue theory, we could take the disjunction of each of the conjunctions of all but one of the families of platitudes. Alternatively, we could exclude a few of the platitudes from within each family.

Fudging in this way makes it easier for the Ramsey sentence to be realized, since the disjunction of conjunctions of most of the platitudes is logically weaker than the straightforward conjunction of all of them. Fudging may end up making it *too* easy, though, such that there are *multiple* realizers of the Ramsey sentence. When this happens, it's up to the theorist to figure out how to strengthen things back up in such a way that there is a unique realizer.

The various responses to the situationist challenge can be seen as different ways of doing this. Everyone recognizes that the un-fudged Ramsey sentence of virtue theory is unrealized. But a sufficiently fudged Ramsey sentence is bound to be multiply realized. It's a theoretical choice exactly how to play things at this point. More traditional virtue theorists such as Joel Kupperman

(2009) favor a fudged version of the Ramsey sentence wherein the virtue prevalence family has been dropped. John Doris (2002) favors a fudged version wherein the virtue/situation and virtue/integration families have been dropped. I (2013a, 2014a) favor a fudged version wherein the virtue/situation family has been dropped and a virtue/social construction family has been added in its place. The statements in the latter family have to do with the ways in which (signals of) social expectations implicitly and explicitly influence behavior. The main idea is that having a virtue is more like having a title or social role (e.g., you're curious because people signal to you their expectations of curiosity) than like having a basic physical or biological property (e.g., being over six feet tall). Christian Miller (2013, 2014) drops the virtue prevalence family and adds a mixed-trait prevalence family in its place, which states that many people possess traits that are neither virtues nor vices, such as the disposition to help others in order to improve one's mood or avoid sliding into a bad mood.

In this short chapter, I don't have the space to argue against all alternatives to my own proposal. Instead, I want to make two main claims. First, the "virtue is rare" dodge advocated by Kupperman and others who drop the virtue prevalence family has costs associated with it. Second, those costs may be steeper than the costs associated with my own way of responding to the situationist challenge.

Researchers in personality and social psychology have documented for decades the tendency of just about everybody to make spontaneous trait inferences, attributing robust character traits on the basis of scant evidence (Ross 1977; Uleman et al. 1996). This indicates that people think that character traits (virtues, vices, and neutral traits, such as extroversion) are prevalent. Zagzebski (1996) concurs, making the somewhat wide-eyed claim that "many of us have known persons whose goodness shines forth from the depths of their being" (p. 83). Furthermore, in a forthcoming paper (Alfano et al., forthcoming), I show that the vast majority of obituaries attribute multiple virtues to the deceased. Not everyone is eulogized in an obituary, of course, but most are (about 55% of Americans, by my calculations). Not all obituaries are sincere, but presumably many are. Absent reason to think that people about whom obituaries differ greatly from people about whom they are not written, we can treat this as evidence that most people think that the people they know have multiple virtues. But of course, if most relations of most people are virtuous, it follows that most people are virtuous. In other words, the virtue-prevalence family is deeply ingrained in folk psychology and folk morality.

Social psychologists think that people are quick to attribute virtues. My own work on obituaries suggests the same. What do philosophers say? Though there are some (Russell 2009) who claim that virtue is rare or even non-existent with a shrug, this is not the predominant opinion. Alasdair MacIntyre (1984) claims that "without allusion to the place that justice and injustice, courage and cowardice play in human life very little will be genuinely explicable" (p. 199). Philippa Foot (2001), following Peter Geach (1977), argues that certain generic statements characterize the human form of life, and that from these generic statements we can infer what humans need and hence will typically have. For the sake of comparison, consider what she says about a different life form, the deer. Foot first points out that the deer's form of defense is flight. Next, she claims that a certain normative statement follows, namely, that deer are naturally or by nature swift. This is not to say that every deer is swift; some are slow. Instead, it's a generic statement that characterizes the nature of the deer. Finally, she says that any deer that fails to be swift—that fails to live up to its nature—is "so far forth defective" (p. 34). The same line of reasoning that she here applies to non-human animals is meant to apply to human animals as well. As she puts it,

> Men and women need to be industrious and tenacious of purpose not only so as to be able to house, clothe, and feed themselves, but also to pursue human ends having to do with love and friendship. They need the ability to form family ties, friendships, and special relations with neighbors. They also need codes of conduct. *And how could they have all these things without virtues such as loyalty, fairness, kindness, and in certain circumstances obedience?* (pp. 44–45, emphasis mine)

In light of these sorts of claims, let's consider again the defense offered by some virtue ethicists that virtue is rare, or even impossible to achieve. If virtues are what humans *need*, but the vast majority of people don't have them, one would have thought that our species would have died out long ago. Consider the analogous claim for deer: although deer *need* to be swift, the vast majority of deer are galumphers. Were that the case, presumably they'd be hunted down and devoured like a bunch of tasty venison treats. Or consider another example of Foot's: she agrees with Geach (1977) that people need virtues like honeybees need stingers. Does it make sense for someone with this attitude to say that most people lack virtues? That would be like saying that, even though bees need stingers, most lack stingers. It's certainly odd to claim that the majority—even the vast majority of a species fails to fulfill its own nature. That's not a contradiction, but it is a cost to be borne by anyone who responds to the situationist challenge by dropping the virtue prevalence family.

One might respond on Foot's behalf that human animals are special: unlike the other species, we have natures that are typically unfulfilled. That would be an interesting claim to make, but I am not aware of anyone who has defended it in print.[8] I conclude, then, that dropping the virtue prevalence family is a significant cost to revising the postulate.

But is it a *more significant* cost than the one imposed on me by replacing the virtue/situation family with a virtue/social construction family? I think it is. This comparative claim is of course hard to adjudicate, so I will rest content merely to emphasize the strength of the virtue/prevalence family.

What would it look like to fudge things in the way I recommend? Essentially, one would end up committed to a version of the hypothesis of extended cognition, a variety of active externalism in the family of the extended mind hypothesis. Clark and Chalmers (1998) argued that the vehicles (not just the contents) of some mental states and processes extend beyond the nervous system and even the skin of the agent whose states they are.[9] If my arguments are on the right track, virtues and vices sometimes extend in the same way: the bearers of someone's moral and intellectual virtues sometimes include asocial aspects of the environment and (more frequently) other people's normative and descriptive expectations. What it takes (among other things) for you to be, for instance, open-minded, on this view is that others think of you as open-minded and signal those thoughts to you. When they do, they prompt you to revise your self-concept, to want to live up to their expectations, to expect them to reward open-mindedness and punish closed-mindedness, to reciprocate displays of open-mindedness, and so on. These are all inducements to conduct yourself in an open-minded way, which they will typically notice. When they do, their initial attribution will be corroborated, leading them to strengthen their commitment to it and perhaps to signal that strengthening to you, which in turn is likely to further induce you to conduct yourself in open-minded ways, which will again corroborate their judgment of you, and so on. Such feedback loops are, on my view, partly constitutive of what it means to have a virtue.[10] The realizer of the fudged Ramsey sentence isn't just what's inside the person who has the virtue but also further things outside that person.

So, can people be virtuous? I hope it isn't too disappointing to answer with, "It depends on what you mean by 'can,' 'people,' and 'virtuous.'" If we're concerned only with abstract possibility, perhaps the answer is affirmative. If we are concerned more with the proximal possibility that figures in people's current deliberations, plans, and hopes, we have reason to worry. If we only care whether more than zero people can be virtuous, the existing, statistical, empirical evidence is pretty much useless. If we instead treat 'people' as a generic referring to human animals (perhaps a majority of them, but at least a substantial plurality), such evidence becomes both important and (again) worrisome. If we insist that being virtuous is something that must inhere entirely within the agent who has the virtue, then evidence from social psychology is damning. If instead we allow for the possibility of external character, there is room for hope.[11]

Ramsify (by all Means)—but Do Not 'Dumb Down' the Moral Virtues

James Montmarquet

The Basic Challenge of Situationist Research

In a number of important publications, Mark Alfano has refined a basically naturalist approach to the theory of moral and epistemic character, attempting to understand these in terms of established research findings in the social sciences.[12] In this general endeavor, of course, he is not alone. The dominant ("pragmatist") strain of philosophy in America has long rejected any strict dichotomy of nature and value—or of ethics and the social and natural sciences. I will turn to Alfano's contributions specifically to this volume in due course. But first it may prove instructive to probe, in somewhat more general terms, the kind of broadly naturalist approach to moral character he would advocate, confronting it, where possible, with what seems a viable alternative—not supernaturalism, mind you, but an approach emphasizing the independence and autonomy of moral philosophy, and insisting that our judgments of moral responsibility are too important to be left to social scientists—or maybe philosophers.

With Plato and Aristotle, let us observe, moral philosophy had begun to display this very autonomy and independence relative both to religion and to natural science—even if in the latter case this was mainly because natural science had hardly begun to break free of philosophy. In fact, we have a remarkable intimation of this breakthrough in Socrates' evidently autobiographical discourse in the *Phaedo* (98b-e). Having been as a young man impressed with the physical sciences, he relates how he later came to learn of the insufficiency of their explanations: Why am I sitting here in prison, he asks, awaiting death? Is it because my muscles, bones, and nerves have arranged themselves in these ways—or is it not because I am committed to certain *values*, for which commitment I freely take responsibility and am willing to die?

In the centuries to follow, challenges to moral philosophy's autonomy have come mainly from the sciences: with each great name in this history (Newton, Darwin, Freud, Einstein), a potential challenge is there, mainly emanating from those enthusiasts, inside or outside of philosophy, who would apply the lessons of the new science to 'old moral thinking.' On the whole, it must be said, moral philosophy has withstood these—though with some pretty good battle scars. But now we come to the latest challenge: many experimental results in social sciences appear to question the very idea—so basic to a broadly Aristotelian approach to ethics and to much of our ordinary moral thinking about ourselves and others—of individuals as possessed of, and having their actions considerably shaped by, *moral character*. According to these results, our actions are, to an unexpected extent, the products of the "situation" in which we find ourselves, and not of distinctive qualities of "moral character."[13] The findings in question are broadly of two kinds:

I. There are ones tending to show that a given situational variable has unexpectedly powerful and largely uniform effects—that is, effects holding largely irrespective of any differences in "moral character" as might have been supposed to exist within the group exposed to this influence.[14]

II. There are also findings tending to show that as one *varies* a situation—but within the confines of what we would take to be a single trait (e.g., honesty), we do not find very much individual consistency.[15] Thus, cheating in one type of educational setting (say, copying another's answers) turns out to be a surprisingly poor predictor of one's cheating in another (say, working past a time deadline).

Such contentions have, to say the least, sparked a lively debate, in which the defenders of traditional virtue ethics have scored their fair share of points.[16] But let me now put my own cards—some of them, those that do not remain up my sleeve—on the table. The situationist's starting point is certain empirical findings and her creed is largely that of "scientific naturalism": roughly, the idea that the findings and methodology of empirical science should be our best guide not just to the nature of the physical universe but in questions of philosophy (of metaphysics and of morality) as well. My starting point, by contrast, is neither science nor a dogmatic adherence to any particular moral outlook or philosophical persuasion; instead I look, initially at least, to the considered moral judgments we make especially concerning moral responsibility (of praise and even more so of blame). Since these judgments are so important, we would like them to be informed by the best, by the most rigorous findings science has to offer; and since questions of moral character are so deeply implicated in these judgments, we would naturally like this science to apply to them. The problem is that insofar as character can be reined in, domesticated and made scientifically serviceable, its most important moral dimensions still have a way of roaming free.

Aristotle's Mixed Legacy

Having indicated the importance I place on the connection between character and responsibility, I immediately yield pride of place briefly to Aristotle, whose ethical theory links praiseworthy and blameworthy conduct to virtuous or vicious dispositions of the agent (*Nicomachean Ethics*, Bk. II, iv-v). Aristotle, however, is also a convenient target for situationists, when he maintains that the virtuous act must reflect a "firm and unchangeable character" (Bk. II, iv). So, for instance, in his early and rather uncompromising statement of situationism, Harman (1999, p. 317) glosses Aristotle's notion of a character trait as a "relatively long-term stable disposition to act in distinctive ways," then proceeds to argue, along the situationist lines sketched earlier, that no such disposition exists.

Now, Aristotle's idea, sympathetically stated, would seem to be this. If an act does not express the right kind of disposition (inner state), even if it succeeds in being the right thing to do, this reflects a kind of luck; just the right non-virtuous factors have helped out. If, however, an act *does* reflect a virtuous inner state, this state will be of sufficient power and stability as to be repeatable—not just in situations narrowly of that type, but across a greater variety.

Arguably, however, this stance involves—not entirely (as we shall see) but in some measure—a "false dichotomy": arguably, that is to say, we need to recognize a *three-*, and not merely a two-fold distinction in this connection. There is such (superficially) good conduct as may result (1) from not much inner virtue at all, conduct that rightly nets faint praise and that is no very good candidate to be repeated. There is good conduct resulting, as Aristotle would wish, from (2) the stable possession of a virtuous (inner) trait. Finally, there is also good conduct resulting from (3) what may be an equally potent, but relatively unstable, expression of such traits. By analogy: there are shots of pure luck by "duffers" in golf; there are shots displaying an excellent, repeatable swing; and there are shots of equal grace and panache pulled off by somewhat erratic young golfers whose swings are not yet consistently good ("grooved").

Of course, there is a kind of "luck" involved in type (3) cases; but this, it also must be pointed out, is not the luck of mere "good fortune." It is good fortune when the duffer's shot hits a rock and bounds out of the hazard, two inches from the pin; and when the coward's act starts a general retreat that ends up saving the army. An act, however, of unusual heroism—performed by a formerly, or just a sometime, very timid soldier—would have been unpredictable, but is not mere good fortune or normally to be described as "mere luck." In fact, this distinction between type (2) and type (3) supports and larger and more significant difference. It is part of the idea of character that it can improve—or worsen—based on what happens in a given case. When this happens, we can in no way judge the moral quality of that display of character according to the *overall* character we suppose this individual to have (or to have had). In the familiar story of *The Red Badge of Courage*,[17] Henry ends up displaying a quality of courage that would have to be heavily, and counter-intuitively, discounted if it were assessed so as to give equal weight to his past cowardice. People grow; people change. As Aristotle himself must recognize, nothing augments one's courage like courage (greater than one's average level to that point): not just doing unusually courageous deeds but with a new inner strength.

Tolstoy and Hume

Our opening discussion has pointed in the direction of a character-based approach to moral responsibility, but emphasizing—what Aristotle does not—the distinction between the praiseworthiness or blameworthiness of a given character exemplification (this courage of Henry's) and that agent's conduct measured over time (Henry's typical level of courage). To this opening, we now add two contrasting (but not incompatible) lines of thought:

(1) *The Tolstoyan Idea*. Character is not well revealed most of the time, but is so in certain especially suitable, often quite difficult, situations. I associate this idea with Tolstoy, as his fiction displays this author's remarkable gift for revealing character by the apt selection of situation and response. Such situations are of an especially challenging nature: to name but one, there is the life-threatening blizzard in his story, *Master and Man* and the quite different responses to it of the rich merchant and his servant.[18] From this standpoint, cases in which it is "easy to be honest" (or where the Russian winter is merely "a bit cold") are hardly worth bothering about; for even if an agent should fail in one of these, this is typically a sign not of amazingly bad character so much as that more is going on than meets the eye.

(2) *Humean Intelligibility*. Even though Hume famously said, we must judge another's conduct not by his acts, which are "temporary and perishing" but by something "durable [and] constant" in his nature—that is, traits of moral character[19]—this does not mean that he must deny that assessments of praise and blame will properly take into consideration differences of situation. Thus, suppose that some English gentleman, known to be scrupulously honest in his business dealings, has been exposed as lying, on a given occasion, to a prostitute. We have found out something new and perhaps a little surprising about him. The Humean point, however, is not just to add this new information on—as though to say, seemingly with Doris, that the man has "business honesty" and "prostitute" (or, if we dare to generalize, "sexual") dishonesty, but to begin to form some revised but still unified picture of "who this man is."[20] We must add, however, that achieving this fuller picture—not just of 'who he is in general' but 'who he has shown himself to be in this case'—is strictly an art, not a science. Those with a penetrating insight into the true moral significance of a given human act (what it truly displays of that agent) are more like a Rembrandt or some other great portraitist than a Newton or an Einstein.

Now both the Tolstoyan and the Humean viewpoints, let us observe, remain broadly 'Aristotelian' in two basic regards:

First, in recognizing that the implications of any given character attribution extend beyond the present act, both would recognize, with Aristotle, the dispositional character of character attributions. Both seek some discovery or understanding of morally 'who one is'—not in general but so far as this is revealed in the present action. But any such judgment must carry implications—tentative and inexact as these may be—for future acts. Thomas Hurka (2006) has remarked, with some justice, that if you see someone kick a dog from an evident desire to hurt the dog just for the pleasure of doing so. Do you say, 'That was a vicious act' or 'That was a vicious act on the condition that it issued from a stable disposition to give similar kicks in similar circumstances'? Surely you say the former. (p. 71)

At a minimum, however, such a display—supposing, with Hurka, that it was of genuine (and not merely apparent) viciousness—would have some implications, however inexact, regarding future displays. We have found out something, something rather unpleasant, about this agent. As long as he is around, we must worry that his viciousness may be around as well. *Pace* Hurka, we do not have to make a prior or an independent discovery of a continuing trait in order to attribute something that would carry implications, to a greater or lesser degree, to that effect. If I see someone lift three hundred pounds, I can call him "strong" without further ado; but again this has implications.

Second, neither point of view rejects the Aristotelian notion that a virtuous act must display *some* suitable connection to one's past character displays. In fact, both will say this of any act for which one has moral responsibility. As in the previous example of the Victorian gentleman, the Humean portrait employs shades often drawn from a past understanding of this agent. It is a composite of past and present. For his part, once the challenge of the situation has been met (or not met) Tolstoy will equally want us to understand 'who this person has shown himself to be'—not in abstraction from the past, but in the present case, using the past to help us understand its meaning. Thus, in another story of his ("Father Sergius"[21]), a proud man passes through a whole series of failures—cadet of the Imperial Guard, suitor, monk, hermit, vagabond—until finally discovering true pride from one possessed of none of his advantages. Little in what happens could have been predicted, but all of it needs to be comprehended under the aspect of his pride and his past.

For both points of view, then, one needs to recognize links to the past and implications regarding the future—neither of which, it is important to emphasize at this point, are altogether satisfactory from a rigorously scientific standpoint. We draw on the past, in a selective, hopefully insightful way, to paint—in what is becoming my central metaphor—a picture of the present, a picture whose implications are in some ways profound, but still profoundly inexact. Thus, to vary our mode of artistic appeal, the reader of such a fine biography as Ron Chernow's *Alexander Hamilton*[22] will assuredly come to have much better understanding of this man than can be gleaned from superficial historical facts concerning him; but I would not suppose that it would help one to predict, or retrodict even, Hamilton's actions in a difficult case. Character is not a terribly good predictor—not because it is ineffectual, but because it is effected (and affected) in such complicated ways. What is the "predictive value" of a Rembrandt?

One last point in this connection, it is helpful to remember that character terms bear much in common with such impolite and obviously unscientific terms of opprobrium as "schmuck" or "bastard." There will be occasions when these are quite the correct terms to characterize what someone has done—as in "You say he did that? What a bastard!"—so it is not as though just 'anything goes' with their use in moral contexts. Still, it must be said that their application is more an art than any part of a science.

Hanna's Question

So far, our preoccupation has been with the loose, the unscientific—but not for that the unimportant—nature of character attributions and their connection to past and future. At this point, however, the situationist may raise a useful objection. 'I could almost agree with what you say concerning the independence, and the limited dependence, of situational evaluation on how well or badly an individual has done in other situations. I do not agree, however, if this is your position, that how well *other* agents would do in a given type of situation is irrelevant to the evaluation of a given agent. Learning how well most people function in Milgram experiments can and arguably should affect our judgments of blameworthiness.'

I feel the force of this concern, and add a reference of my own. As an admirer in general of contemporary cinema and of Kate Winslet in particular, I am reminded of the former concentration camp guard, Hanna's, question in the film, *The Reader*: confronted with her own crime of not unlocking the inmates caught in the burning church, she asks her main accuser, the presiding judge: "What would you have done?" There is no answer.

Again, following our usual practice, we will distinguish two different views on the relevance of what others have done or would do, in a given situation:

In a spirit of Tolstoyan—now become Kantian—boldness, it might be urged that we are free, guided only by reason and a sense of what is possible, to set the bar as high as we like, whatever empirical evidences indicates regarding 'normal performance.' (Even in golf, par is not set by the average number of strokes on a hole.) Thus, the judge might have informed Hanna: 'I would hope that I wouldn't have acted as you did, but if I did act in that way, then I must be judged guilty.'

The Humean is able to craft a more nuanced position. If we are talking somewhat superficially about kinds of action, I will agree that one's estimation of how bad (or good) a given kind is, would take into account what the norm would be regarding its performance. But that is not the same thing as the question of how a given agent would properly be evaluated—more fully, in more detail—if he were to do a given act. In the case of keeping the prisoners locked up, if the judge were to have done it, this would have quite a different moral significance than Hanna's act. Basically, the more we keep of the judge's present moral make-up, knowledge, and sophistication—the worse becomes his offense, the more it becomes an expression of sheer cowardice. As to the Milgram case, the Humean might say this: the behavior of others will to a point help us to understand what a given agent does, but so far as excusing, or even just diminishing the moral badness of, that behavior is concerned—this is neither necessary nor sufficient. The more deeply we understand, the more deeply we penetrate into the motives and moral personality of a given agent, the less we should need to rely on the inevitably different story concerning others.

Finally, by way of comparison, we turn to a situationism-influenced ethicist who has worked out in some detail a conception not only of moral character but of moral responsibility: John Doris (2002). Helpfully, Doris begins his account of responsibility by distinguishing the "intensity" and "frequency" aspects of a possible excusing condition, noting that even if we can isolate a certain situational variable as causally salient, this does not mean that it possesses the kind of intensity—the quality of being "difficult to resist"—which ought to excuse (p. 135). Still, he points to the fact that situationist research may uncover certain "unobtrusive high-intensity stimuli" that seemingly do exert a decisive effect on behavior and thus bid fair to be counted as "undetected excusing conditions" (p. 136). Doris addresses this possibility as, first, a worry concerning "normative competence": our capacity to recognize, reason, and act on morally relevant features of one's situation. Ultimately, though, it becomes a problem concerning "identification": insofar as these variables are hidden, we do not identify with them, thus, seemingly, cannot be held responsible for acting upon them (p. 140).

This, if it had been Doris's conclusion, would have been clear, illuminating, and fairly radical in the extent to which it upsets our common sense, folk psychological notions of responsibility. Doris, however, elects not to go this route. Instead, he argues that even if one is unaware of a situational factor, it may be possible to work up a "narrative" (pp. 142–143) underlying one's action with which one plausibly would identify. Thus, Doris maintains that, in the Darley and Batson, "Good Samaritan"—in which those who were late tended not to stop to help a man apparently in distress—"even where a person fails to identify with the callousness that resulted from haste, he might yet embrace having the sort of packed schedule that induces haste" (p. 144). We may, in other words, find grounds for holding him responsible (morally blameworthy) after all.

I find it most interesting, then, that Doris's bold naturalism when the topic is "virtue ethics" turns into a cautious conservatism when it comes to offering widespread exemption from moral responsibility. (This is not an unusual combination in the history of moral philosophy: attacking the received grounds for moral responsibility, but feeling pressed in the end to supply replacement grounds of one's own.) Doris has in any case worked his way around—as he may choose—to either the Kantian or the Humean position. One may find in the story of Hanna's life times enough of a humanitarian narrative for her to identify with—so that she may be held to quite a high moral standard. There will also, however, be competing narratives, running closer to the motivations actually at work in this case, whose effect would be exculpatory. In the end, the choice simply lies with us (including the judge) as moral observers. We would *like* assistance from social science—or religion, or philosophy, or something—but it is not clear that anything altogether helpful is available.

An Irenic Approach, Initially

In his contribution to the present volume, Mark Alfano has offered what seems initially a peaceable approach to these situationist wars, an analytical framework with respect to which various approaches (including but by no means limited to his own) can be represented. On this view, we characterize 'moral character traits' as a kind of theoretical entity able to satisfy various types, and combinations of types, of open sentences. These sentences will collect some of the more important truths, or putative truths ("platitudes") concerning a given trait of moral character. Interestingly, it will treat not only character terms ('courage,' 'moral character,' etc.), but "persons" as theoretical terms, implicitly defined by the theory.

Now, as a device, this seems a fair and neutral way of representing certain possible views of moral character; but of course controversial claims may be, as Alfano points out, built into it one or another selection of platitudes. So, for instance, the claim that "if a person has courage, then she will typically be unaffected by situational factors that are neither reasons for nor reasons against overcoming a threat"; coupled with the claim that "many people have courage" would be, for some situationists, "fighting words." But let me focus on two aspects of particular relevance to the foregoing discussion.

First, the notion of "sufficient reasons" figures in a very prominent way in these partial characterizations. Thus, it is said that a courageous person will act in certain ways, will feel certain things, will be unaffected by situational factors—all when there is "sufficient reason" for this. But apply this back to the case of Hanna: Is the situation that one is a concentration camp guard a sufficient reason to omit what would otherwise count as simple kindness and benevolence, etc.? If our notion of sufficiency is sharply Kantian ("of *course* she had sufficient reason to help"), many, even most, people will ultimately prove unkind and not very benevolent. If it is not, we will get a different verdict. In short, the notion of 'sufficient reason,' as it figures in these collections, threatens but to recapitulate the most troubling aspects of cases like Hanna's (or the Milgram subjects').

Second, there seems one notable difference between the Lewis and Alfano projects. In Lewis's case, the interesting development is that, for all the different things believed about these inner states, it turns out (arguably) that they are brain states. What, comparably, may we discover through Ramsification concerning what moral character turns out to be? Nothing equally surprising or exciting, some may think—but Alfano, I think, would disagree. According to his particular conception of moral character, at least, it turns out that what realizes the relevant Ramsey sentence includes things not going on solely "inside the person who has the virtue" (p. 225).

This, it could be supposed, is both surprising and exciting, but I remain a bit skeptical. Here we must distinguish the full reference of our theory of character, which may include all sorts of things (persons, states of persons, features of the environment, situations, and so forth), and what is referred to by such discourse as "my courage" or "her patience"—or what Alfano himself, in the passage just quoted, speaks of as the person "who has" a given virtue. I am not sure that Alfano is altogether clear in his way of putting this matter. He will say, at the very end (p. 226), that according to some very good social psychology, "being virtuous" does not "inhere entirely within the agent" (again "the agent that has that virtue"). This strikes me as either a truism (that the full range of what must be the case in order to "have a virtue" will include much that is outside of oneself)—or what hardly seems a truism, or true at all, that when Jones is praised for her courage (the courage she "has"), she is being praised for something which is located all over the place (including wherever those people or situations that have helped to encourage this behavior are located). Perhaps Alfano will say that we cannot properly make this distinction (between the full reference of the theory and what things like "Jones's courage" pick out); he might say that this is like asking what the relation is between the reference of Lewis's Ramsification (brain states) and what we meant to refer to in our old folk psychological talk. I will in any case return later to this important topic: the relation between moral praise for courage and what social science may teach us about such qualities.

Virtue Prevalence and Social Construction

I turn, first, to another important concern of Alfano's, which has been to emphasize the price to be paid for giving up, as some character theorists wish to do, "virtue prevalence"—that is, the thesis that virtues are quite widespread throughout the moral community, and are not merely the possession of a few moral heroes. Along these lines, Alfano seizes on a point of Philippa Foot, who makes much of the virtues as being qualities that we "need" as much as the deer needs speed or the bee its stinger. He observes, ironically, that if the virtues were both this necessary and as rare as some suggest, "one would have thought that our species would have died out long ago" (p. 224).

I hold no particular brief for Foot, but would simply draw an analogy here between situationist findings concerning the non-prevalence of virtue, and discouraging test results concerning American students in science and mathematics. Of course, the latter hardly show that the skills measured by such tests are not important. Likewise, it could be argued, virtue ethicists are entitled to hold that the virtues (and especially the vices) remain important despite the discouraging test results of social science. An ethics of virtue does not hold that we will "test well" for these, so much as that if we do not, this is important—and disturbing. Thus, concern over Milgram's results, like concern with standardized test results, shows how important we take the virtues and vices to be. Moreover, to extend the analogy, we need not deny that these qualities—be they moral, mathematical, or scientific—are broadly necessary for "survival"—but of course we cannot maintain in either case that, at their current, admittedly low levels, we are faced with imminent extinction. Luckily, speed in mathematics is not quite as important for us as speed of foot is for the deer. For that matter, "obedience to authority" may have, or have had, (*pace* Milgram) greater survival value than "moral independence."

To continue the previous thought, it seems evident that certain kinds and levels of virtue are required for—call it, "social solidarity" but that these may not agree with qualities morally sensitive people praise and claim to value. Again, it may be that getting to one's assigned place on time has greater survival value than helping strangers (who may be planning an ambush). It may be that the limitations social scientists have uncovered in our moral characters are actually evolutionary virtues of sorts.

"Fair enough," Alfano may say, "I have just the conception you need for your 'social solidarity' and it is my 'social construction' conception you took swipe at earlier." In fact, that previous discussion notwithstanding, I will agree—partly. It may well be that what survival demands are more or less the very qualities good social science picks out as highly prevalent. Now, his social construction view Alfano describes in these terms:

> What it takes (among other things) for you to be, for instance, open-minded ... is that others think of you as open-minded and signal those thoughts to you. When they do, they prompt you to revise your self-concept, to want to live up to their expectations, to expect them to reward open-mindedness and punish closed-mindedness, and so on. These are all inducements to think in an open-minded way, which they will typically notice. When they do, their initial attribution will be corroborated, leading them to strengthen their commitment to it, and perhaps to signal that strengthening to you ... Such feedback loops are, on my view, partly constitutive of what it means to have a virtue.

I would like to probe two areas of possible difficulty for such a view, the second of which will take us back to the main theme of my discussion.

First, there are important questions concerning the *vices*. Are these, too, socially induced by the same kind of feedback loops? Or do they mark, to the contrary, merely failed (positive) loops? It is, let me say in passing, characteristic of the literature on situationism that questions of the virtues, their consistency, and prevalence entirely dominate questions of vice (their consistency and prevalence)—which in a way is strange, inasmuch as questions of blame, not praise, dominate whole other areas of moral philosophy. Now, for his part, Alfano refers to the fact that "social scientists think that people are quick to attribute virtues"; but this tendency would surely suggest that we are quick, perhaps even quicker, to attribute vices. If that is correct, we have some fairly substantial grounds for thinking of the vices as, in great part, acquired via the same social influences as generate, and partly constitute, the virtues. The danger for Alfano, I submit, is now the very distinction between virtue and vice, good and bad, looks to be entirely external to the theory—almost as though it were an afterthought. Of course, this problem does not arise—not in such an acute way—if we think of the vices according to the other suggestion (as failed virtues); but now we seem to be going against the grain of what social science is telling us concerning the acquisition of all qualities (good and bad); moreover, there is also the question of whether, or how, the mere failure of a "feedback loop" would be morally blameworthy.

Second, and most importantly, there is the issue with which we began: Aristotle's formative claim that we are to be praised and blamed primarily for our virtues and vices. The issue becomes this. If we follow social science, we will arrive at a variety of conceptions, one of which is Alfano's 'social construction' view. To extend my earlier comparison, these conceptions would be like attempts to redefine ("dumb down") mathematical and scientific skills in such a way that it turns out that most children *do* have these to a satisfactory degree after all (much relief all around!). However, just as rethinking mathematical ability does not make anyone better at solving mathematics problems, redefinitions of 'virtue' do not actually make any one morally better—just ask someone who is lying along the road, waiting for a Good Samaritan to come along.

But I want to be fair to the social sciences: let us allow that when I refer to courage, I may in some sense be referring to a trait whose nature is such as to be characteristically induced by certain types of social cues, expectations, and feedback loops of the sort Alfano describes. Again, though, the fundamental limitation of this conception is that there is nothing terribly praiseworthy about responding to such social indicators—not as such. Rather, one must suppose that the praiseworthiness of courage lies in the fact that sometimes it is very *difficult* to respond to such indicators (think of the soldiers comprising "The Charge of the Light Brigade"). If you like, sometimes it takes real courage to exhibit this kind of "social courage." Likewise, real generosity and helpfulness would begin where socially cued generosity and helpfulness leave off. By the same token, the former would be rare; the latter, prevalent.

So, in the end, we can have our cake and eat it too—just so long as we do not confuse those parts of it that are real, and rare, from those parts that are mass produced. We can frame, as Mark Alfano is doing, a sophisticated philosophical notion, drawn from social science research. We can also reflect on what is genuinely praiseworthy and genuinely blameworthy; but this, I want to say, will carry us beyond questions of social science, evolution, and survival.

Socrates' Unanswered Question

"Thou shalt not sit/with statisticians nor commit/A social science," warned a noted poet.[23] We will adopt a somewhat more forgiving stance. There is certainly a role for the social and biological sciences in understanding moral character and morality generally. The giants of our subject—Aristotle, Kant, Mill—have generally kept clear of explaining moral conduct (sociologically, psychologically, biologically), recognizing that explaining it would run the extreme risk of explaining it away. There is another way of putting these matters, which hearkens back to what I said at the outset. We would like the most important things to be studied in the best of ways. Science has proven itself to be the best, so we would like to study moral character and responsibility scientifically. We would like what is most important to us to be very clear to us. All the same, Socrates' question—what am I doing here (in prison)?—seems no more answerable by today's than by the sciences of his day. If its answer is clear (to him), answers to comparable questions (including Hanna's) are anything but.

Study Questions

1. Is someone's character better revealed by how they live their life in ordinary circumstances or how they respond to extraordinary circumstances?
2. Arguably, Aristotle thought that friendship was "extended" in the way Alfano says all virtues are extended. Do you think virtues such as trustworthiness are extended? Explain.
3. How well would you need to know someone to be able to paint a Humean picture of their character? How many people do you know that well (including yourself)? Would it be a problem if we never knew each other or ourselves this well?
4. What does Alfano mean by saying that "the bearers of someone's moral and intellectual virtues sometimes include asocial aspects of the environment and (more frequently) other people's normative and descriptive expectations"?

5. Ethical naturalism is endorsed by some of the authors in this volume, especially Snow, Russell, Miller, and Alfano; it's rejected by others, especially Montmarquet. What's the best argument in favor of ethical naturalism? What's the best argument against it?
6. How would Alfano likely address Montmarquet's worry that in explaining moral character and responsibility in ways suggested by the social sciences, we run the risk of explaining them away?

Notes

1. Nathan is also using an extended metaphor. My point is clear nevertheless.
2. An alternative is the "psycho-functionalist" method, which disregards common sense in favor of (solely) highly corroborated scientific claims. See Kim (2011) for an overview. For my purposes, psycho-functionalism is less appropriate, since (among other things) it is more in danger of changing the topic.
3. See, for instance, Zagzebski (1996, p. 112): "It does count against a person's virtue, however, if stractions or persuasions lead him to fail to exercise it."
4. I seem to be in disagreement on this point with Christian Miller (this volume), who worries that people may not be motivated to be or become virtuous. In general, I'm even more skeptical than Miller about the prospects of virtue theory, but in this case I find myself playing the part of the optimist.
5. I am here indebted to Gideon Rosen.
6. It might also be possible to circumvent this difficulty, which anyway troubles Lewis's application of Ramsification to the mind-brain identity theory, by using only *de re* formulations of the relevant statements. See Fitting and Mendelsohn (1999) for a discussion of how to do so.
7. Experimental philosophers have started to fill this gap, but not in any systematic or consensus-based way.
8. Micah Lott (personal communication) has told me that he endorses this claim, though he has a related worry. In short, his concern is to explain how, given the alleged rarity of virtue, most people manage to live decent enough lives.
9. For an overview of the varieties of externalism, see Carter et al. (2014).
10. I spell out this view in more detail in Alfano (forthcoming) and Alfano and Skorburg (forthcoming). For a treatment of the feedback-loops model in the context of the extended mind rather than the character debate, see Palermos (2014).
11. I am grateful to J. Adam Carter, Orestis Palermos, and Micah Lott for comments on a draft of this chapter.
12. See mainly (Alfano 2013a), especially his description of his approach to ethics involving reasoning in an "abductive" way (p. 5) from scientific findings to what must be the case, philosophically, for those to be true. This general viewpoint informs his treatment of epistemic character in (Alfano 2012).
13. For important discussion of these results (and defense of what has come to be called the situationist viewpoint regarding moral character), see Harman (1999, 2000) and Doris (1998), but especially Doris's extended and extraordinarily valuable treatment of these issues in *Lack of Character: Personality and Moral Behavior* (2002).
14. Among the best known of these are, respectively, the work of Isen and Levin (1972)—in which the remarkable effects of a found dime on helping behavior are demonstrated; Darley and Batson (1973)—in which the effects of 'being in a hurry because late' on Good Samaritan behavior are presented, and, finally, the famous Milgram (1974) experiments concerning obedience to authority.

15. Most commonly cited here would be Hartshorne and May (1928), in which it was shown how the likelihood of dishonesty or cheating among school children tended to vary, for any given individual, considerably from situation to situation.
16. See, for example, Kupperman (2001), Sreenivasan (2002), Montmarquet (2003), Kamtekar (2004), Sabini and Silver (2005), and Adams (2006).
17. Stephen Crane (New York: Dover, 1990).
18. In *Great Short Works of Tolstoy* (New York: Harper and Row, 1967).
19. *Treatise of Human Nature*, Bk. II, Section II.
20. For Hume (1975/2007, 8.10), the "uniformity of human action" must take account of the "diversity of characters, prejudices, and opinions." Here he adds, tellingly, that even if an action occurred with "no regular connection to any known motive"—this would provoke no very clear or definite judgment from the observer—except wonder.
21. Also in *Great Short Works of Tolstoy*.
22. (New York: Penguin, 2005).
23. W. H. Auden in *Under Which Lyre: A Reactionary Tract for the Times*.

CHAPTER 6

A Brief Introduction to Other Virtue Theoretic Controversies

Our authors have attempted to advance the debate on five controversies in virtue theory:

1. What is a virtue?
2. Does virtue contribute to flourishing?
3. How are ethical and epistemic virtues related?
4. How are virtues acquired?
5. Can people be virtuous?

Naturally, there are other unsettled questions that could not be addressed between the covers of this volume. In this closing section of the book, I list just a few, along with a brief discussion of each.

6. Why attribute virtues and vices to other people and ourselves?

What is the *point* of attributing virtues and vices? Ordinarily, ascriptions of dispositions are meant to explain and predict. We say that gasoline is combustible because that disposition helps to explain why engines work. We say that a chair is rickety because that disposition helps us to predict whether it will break if someone sits on it. Do virtue and vice attributions function in the same way? Do we call someone curious because that disposition helps to explain why she investigates things in a particular way? Do we call someone untrustworthy because that disposition helps to predict whether he will take advantage of us? Intuitively, the answer is yes. Are there further uses of virtue and vice attributions? Many philosophers admit other uses. For instance, it's plausible to think that the function of virtue and vice attributions is to evaluate. To call someone open-minded is to say that she's good in a certain way; to call someone dogmatic is to say that he's bad in a certain way. Another potential function of virtue and vice attributions is control—and in multiple ways. For instance, it's plausible to think that blaming someone for being vicious or engaging in vicious conduct is a way of prompting him to act differently in the future. It's also plausible to think that blaming someone for being vicious or engaging in vicious conduct is a way of committing *oneself* not to acting in that way (at the risk of being a hypocrite and losing one's integrity). It's also plausible to think that blaming someone for being vicious or engaging in vicious conduct is a way of deterring other people from engaging in such conduct, since they now know that they're likely to be blamed for it. Similar points could be made about praising someone for virtue or virtuous conduct. It's plausible to think that praising someone for being virtuous or engaging in virtuous conduct is a way of prompting her to continue acting in the same way in the future. It's also plausible to think that praising someone for being virtuous or engaging in virtuous conduct is a way of committing oneself to acting in the same way in the future, and also a way of prompting others to engage in such conduct (in pursuit of your praise, esteem, or reward). Which, if any, of the alleged functions of virtue and vice ascriptions is essential? Which, if any, of the alleged functions of virtue and vice ascriptions is antithetical to a virtue-theoretic approach to ethics and epistemology? These questions remain unanswered.

7. Does the scholarship on epistemic injustice point to a departure from Aristotelian conceptions of virtue?

Epistemic injustice is particular kind of harm: harm to someone specifically in their capacity as a (potential) knower (Fricker 2007). There are multiple manifestations of epistemic injustice at the level of the act, the agent, and the group or institution. Testimonial injustice, for instance, occurs when someone is treated as less credible than she deserves simply because of her sex. Miranda Fricker (2007) explores such injustice in some depth. She points out that such injustice can be practiced by a particular person to such an extent that it constitutes a vice in that person. Opposed to this vice are two different kinds of epistemic justice: a kind of naïve epistemic justice, which someone can have if they've never imbibed and internalized various negative stereotypes and thus has no disposition to discount their views, and a corrective epistemic justice, which someone can have if they've realized that they are biased but actively attempt to correct for that bias. Epistemic injustice can also occur even if no particular person is sufficiently biased to count as vicious—provided that enough people are just slightly biased, the effect will still be pernicious. Thus, there exists a form of social or institutional injustice as an emergent phenomenon that does not depend on any particular person to be unjust. Why might the literature on epistemic injustice challenge Aristotelian conceptions of virtue? One main way is that it seems that the solution to epistemic injustice in many instances cannot be achieved at the level of the individual. If epistemic injustice can occur even when no one is unjust, there needs to be a higher-level way of practicing epistemic justice, one which operates on groups and institutions rather than just individuals. To the extent that Aristotelian virtue theory locates virtues solely in the agent, it cannot solve this problem. But perhaps a few extremely just and vocal people can prompt others to develop the corrective form of epistemic justice, making such institutional solutions unnecessary. Further research is required.

8. What kind of practical guidance can virtue ethics provide on difficult moral issues, especially in applied ethics?

Anscombe (1958) claims that while it may be unclear what to do when one asks the question "Is this right or wrong?" asking the more specific and virtue-involving question whether a particular action is, for instance, *unjust* can make the answer "clear at once." Is this always the case? How much practical guidance can virtue ethics provide in especially thorny dilemmas? There are reasons to worry. In particular, in thorny problems, there are almost always relevant virtues that point in different directions. For instance, consider a case in which a parent shows up at a clinic with their child, whom they adamantly refuse to immunize for measles, mumps, and rubella—claiming a religious or ideological exemption. On the one hand, the nurse or doctor knows that there is no good reason not immunize. Additionally, the clinician knows that reducing the vaccination rate is potentially harmful not only to unvaccinated children (who, because of their age, are incapable of consenting either to vaccination or to non-vaccination), but also to others because it reduces herd immunity to potentially deadly diseases. This is an issue of non-malevolence, a core value in medicine. On the other hand, the clinician is obligated to respect the parent's autonomy—also an issue of justice and respect for autonomy. Will it be clear at once to the clinician (or a legislator or judge considering how to handle such cases) what the right thing to do is? One might worry that thinking of virtues without any way of weighting them will only lead to further consternation, not enlightenment. For more on applied virtue theory, see Austin (2014).

9. Are seemingly vicious traits needed or even virtuous in an oppressive society?

In Ferguson, Missouri, in the summer of 2014, a police officer shot and killed Michael Brown, an unarmed man who was holding his hands up in a signal of surrender. Such events are shockingly common in the United States. When protesters demanded justice in the form of an open investigation of the shooting, they were attacked multiple times by police officers equipped with riot gear, MRAPs (mine-resistant ambush protected military vehicles that are designed for use in war), sniper rifles, tear gas, and so on. In addition to the violent response, officials in Ferguson attempted in various ways to defame the deceased, for instance by implying falsely that he'd been involved in a robbery the same day he was killed. How should someone in this society, teeming as it is with brutality, manipulation, and repression, respond? What dispositions are appropriate here? One might think that dispositional anger and cynicism are always vices, but arguably in sufficiently unjust societies rage and skepticism toward those in power is justified—even virtuous. This raises the question whether there can be a culture-invariant catalogue and ranking of virtues.

References

Abernathy, C.M. and R.M. Hamm. (1994). *Surgical Scripts: Master Surgeons Think Aloud about 43 Common Surgical Problems*. Philadelphia: Hanley and Belfus.

Adams, R.M. (2006). *A Theory of Virtue*. Oxford: Oxford University Press.

Alfano, M. (2011). Explaining away intuitions about traits: Why virtue ethics seems plausible (even if it isn't). *Review of Philosophy and Psychology*, 2:1, 121–136.

Alfano, M. (2012). Extending the situationist challenge to responsibilist virtue epistemology. *Philosophical Quarterly*, 62:247, 223–249.

Alfano, M. (2013a). *Character as Moral Fiction*. Cambridge: Cambridge University Press.

Alfano, M. (2013b). Identifying and defending the hard core of virtue ethics. *Journal of Philosophical Research*, 38, 233–260.

Alfano, M. (2014a). What are the bearers of virtues? In H. Sarkissian and J. Wright (eds.), *Advances in Moral Psychology*. New York: Continuum.

Alfano, M. (2014b). Extending the situationist challenge to reliabilism about inference. In A. Fairweather (ed.), *Virtue Epistemology Naturalized: Bridges Between Virtue Epistemology and Philosophy of Science*. Dordrecht: Synthese Library.

Alfano, M. (forthcoming). Friendship and the structure of trust. In J. Webber and A. Masala (eds.), *From Personality to Virtue: Essays in the Psychology and Ethics of Character*. Oxford: Oxford University Press.

Alfano, M., A. Higgins, and J. Levernier. (forthcoming). Mapping human values: An analysis of obituaries. In L. Kahle (ed.), Social and Cultural Values in a Global and Digital Age.

Alfano, M. and D. Loeb. (Summer 2014 edition). Experimental moral philosophy. In Edward Zalta (ed.), *The Stanford Encyclopedia of Philosophy*. Retrieved from http://plato.stanford.edu/archives/sum2014/entries/experimental-moral/

Alfano, M. and G. Skorburg. (forthcoming). The extended character hypothesis. In J. Kilverstein (ed.), *Philosophy of the Social Mind*. New York: Routledge.

Alston, W. (2005). *Beyond "Justification": Dimensions of Epistemic Justification*. Ithaca, NY: Cornell University Press.

Annas, J. (2003). The structure of virtue. In Michael DePaul and Linda Zagzebski (eds.), *Intellectual Virtue* (pp. 15–33). New York: Oxford University Press, 15–33.

Annas, J. (2011). *Intelligent Virtue*. Oxford: Oxford University Press.

Appiah, K. (2008). *Experiments in Ethics*. Cambridge: Harvard University Press.

References • 155

Aquinas, T. (1947). *Summa Theologica*. Translated by Fathers of the English Dominican Province. New York: Benziger Brothers.
Aristotle. (1980). *Nicomachean Ethics*. Translated by W.D. Ross and revised by J.L. Ackrill and J.O. Urmson. Oxford: Oxford University Press.
Aristotle. (1985). *Nicomachean Ethics*. Trans. T. Irwin. Indianapolis: Hackett Publishing Company.
Arjoon, S. (2008). Reconciling situational social psychology with virtue ethics. *International Journal of Management Reviews*, 10, 221–243.
Austin, M. (2014). *Virtues in Action: New Essays in Applied Virtue Ethics*. New York: Palgrave.
Badhwar, N. (2009). The Milgram experiments, learned helplessness, and character traits. *The Journal of Ethics*, 13, 257–289.
Baehr, J. (2011). *The Inquiring Mind: On Intellectual Virtues and Virtue Epistemology*. Oxford: Oxford University Press.
Baehr, J. (2013). The cognitive demands of intellectual virtue. In David Schweikard and Tim Henning (eds.), *Knowledge Virtue and Action* (pp. 99–118). London: Routledge.
Bargh, J.A. (1989). Conditional automaticity: Varieties of automatic influence in social perception and cognition. In J.S. Uleman and J.A. Bargh (eds.), *Unintended Thought*. New York: Guilford.
Batson, D. (2011). *Altruism in Humans*. Oxford: Oxford University Press.
Battaly, H. (2001). Thin concepts to the rescue. In Abrol Fairweather and Linda Zagzebski (eds.), *Virtue Epistemology* (pp. 98–116). Oxford: Oxford University Press.
Battaly, H. (2011). Is empathy a virtue? In Amy Coplan and Peter Goldie (eds.), *Empathy: Philosophical and Psychological Perspectives* (pp. 277–301). Oxford: Oxford University Press.
Battaly, H. (2014). Acquiring epistemic virtue: Emotions, situations, and education. In O. Flanagan and A. Fairweather (eds.), *Naturalizing Epistemic Virtue*. Cambridge: Cambridge University Press.
Battaly, H. (forthcoming). *Virtue*. Cambridge: Polity Press.
Baumeister, R., L. Smart, and J. Boden. (1996). Relation of threatened egoism to violence and aggression: The dark side of high self-esteem. *Psychological Review*, 103, 5–33.
Bazelon, E. (2013). *Sticks and Stones: Defeating the Culture of Bullying and Rediscovering the Power of Character and Empathy*. New York: Random House.
Bazerman, M.H. and A.E. Tenbrunsel. (2011). *Blind Spots: Why We Fail to Do What's Right and What to Do about It*. Princeton: Princeton University Press.
Beaman, A., P. Barnes, B. Klentz, and B. McQuirk. (1978). Increasing helping rates through information dissemination: Teaching pays. *Personality and Social Psychology Bulletin*, 4, 406–411.
Berlin, I. (2003). *Generations of Captivity: A History of African American Slaves*. Cambridge, MA: The Belknap Press of Harvard University Press.
Bierbrauer, G. (1979). Why did he do it? Attribution of obedience and the phenomenon of dispositional bias. *European Journal of Social Psychology*, 9, 67–84.
Blasi, A. (1984). Moral identity: Its role in moral functioning. In W.M. Kurtines and J.L. Gewirtz (eds.), *Morality, Moral Behavior, and Moral Development*. New York: John Wiley and Sons.
Blasi, A. (2005). Moral character: A psychological approach. In D.K. Lapsley and F.C. Power (eds.), *Character Psychology and Character Education*. South Bend: University of Notre Dame Press.
Bloodgood, J., W. Turnley, and P. Mudrack. (2008). The influence of ethics instruction, religiosity, and intelligence on cheating behavior. *Journal of Business Ethics*, 82, 557–571.
Cann, A. and J. Blackwelder. (1984). Compliance and mood: A field investigation of the impact of embarrassment. *The Journal of Psychology*, 117, 221–226.
Cantor, N. (1990). From thought to behavior: 'Having' and 'doing' in the study of personality and cognition. *American Psychologist*, 45, 735–250.
Carlson, M., V. Charlin, and N. Miller. (1988). Positive mood and helping behavior: A test of six hypotheses. *Journal of Personality and Social Psychology*, 55, 211–229.
Carter, J.A., J. Kallestrup, S. O. Palermos, and D. Pritchard. (2014). Varieties of externalism. *Philosophical Issues*, 24:1, 63–109.

Cervone, D. and Y. Shoda. (1999). Social-cognitive theories and the coherence of personality. In D. Cervone and Y. Shoda (eds.), *The Coherence of Personality: Social-Cognitive Bases of Personality Consistency, Variability, and Organization*. New York: Guilford.

Chase, W.G. and H.A. Simon. (1973a). The mind's eye in chess. In W.G. Chase (ed.), *Visual Information Processing*. New York: Academic Press.

Chase, W.G. and H.A. Simon. (1973b). Perception in chess. *Cognitive Psychology*, 4, 55–81.

Clark, A. and D. Chalmers. (1998). The extended mind. *Analysis*, 58, 7–19.

Coates, T.-N. (2014). The case for reparations. *The Atlantic*.

Crane, S. (1990). *The Red Badge of Courage*. New York: Dover.

Darley, J. and C.D. Batson. (1973). "From Jerusalem to Jericho": A study of situational and dispositional variables in helping behavior. *Journal of Personality and Social Psychology*, 27, 100–108.

Doris, J. (1998). Persons, situations, and virtue ethics. *Nous*, 32, 121–136.

Doris, J. (2002). *Lack of character: Personality and moral behavior*. Cambridge: Cambridge University Press.

Dreyfus, H. and S. Dreyfus. (1990). What is morality? A phenomenological account of the development of ethical expertise. In David Rasmussen (ed.), *Universalism vs. Communitarianism: Contemporary Debates in Ethics* (pp. 237–264). Cambridge: The MIT Press.

Driver, J. (2000). Moral and epistemic virtue. In Guy Axtell (ed.), *Knowledge, Belief, and Character* (pp. 123–134). Lanham, MD: Rowman and Littlefield.

Driver, J. (2001). *Uneasy Virtue*. New York: Cambridge University Press.

Fitting, M. and R. Mendelsohn. (1999). *First-order Modal Logic*. Dordrecht: Kluwer Academic Publishers.

Flanagan, Owen. (1991). *Varieties of Moral Personality*. Cambridge: Harvard University Press.

Foot, P. (1978). Virtues and vices. In *Virtues and Vices*. Berkeley: University of California Press.

Foot, P. (2001). *Natural Goodness*. Oxford: Oxford University Press.

Fossheim, H.J. (2014). Virtue ethics and everyday strategies. *International Journal of Philosophical Studies*, 267, 65–82.

Frederickson, G.M. (1971). *The Black Image in the White Mind: The Debate on Afro-American Character and Destiny, 1817–1914*. New York: Harper & Row.

Fricker, M. (2007). *Epistemic Injustice*. Oxford: Oxford University Press.

Geach, P. (1977). *The Virtues*. Cambridge: Cambridge University Press.

Genovese, E.D. (1974). *Roll, Jordan, Roll: The World the Slaves Made*. New York: Pantheon Books.

Gilbert, D. (2007). *Stumbling on Happiness*. New York: Vintage.

Goldman, A. (1992). *Liaisons: Philosophy Meets the Cognitive and Social Sciences*. Cambridge, MA: MIT Press.

Graves, J.L. (2001). *The Emperor's New Clothes: Biological Theories of Race at the Millennium*. New Brunswick, NJ: Rutgers University Press.

Harman, G. (1999). Moral philosophy meets social psychology: Virtue ethics and the fundamental attribution error. *Proceedings of the Aristotelian Society*, New Series 119, 316–331.

Harman, G. (2000). The Nonexistence of Character Traits. *Proceedings of the Aristotelian Society*, 100, 223–226.

Hartshorne, H. and M. May. (1928). *Studies in the Nature of Character*. New York: Macmillan.

Hogarth, R.M. (2001). *Educating Intuition*. Chicago.

Hookway, C. (2003). How to be a virtue epistemology. In *Intellectual Virtue: Perspectives from Ethics and Epistemology* (pp. 149–160). Oxford: Oxford University Press.

Hume, D. (1966). *An Enquiry Concerning the Principles of Morals*. La Salle, Illinois: Open Court.

Hume, D. (1978). *A Treatise of Human Nature*, 2nd ed. Edited by P.H. Nidditch. Oxford: Clarendon Press.

Hume, D. (1748/2007). *Enquiry Concerning Human Understanding*. Edited by S. Buckle. Cambridge University Press.

Hurka, T. (2006). Virtuous act, virtuous dispositions. *Analysis* 66.

Hursthouse, Rosalind. (1999). *On Virtue Ethics*. Oxford: Oxford University Press.

Isen, A. and P. Levin. (1972). Effect of feeling good on helping: Cookies and kindness. *Journal of Personality and Social Psychology,* 21, 384–388.
Jackson, F. (1998), *From Metaphysics to Ethics.* Oxford: Oxford University Press.
Jacobson, D. (2005). Seeing by feeling: Virtues, skills, and moral perception. *Ethical Theory and Moral Practice,* 8, 387–409.
Kahneman, D. (2011). *Thinking, Fast and Slow.* New York: Penguin.
Kamtekar, R. (2004). Situationism and virtue ethics on the content of our character. *Ethics,* 114, 458–491
Kim, J. (2011). *Philosophy of Mind,* 3rd ed. New York: Westview Press.
Kohlberg, L., C. Levine, and A. Hewer. (1983). Moral stages: A current formulation and a response to critics. In J.A. Meacham (ed.), *Contributions to Human Development* (Vol. 10). New York: Karger.
Kraftl, P. (2008). Young people, hope, and childhood-hope. *Space and Culture,* 11:2, 81–92.
Kristjánson, K. (2004). Empathy, sympathy, and justice in the child. *Journal of Moral Education,* 33:3, 291–305.
Kunda, Z. and R. Nisbett. (1986). The psychometrics of everyday life. *Cognitive Psychology,* 18: 195–224.
Kupperman, J. (2001). The indispensability of character. *Philosophy,* 76.
Kupperman, J. (2009). Character in virtue ethics. *Ethics,* 13:2–3, 243–255.
Lapsley, D.K. and D. Narvaez. (2004). A social-cognitive approach to the moral personality. In D. Lapsley and D. Narvaez (eds.), *Moral Development: Self and Identity.* Mahwah, NJ: Lawrence Erlbaum Associates.
Lapsley, D.K. and D. Narvaez. (2005). Moral Psychology at the Crossroads. In D.K. Lapsley and F.C. Power, (eds.), *Character Psychology and Character Education.* South Bend: University of Notre Dame Press.
Latané, B. and J. Darley. (1970). *The Unresponsive Bystander: Why Doesn't He Help?* New York: Appleton-Century-Crofts.
Latané, B. and J. Rodin. (1969). A lady in distress: Inhibiting effects of friends and strangers on bystander intervention. *Journal of Experimental Social Psychology,* 5, 189–202.
Leslie, S.J. (2008). Generics: Cognition and acquisition. *Philosophical Review,* 117:1, 1–47.
Lewis, D. (1966). An argument for the identity theory. *The Journal of Philosophy,* 63:1, 17–25.
Lewis, D. (1970). How to define theoretical terms. *The Journal of Philosophy,* 67:13, 427–446.
Lewis, D. (1972). Psychophysical and theoretical identifications. *Australasian Journal of Philosophy,* 50, 249–258.
Logan, G.D. (1989). Automaticity and cognitive control. In J.S. Uleman and J.A. Bargh (eds.), *Unintended Thought.* New York: Guilford.
Lynch, M.P. (1998). *Truth in Context.* Cambridge, MA: The MIT Press.
MacIntyre, A. (1984). *After Virtue: A Study in Moral Theory.* University of Notre Dame Press.
Mazar, N., O. Amir, and D. Ariely. (2008). The dishonesty of honest people: A theory of self-concept maintenance. *Journal of Marketing Research,* 45: 633–644.
Mele, A. and J. Shepherd. (2013). Situationism and agency. *Journal of Practical Ethics,* 1: 62–83.
Merritt, M. (2000). Virtue ethics and situationist personality psychology. *Ethical Theory and Moral Practice,* 3, 365–383.
Merritt, M., J. Doris, and G. Harman. (2010). Character. In J. Doris and the Moral Psychology Research Group (eds.), *The Moral Psychology Handbook* (pp. 355–401). Oxford: Oxford University Press.
Milgram, S. (1965). Some conditions of obedience and disobedience to authority. *Human Relations,* 18, 259–276.
Milgram, S. (1974). *Obedience to Authority: An Experimental View.* New York: Harper & Row.
Mill, J.S. (1869/2002). The subjection of women. *The Basic Writings of John Stuart Mill.* New York: The Modern Library.
Miller, C. (2013). *Moral Character: An Empirical Theory.* Oxford: Oxford University Press.
Miller, C. (2014). *Character and Moral Psychology.* Oxford: Oxford University Press.

References

Mischel, W. (1973). Toward a cognitive social learning reconceptualization of personality. *Psychological Review*, 80, 252–283.
Mischel, W. (1999). Personality Coherence and Dispositions in a Cognitive-Affective Processing System (CAPS) approach. In D. Cervone and Y. Shoda (eds.), *The Coherence of Personality: Social-Cognitive Bases of Personality Consistency, Variability, and Organization*. New York: Guilford.
Mischel, W. and Y. Shoda. (1995). A cognitive-affective system theory of personality: Reconceptualizing situations, dispositions, dynamics, and invariance in personality structure. *Psychological Review*, 102, 246–268.
Montmarquet, J. (1993). *Epistemic Virtue and Doxastic Responsibility*. Lanham, MD: Rowman & Littlefield Publishers.
Montmarquet, J. (2003). Moral character and social science research. *Philosophy*, 78, 355–368.
Myles-Worsley, M., W. Johnston, and M.A. Simons. (1988). The influence of expertise on X-ray image processing. *Journal of Experimental Psychology: Learning, Memory, and Cognition*, 14, 553–557.
Nahmias, E. (2007). Autonomous agency and social psychology. In Massimo Marraffa, Mario De Caro, and Francesco Ferretti (eds.), *Cartographies of the Mind* (Vol. 4, pp. 169–185). Dordrecht: Springer.
Narvaez, D. and D.K. Lapsley. (2005). The psychological foundations of everyday morality and moral expertise. In D.K. Lapsley and F.C. Power (eds.), *Character Psychology and Character Education*. University of Notre Dame Press.
Neisser, U. (1979). The concept of intelligence. *Intelligence*, 3, 217–227.
Nietzsche, F. (1881/1997). *Daybreak*. Edited by M. Clark & B. Leiter. Translated by R. J. Hollingdale. Cambridge: Cambridge University Press.
Nozick, R. (1974). *Anarchy, State, and Utopia*. New York: Basic Books.
Nussbaum, M. (2001). *Upheavals of Thought*. Cambridge: Cambridge University Press.
Olin, L. and J. Doris. (2014). Vicious minds: Virtue epistemology, cognition, and skepticism. *Philosophical Studies*, 168:3, 665–692.
Palermos, S.O. (2014). Loops, constitution, and cognitive extension. *Cognitive Systems Research*, 27, 25–41.
Pietromonaco, P. and R. Nisbett. (1982). Swimming upstream against the fundamental attribution error: Subjects' weak generalizations from the Darley and Batson study. *Social Behavior and Personality*, 10: 1–4.
Pinsent, A. (2012). Humility. In Michael W. Austin and R. Douglas Geivett (eds.), *Being Good: Christian Virtues for Everyday Life*. Grand Rapids: Eerdmans.
Plato. (1992). *Republic*. Trans. G.M.A. Grube. Indianapolis: Hackett Publishing Company, Inc.
Plato. (1997). *Complete Works*. Edited by John. M. Cooper. Indianapolis: Hackett.
Putnam, D. (1995). The primacy of virtue in children's moral development. *Journal of Moral Education*, 24:2, 175–183.
Ramsey, F. (1931). Theories. In R.B. Braithwaite (ed.), *The Foundations of Mathematics*. London: Routledge & Kegan Paul.
Roberts, R. (1984). Will power and the virtues. *The Philosophical Review*, 93, 227–247.
Ross, L. (1977). The intuitive psychologist and his shortcomings. In Berkowitz (ed.), *Advances in Experimental Psychology* (Vol. X, pp. 174–214). New York: Academic Press.
Ross, L. and R. Nisbett. (1991). *The Person and the Situation: Perspectives of Social Psychology*. New York: McGraw-Hill.
Rousseau, J.-J. (1911). *Emile*. Trans. by Barbara Foxley. London: J.M. Dent & Sons.
Russell, D. (2009). *Practical Intelligence and the Virtues*. Oxford: Clarendon Press.
Russell, D. (2012). *Happiness for Humans*. New York: Oxford University Press.
Russell, D. (2014a). Aristotle on cultivating virtue. In N. Snow (ed.), *Virtue Cultivation: Multiple Perspectives*. Oxford: Oxford University Press.
Russell, D. (2014b). Phronesis and the Virtues: *Nicomachean Ethics* VI.12–13. In R. Polansky, ed., *The Cambridge Companion to Aristotle's Nicomachean Ethics*. Cambridge University Press.
Russell, D. (2014c). What virtue ethics can learn from utilitarianism. In B. Eggleston and D. Miller, eds., *The Cambridge Companion to Utilitarianism*. Cambridge University Press.

Russell, L. (2007). What even consequentialists should say about the virtues. *Utilitas*, 19(4), 466–486.
Russell, L. (2009). Is situationism all bad news? *Utilitas*, 21: 443–463.
Sabini, J. and M. Silver. (2005). Lack of character? Situationism critiqued. *Ethics*, 115, 535–562.
Samuels, Steven and William Casebeer. (2005). A social psychological view of morality: Why knowledge of situational influences on behaviour can improve character development practices. *Journal of Moral Education*, 34: 73–87.
Schmidtz, D. (2006). *Elements of Justice*. Cambridge: Cambridge University Press.
Seligman, M. (2002). *Authentic Happiness*. New York: The Free Press.
Slote, M. (1983). *Goods and Virtues*. Oxford: Clarendon Press.
Slote, M. (2001). *Morals from Motives*. Oxford: Oxford University Press.
Slote, M. (2010). *Moral Sentimentalism*. New York: Oxford University Press.
Snow, N. (2002). Virtue and the oppression of women. In Samantha Brennan (ed.), *Feminist Moral Philosophy* (pp. 33–61). Calgary, Alberta, Canada: University of Calgary Press.
Snow, N. (2004). Virtue and the oppression of African Americans. *Public Affairs Quarterly*, 18:1, 57–74.
Snow, N. (2010). *Virtue as Social Intelligence: An Empirically Grounded Theory*. New York: Routledge Press.
Sosa, E. (1980). The raft and the pyramid: Coherence versus foundations in the theory of knowledge," *Midwest Studies of Philosophy*, 5, 3–26.
Sosa, E. (1991). *Knowledge in Perspective*. Cambridge: Cambridge University Press.
Sosa, E. (2003). The place of truth in epistemology. In Michael DePaul and Linda Zagzebski (eds.), *Intellectual Virtue* (pp. 155–179). New York: Oxford University Press.
Sosa, E. (2007). *A Virtue Epistemology*. Oxford: Oxford University Press.
Sosa, E. (2009). Situations against virtues: The situationist attack on virtue theory. In C. Mantzavinos (ed.), *Philosophy of the Social Sciences*. Cambridge: Cambridge University Press.
Sosa, E. (2011). *Knowing Full Well*. Princeton: Princeton University Press.
Sreenivasan, G. (2002). Errors about errors: Virtue theory and trait attribution. *Mind*, 111.
Staub, Ervin. (1974). Helping a distressed person: Social, personality, and stimulus determinants. In L. Berkowitz (ed.), *Advances in Experimental Social Psychology* (Vol. 7, pp. 293–341). New York: Academic Press.
Sternberg, R.J. (1998). Abilities are forms of developing expertise. *Educational Researcher* 3, 22–35.
Swanton, C. (2003). *Virtue Ethics: A Pluralistic View*. Oxford: Oxford University Press.
Taylor, C. (1985). *Philosophical Papers 1*. Cambridge: Cambridge University Press.
Taylor, C. (2007). *A Secular Age*. Harvard: Harvard University Press.
Tessman, L. (2005). *Burdened Virtues: Virtue Ethics for Liberatory Struggles*. New York: Oxford University Press.
Uleman, J. et al. (1996). People as flexible interpreters: Evidence and issues from spontaneous trait inference. In Zanna (ed.), *Advances in Experimental Social Psychology* (Vol. XXVII, pp. 211–280). San Diego: Academic Press.
Van IJzendoorn, M., M. Bakermans-Kranenburg, F. Pannebakker, and D. Out. (2010). In defence of situational morality: Genetic, dispositional and situational determinants of children's donating to charity. *Journal of Moral Education*, 39, 1–20.
Vranas, P. (2005). The indeterminacy paradox: Character evaluations and human psychology. *Noûs*, 39, 1–42.
Wallace, J. (1978). *Virtues and Vices*. Ithaca, NY: Cornell University Press.
Warren, M.A. (1980). *The Nature of Woman: An Encyclopedia & Guide to the Literature*. Inverness, CA: Edgepress.
West, R. (in progress). A critique of pure reasons-based virtue individuation.
Wollstonecraft, M. (1975). *A Vindication of the Rights of Woman: An Authoritative Text, Backgrounds, Criticism*. Edited by Carol H. Poston. New York: W.W. Norton.
Wolterstorff, N. (2008). *Justice: Rights and Wrongs*. Princeton: Princeton University Press.
Zagzebski, L. (1996). *Virtues of the Mind*. Cambridge: Cambridge University Press.
Zagzebski, L. (2008). *On Epistemology*. New York: Cengage.

Index

aggression 111–12
Alfano, Mark, introduction, 1–5, 16, 123–35, 143–7
Annas, Julia 16, 24, 107–8,
Aristotle 10–16, 22, 30, 39–45, 50–3, 84, 92, 100–4, 113, 137–40, 146–7
Austen, Jane 53
autonomy 47–9, 152

Baehr, Jason 61–87
Batson, Daniel 114–15, 142
Battaly, Heather 7–33
blame 14–17, 21–2, 127, 137–42, 146–7; see also praise
Blasi, Augusto 94–5

Cantor, Nancy 93
children 14, 27, 36–40, 46–51, 56–9, 146
Christianity 43–9, 54–5
competence 62–74, 76–7, 80–3

Darley, John 114, 142
Doris, John 125, 133, 139, 142
Driver, Julia 13, 19–22, 25–6, 32, 79

Eliot, George 53
experience machine 38–43

family 18, 38–41, 54–5
flourishing 31, 36–7, 42–4, 48–56, 71, 85–6
Foot, Philippa 108, 134, 144
Fricker, Miranda 151
friendship 18, 36–40, 98–105, 134

gender 19, 26, 50–4, 151–2
Gilbert, Daniel 37–41
Goldman, Alvin 76
Greco, John 66, 76

happiness see flourishing
Harman, Gilbert 125, 137
Hogarth, Robin 101–3, 114
human nature 36, 47–55
Hume, David 7–8, 52–3, 139–43
Hurka, Thomas 139–40
Hursthouse, Rosalind 16–19, 31–2

Kahneman, Daniel 101
Kant, Immanuel 47–9
Kohlberg, Lawrence 104
Kraftl, Peter 57–8

Lapsley, Daniel 94–5
Latané, Bibb 110–14
Lewis, David 125–32, 143–4

Milgram, Stanley 48, 97, 115, 141–5
Mill, John Stuart 53
Miller, Christian 96, 106–117, 133
Montmarquet, James 17–19, 30, 136–47

Narvaez, Darcia 94–5
Nietzsche, Friedrich 45–6
Nisbett, Richard 114
Nozick, Robert 38
Nussbaum, Martha 44–6

oppression 9, 15, 21, 29, 49–59, 152–3

pain 38–46, 97, 110–13, 126; *see also* pleasure
Pieper, Josef 55
Plato 11–12, 67
pleasure 36–40, 113; *see also* pain
praise 14–17, 21–4, 47, 111, 124, 127–8, 137–9, 144–7; *see also* blame

race 54–6
Ramsey, Frank 125–35, 144
reliability 9–20, 23–33, 62–9, 71–4, 75–84, 92, 107, 128
responsibility 10, 44, 62–72, 76–8, 83–4, 124, 136–8, 142
Roberts, Robert 36–50
Roberts, Samuel 55
Rousseau, Jean-Jacques 52–3
Russell, Daniel 92–106, 108–9, 116, 133

Seligman, Martin 42
slavery 50–6
Slote, Michael 18–20, 26, 57
Snow, Nancy 49–58, 107
Socrates 44, 51, 147

Sosa, Ernest 12–13, 19–20, 62–85, 107

Taylor, Charles 41
Tolstoy, Lev 139–41

Van Zyl, Liezl 22–33
virtues and vices: benevolence 8–10, 13–15, 22–9, 33, 54, 143; cheating 96, 110–12, 127, 137; compassion 30, 42–7, 51, 94, 107; courage 7–17, 19, 25–31, 51, 66–9, 75–7, 83–4, 127–34, 138–9, 143–6; cowardice 8, 83, 127, 134, 138; curiosity 124–33; empathy 7–8, 18, 24, 116; fairness 24, 30, 41–3, 79, 83, 94–6, 104–5, 116, 134; fortitude 55–6; generosity 24, 29, 38–41, 92–6, 100–4, 127–30; gratitude 54; honesty 57, 79, 82–6, 127–32, 139; hope 36–7, 55–9; humility 43–9, 129; industry 54, 134; justice 11–16, 41–2, 55–8, 151; loyalty 54–5, 127, 134; malevolence 111, 152; modesty 32, 129; obedience 29, 47–8, 51–5, 97, 134, 145; open-mindedness 7–8, 17–19, 24–31, 59, 66–9, 75–80, 82–6, 129, 135, 145; prudence 55–7; self-control 42, 53; selfishness 13–14, 27–33; temperance 11–12, 51, 55–6; thrift 54–5; trust 56–8, 70, 150; wisdom 11–15, 29–31

Wollstonecraft, Mary 53

Zagzebski, Linda 17–19, 24, 30–2, 63, 69–70, 78, 133